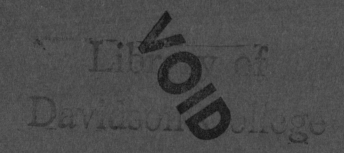

The Latin Americans

MODERN LATIN AMERICA

THE LATIN AMERICANS
Their Heritage and Their Destiny

Ronald Hilton
Stanford University

J. B. LIPPINCOTT COMPANY

Philadelphia

New York   Toronto

918
H656l

Paperbound: ISBN-0-397-47283-8

Clothbound: ISBN-0-397-47288-9

Library of Congress Catalog Card Number 73-4320

Printed in the United States of America

1 3 5 7 9 8 6 4 2

Library of Congress Cataloging in Publication Data

Hilton, Ronald, 1911—
    The Latin Americans.   75-1964
    Bibliography: p.
    1. Latin America. I. Title.

F1408.H635   918'.03   73-4320

Paperbound: ISBN-0-397-47283-8

Clothbound: ISBN-0-397-47288-9

The Destiny of Latin America

"The Kingdom of *Chile* is deſtined, by the nature of its location, by the ſimple and virtuous character of its people, and by the example of its neighbors, the proud *republicans* of Arauco, to enjoy the bleſſings that flow from the juſt and gentle laws of a republic. If any American republic is to have a long life, I am inclined to believe it will be Chile. There the ſpirit of *liberty* has never been extinguiſhed; the vices of Europe and Aſia arrived too late or not at all to corrupt the cuſtoms of that diſtant corner of the World. Its area is limited; and, as it is remote from other peoples, it will always remain free from *contamination*. Chile will not alter her laws, ways, and practices. She will preſerve her uniform political and religious views. In a word, it is poſſible for Chile to be *free*."

This paragraph comes from the "Reply of a South American to a Gentleman of this Island," which Simón Bolívar wrote in Kingston Jamaica, on September 6, 1815. In this famous letter surveying the past, present, and future of what was later to be known as "Latin America," the Liberator with singular insight and a certain rashness engaged in the now blossoming "science" of futurology. How correct was Bolívar in his predictions? The remoteness of Chile was very real until the advent of jet planes. Now Santiago is linked with Moscow, and its isolation is only relative. There is still disagreement about the past. An informed and dispassionate discussion of the present is a rarity. Only certain theoreticians believe that futurology is or ever can be a science.

Contents

Illustrations

Foreword

A small book on Latin America must leave a lot unsaid. It is often necessary to make statements without the supporting evidence. The reader may be assured that no statement in this book is made lightly; it is backed up not only by data but also by a lifetime of travel and observation in all the countries of Latin America. This does not mean that the reader must agree with the judgments expressed. The author himself revises his opinions constantly in the light of new evidence and further reflection on the problems considered. Indeed, he hopes that this book will stimulate a candid and intelligent discussion rather than a curt rejection of unwelcome ideas.

The book contains, in addition to information, considerations on controversial, important, and sensitive issues. These are discussed candidly, without the jargon behind which some scholars like to hide and without the parochialism which makes some subjects and values taboo. The current demand for relevance is justified if it means that the immensely important issues which confront us must be faced honestly. No one discipline is competent to embrace all the subjects discussed, and the book is addressed to a wide audience with a variety of interests.

This is not a textbook of Latin American geography, history, economics, literature, or of any one of the established "disciplines"; rather is it a synthesis of all of them. No attempt is made to cover each field. It is indeed difficult to distinguish between fields; they are all related and intertwined, and the same subject may thus reappear in a different context in various chapters. The stress is on those significant and relevant matters which are important for the understanding of the total picture. Hopefully, the interest thus aroused will be translated into a more detailed study of those areas in which the reader wishes to go deeper and in which the bibliography will provide guidance.

Ronald Hilton

1 • A World of Regions: Latin America, the Name and the Place

How should the world be organized? This is the basic question in international relations. In the old isolationist days we had a simplistic answer. There was the Western Hemisphere, which the United States dominated through the Pan American system, and there was the Old World, on which Americans had turned their backs. The New World was virtuous, the Old World was corrupt, and it was unfortunate that we were ever dragged into its affairs. World War I and especially World War II shattered that smug illusion. Neither in area, nor population, nor even importance is America a hemisphere, i.e. half of the world, and America cannot disentangle itself from the Old World.

During the euphoria which followed World War II, we spoke of "one world," in which it was tacitly assumed that the United States would provide the leadership. The Cold War, and later the Vietnamese War, shattered that illusion too. The United States is now reconciled to life in a world of regions, in which each region will lead its own life. We encouraged Western Europe to unite in order to survive, and we now assume that in the future there will be five power centers: the United States, Western Europe, the Soviet bloc, China, and Japan.

All these power centers are in the Northern Hemisphere. What about the areas, like Latin America, which lie primarily in the Southern Hemisphere? It has been argued that the old antitheses between the Western Hemisphere and the Old World, between the capitalist and the communist worlds, no longer have major importance. The main antithesis is between the industrialized North and the underdeveloped South of the world.

One striking development is that we have modified our belief in a united Western Hemisphere. Until a few years ago, it was subversive to suggest that there should be a united Latin America, indeed, that there was such a thing as "Latin America." The sudden change in Washington's attitude has several explanations. Our global planners were thinking of a world of regions in which each region would settle its own problems without, if possible, involving the United States. Following the example of the United Nations, which had created the Economic Commission for Latin America (ECLA), the United States recognized Latin America as one such region. The keystone of our foreign policy was NATO, and Latin America was outside of that. The sudden change was a typical Washington phenomenon, like President Nixon's reconciliation with China and the Soviet Union; we have a tendency to change policies to give the impression that we are making progress. With U. S. industry becoming less and less competitive in world markets, our policy has been to encourage the development of large common markets where U. S.-financed industries could develop economies of scale. Thus, Latin America, which in the past had been merely a descriptive phrase, became a reality. Or did it?

The problem took a curious new shape at the Conference on European Security and Cooperation held in Helsinki in late 1972, with the participation of the United States and Canada. The *New York Times* ran a headline: "Helsinki Talk Redefining 'Europe'— North America Is 'Europe'." One U.S. representative remarked, "The surprising thing is how easily we and the Canadians are accepted as Europeans." Latin America often prides itself on its close ties with Europe, but it was not included in the conference. The Helsinki conference may shape the world of the future. In a negative way it reinforced the existence of "Latin America."

Is There a Latin America?

What is Latin America? Is there such a thing? The term "Anglo-America" applied to the United States and Canada designates the area north of "Latin America," but it is not widely used and it also presents difficulties. Latin Americans object to our using the term "America" to refer to the United States (which is also not too precise a name). We have begun to pick up from Spanish usage the term "North America," which is unsatisfactory because it should include Canada and, from the strictly geographical viewpoint, Mexico.

The attempt to divide the world into areas, each with its label, is an unending source of difficulty. The term "Latin America" is as confusing as the terms "Europe" or "Africa." Traditionally, the eastern limits of Europe were the Ural Mountains and the Bosporus, but in these days of a highly centralized Russia, with good air communications, the Urals are not a barrier. The Soviet Union is essentially a European empire, but the Soviets in their desire to achieve hegemony in Asia are wont to say that over half of the USSR is in Asia. A bridge is being built across the Bosporus at Istanbul, where "Asia" is to "Europe" what Jersey City is to New York City. Under Islam, Turkey was definitely not "European," even though its capital was European Constantinople (now Istanbul). Kemal Ataturk Europeanized Turkey, but he moved the capital to Ankara in Asia. Turkey is a key member of the North Atlantic Treaty Organization, and most Turks are oriented toward Europe, but the older generation looks toward Mecca, and the young leftists identify themselves with the peoples of Asia and Africa, i.e. the Third World.

A similar schizophrenia has been evident in Spain. A popular saying holds that "Africa begins in the Pyrenees," but most Spaniards today regard themselves as Europeans, although Spain belongs neither to NATO nor to the European Economic Community. Some older Spaniards think that their most important ties are with America, South and North, just as the older generation of Britishers regard their connections with the Commonwealth and the United States as more significant than those with Europe. What, in any case, is Europe? Is it Roman Catholic and conservative, or agnostic and liberal? Does it include the Soviet Union, or is it a group of nations striving to maintain their independence from Moscow?

The term "Asia" likewise masks a confusion of diversities. Is it Islamic, communist, or capitalist? Asia has no racial or cultural common denominators. The rivalry between the Soviet Union and China is largely for hegemony in this area teeming with humanity and contradictions.

"Africa" is an equally imprecise label. It is at best a geographical expression, but even so the unfortunate Suez Canal, like the Bosporus, allegedly separates one continent from another, cutting a country in two. Except in geographical terms, the label "Africa" means nothing. Addis Ababa is the headquarters of the Organization for African Unity, but African unity is a myth. The continent consists of three zones: the Arab north which belongs to the Arab world (Mecca is not in Africa!); the black middle zone; and the

THE POPULATION AND AREA OF THE COUNTRIES OF LATIN AMERICA

Region or Country	Capital	Area (sq. mi.)	Population Estimates Mid-1972 (millions)	Annual Births per 1,000 Population	Annual Deaths per 1,000 Population
LATIN AMERICA	—	—	300	38	10
MIDDLE AMERICA	—	—	72	43	11
Costa Rica	San José	19,575	1.9	34	7
El Salvador	San Salvador	8,260	3.7	40	17
Guatemala	Guatemala City	42,042	5.4	43	17
Honduras	Tegucigalpa	43,277	2.9	49	17
Mexico	Mexico City	761,602	54.3	43	10
Nicaragua	Managua	50,193	2.2	46	17
Panama	Panama	29,205	1.6	38	9
CARIBBEAN	—	—	27	33	11
Barbados	Bridgetown	166	0.3	21	8
Cuba	Havana	44,218	8.7	27	8
Dominican Republic	Santo Domingo	18,816	4.6	49	15
Guadeloupe	Basse-Terre	687	0.4	30	8
Haiti	Port-au-Prince	10,714	5.5	44	20
Jamaica	Kingston	4,232	2.1	33	8
Martinique	Fort-de-France	425	0.4	27	8
Puerto Rico	San Juan	3,435	2.9	25	7
Trinidad & Tobago	Port of Spain	1,980	1.1	23	7
TROPICAL SOUTH AMERICA	—	—	160	40	10
Bolivia	La Paz	424,163	4.9	44	19
Brazil	Brasília	3,286,478	98.4	38	10
Colombia	Bogotá	439,736	22.9	44	11
Ecuador	Quito	109,483	6.5	45	11
Guyana	Georgetown	83,000	0.8	36	8
Peru	Lima	496,223	14.5	42	11
Surinam	Paramaribo	63,000	0.4	41	7
Venezuela	Caracas	352,143	11.5	41	8
TEMPERATE SOUTH AMERICA	—	—	41	25	9
Argentina	Buenos Aires	1,072,158	25.0	22	9
Chile	Santiago	292,259	10.2	28	9
Paraguay	Asunción	157,047	2.6	45	11
Uruguay	Montevideo	68,536	3.0	21	9

Source: World Population Data Sheet. Population Reference Bureau.

The countries of Latin America vary enormously in size and population. Brazil is larger than the continental United States and has a population of about 100 million. Argentina is only a third of the size, but it has a far higher percentage of good land. Mexico is four times as large as Spain, one of the largest countries in Europe. Peru, Colombia, and

Annual Deaths to Infants under One Year of Age per 1,000 Live Births	Population under 15 Years (percent)	Population over 64 Years (percent)	Percent of Population in Cities of 100,000	Per Capita Gross National Product (US $)	Annual Rate of Population Growth (percent)	Number of Years to Double Population	Population Projections to 1985 (millions)
—	42	4	31	—	2.8	25	435
—	46	3	20	—	3.2	22	112
67	48	L*	25	510	2.7	26	3.2
67	45	L	14	290	3.0	23	5.9
92	46	L	15	350	2.6	27	7.9
—	47	L	10	260	3.2	22	4.6
69	46	L	21	580	3.3	21	84.4
—	48	L	18	380	2.9	24	3.3
41	44	L	30	660	2.9	24	2.5
—	40	4	21	—	2.2	32	36
42	36	7	N.A.†	500	0.8	87	0.3
48	31	6	31	280	1.9	37	11.0
64	47	L	18	280	3.4	21	7.3
45	43	5	N.A.	540	2.2	32	0.5
—	38	L	8	P**	2.4	29	7.9
39	46	L	28	550	2.1	33	2.6
35	43	5	N.A.	690	1.6	44	0.5
26	37	7	33	1,410	1.4	50	3.4
37	42	L	N.A.	890	1.1	63	1.3
—	43	3	32	—	3.0	23	236
—	42	L	15	160	2.4	29	6.8
—	43	L	34	270	2.8	25	142.6
76	47	L	35	290	3.4	21	35.6
91	48	L	21	240	3.4	21	10.1
40	45	L	27	340	2.8	25	1.1
72	45	L	22	330	3.1	23	21.6
30	46	L	34	560	3.2	22	0.6
47	47	L	37	1,000	3.4	21	17.4
—	32	7	52	—	1.7	41	51
58	30	7	61	1,060	1.5	47	29.6
92	39	5	37	510	1.9	37	13.6
67	46	L	19	240	3.4	21	4.1
49	28	8	53	560	1.2	58	3.4

*L=Estimated to be less than 5 percent
†N.A.=Not applicable; country has no urban community over 100,000
**P=Estimated to be less than U. S. $100

Bolivia are all more than twice as large as France. In contrast, El Salvador is the size of Massachusetts. Now several ministates—Barbados, Jamaica, and Trinidad and Tobago—have joined the Organization of American States and the United Nations, raising the touchy question of the role of ministates in the world concert.

white-controlled southern zone. The Organization for African Unity is an instrument of black power politics. The Arab north and black Africa cooperate when it is mutually convenient, but the Arab states have oppressed the blacks, and the Sudan has been the scene of a bloody civil war between the Arab north and the black south. Black Africa and southern Africa are in a state of permanent confrontation.

"Latin America"

Let us return now to the concept of "Latin America." Here, again, it is difficult to establish precise boundaries. Spanish traditionalists regard California, Arizona, New Mexico, Texas, and Florida as still part of the Hispanic world, and the strong Spanish-speaking minorities in those states have in recent years defiantly asserted their ancient links. What about the Caribbean? The term "Latin America," which the U.S. Government has traditionally avoided using because of the problems it presents, has finally been accepted and is defined as all the members of the Organization of American States (OAS) except the United States. The English-speaking territories which have joined the OAS resent being lumped together with "Latin America." Cuba's membership in the OAS has been suspended. Some organizations still use the expression "Latin America and the Caribbean."

The eastern limits of "Latin America" likewise present a problem. Brazil has a Portuguese and not a Spanish tradition, and it rejects the term "Hispanic America." It accepts unenthusiastically the terms "Latin America" or even "Ibero-America." However, it regards itself as a world power and looks with indifference or disdain at the countries behind its back, especially the *republiquetas* (banana republics) of Central America. Brazilians pride themselves as being more than "Latin Americans." This was traditionally the attitude of Argentinians, who stressed their ties with Europe and looked superciliously at the mixed breeds to the north. Decades of crisis have weakened Argentina; now, it would be happy if it could at least have hegemony in Latin America, but even this dream eludes it.

The southern limits of "Latin America" are in dispute, since Argentina and Chile claim sovereignty as far as the South Pole, but internationally no claims to sovereignty in Antarctica are recognized. The Argentinians likewise claim sovereignty over the British-owned Falkland Islands, but the Falkland Islanders reject vigorously any attempt to annex them to "Latin America." The

Pacific Coast gives Latin America a fairly definite western boundary, but since the Galapagos Islands belong to Ecuador and Easter Island to Chile, they, too, are technically part of "Latin America." We could even raise the question of Canada, since some French Canadians describe themselves as "Latins of America," and they certainly are more Latin than the Indians and blacks of "Latin America."

In view of all these difficulties, it would be simpler to talk of North America (the United States and Canada), Middle America (Mexico, Central America, Panama, and the Caribbean islands), and South America. Latin America would then consist of Middle and South America, and that is the area to which this book is devoted.

The use of the terms "Middle" and "South" America would avoid the sensitive issues raised by the use of cultural terms such as "Latin," "Hispanic," or "Iberian." The U.S. Government has traditionally said "American Republics," "inter-American," or "Pan American." Each of these terms is questionable, the first because the former British colonies are now sovereign and independent, but, with the exception of Guyana, they are not republics, although they are free to become so within the Commonwealth. "Inter-American" should include Canada and the French and Dutch territories of the Caribbean, which are not sovereign. "Pan American" recalls the days of "Pan Germanism," and "Pan Slavism," when the world was grouping itself into antagonistic racial blocs. The Western Hemisphere organization, formerly known as the Pan American Union, is now the Organization of American States, a much less totalitarian expression.

The Name

The name "Latin America" is accepted for lack of anything better, despite its geographical imprecision and its cultural coloration. The initial difficulty arose with the term "America." The Spaniards called the New World "the Indies," because Christopher Columbus thought he had reached India. Even after the Pacific was discovered and the Spaniards realized their error, the term continued to be used. *Un indio* was a native of the New World, un *indiano* was a Spaniard who had made a fortune there and returned to live in Spain, often with conspicuous wealth. The British spoke of the "West Indies," and the term is still used to describe the Antilles. The name "America" is almost an accident. The cartographer Martin Waldseemüller was a friend of Amerigo

Vespucci (who was of secondary importance in the discovery of the New World) and called the continent "America." The fact that the name stuck is more a tribute to Waldseemüller's reputation than to Vespucci's.

During the Romantic period, Columbus became the archtype of the misunderstood and unappreciated great man, tragically superior to Vespucci, who had usurped his glory. There was an attempt to rename the continent Columbia. Traces of the campaign are evident in such names as British Columbia, Columbia University (formerly King's College), and Colombia (formerly New Granada), but it failed—the name America was already too well established. Although it is now generally accepted, the word is still ambiguous. We use the term to mean the United States (US!), whereas in Spanish it refers, or referred, to "Latin" America. The Spaniards thought they had a God-given destiny to run the continent, and even Simón Bolívar declared that "America is Catholic and speaks Spanish." Brazil was then confined to the east coast of South America and was looked upon as a minor accident.

The liberals admired George Washington much as some leftists today admire Fidel Castro, and the idea that the United States would assert its continental hegemony was looked upon as we would a claim by Cuba to control of the Western Hemisphere. The United States promoted the doctrine of "manifest destiny," which was a reincarnation of the Spaniards' claim to be the agents of God. The Monroe Doctrine virtually reduced the Latin American countries to the status of protectorates and is, therefore, resented in Latin America in a way which puzzles "Americans"; the Soviets must likewise think that their East European satellites are not properly grateful for the Brezhnev doctrine. Now we seem reconciled to the fact that both claims to a divine mission to run "the Americas" were exaggerated, and we have accepted the division of the continent into what may be called "Anglo-America" and "Latin America." Verbally, we may have won the battle; our soldiers and tourists have gone around the world proclaiming themselves "Americans," and even the Spaniards are now beginning to use the word "americanos" to mean US. However, for most Latin Americans we are still "North Americans."

More significant has been the argument about the adjective "Latin." As it became necessary to distinguish between the two parts of the continent, the Spaniards spoke of "Hispanoamérica," and the expression "Hispanic America" was taken up in English.

It is still used in certain scholarly references instead of "Latin America," but it is resented by the Brazilians except as a synonym for Spanish America. They regard the Spanish argument that in Latin the term "Hispania" referred to the whole Iberian Peninsula as an expression of the Spanish claim to a manifest destiny which led to the "Babylonian captivity" of 1580-1640, when Spain controlled Portugal. Portugal claims to be the successor to "Lusitania," and the Brazilians sometimes use "Luso-America" as we say "Anglo-America."

The term "Hispanic America" having been rejected by Brazil, the Spaniards promoted the term "Ibero-America," since "Iberia" referred to the whole peninsula but did not suggest Spanish hegemony. This reference to remote ancestors who once occupied part of the peninsula was paralleled by references to Americans (US) as "Anglo-Saxons," but neither term has been adopted in common usage. Following the wars of independence, the Spanish and Portuguese conquests were rejected by some intellectuals (not Indians themselves) who said that the real Americans were the Indians and that the continent should be called "Indo-America." However, this term could at best be applied to a few countries such as Ecuador, Peru, and Bolivia, where the heirs of the Incas still form the bulk of the Andean population. The term is not even used in Mexico, which is proud of its Aztec and Mayan origins. The concept of *négritude,* which President Senghor of Senegal has made popular in black Africa, was concocted by a French Antillean writer, André Césaire of Martinique, and some Latin Americans have spoken of "Afro-America," but this name has not been accepted, since it could refer to only a few areas of the continent; Fidel Castro, who claims to be a defender of the black cause, for a time spoke of "Africanía."

The modern name "Latin America" was invented by the French in the second half of the last century, when they promoted the concept of a Paris-centered "Latin world" to compete with the Pan Germanic, Pan Slavic, and Anglo-Saxon blocs. At the time, French culture was at the height of its prestige, and the former Spanish and Portuguese colonies, which wished to achieve their cultural as well as their political independence, aped everything French. The term "Latin America" was resented by the conservatives of Spain and Latin America, who regarded it as an affront to the Spanish tradition. It was accepted without much difficulty in Argentina and Uruguay, where the Spanish colonial tradition was weak and where Italian immigration had been especially numerous.

The term "Hispanic America" was still commonly used in Spanish America until it received an unhappy political coloration during World War II. The Spanish regime of Generalissimo Franco, expecting that the Axis would win the war, promoted the cult of "Hispanidad." This was a mystic belief in the Spanish tradition, combined with the expectation that, following the defeat of the Western democracies, Spain would resume its rightful place in the sun. California, Arizona, New Mexico, Texas, and Florida would be restored to "Hispanidad." When the Allies defeated the Axis, the Franco government did everything possible to hide its earlier sympathies for the Axis, and the "Hispanidad" doctrine was quietly buried. Even so, the Franco government won only a modest degree of acceptance in Spanish America, and the affection for Old Spain implicit in the term "Hispanoamérica" was diminished. This led to a more general acceptance of the term "Latin America."* There has been, as we shall see later, a movement toward the integration of Latin America, and since its core was Brazil, Argentina, and Uruguay, where there is a heavy infusion of Italian population, it was natural that the organization that developed out of this movement should have been called the Latin American Free Trade Association (LAFTA). The United Nations has begun to use the name in titles such as the Economic Commission for Latin America (ECLA). So, despite all the reservations about both words, we shall speak of "Latin America."

Geography

Geographically, Latin America is a vast and complex area. Brazil alone is larger than the continental United States. Spanish America stretches from Tijuana, just across the Mexican border from San Diego, to Tierra del Fuego, or even to the South Pole. Brazil forms a geographical unit, but Spanish America does not. It is an extremely long and generally mountainous band of territory. Its two principal cities, Mexico City and Buenos Aires, are almost at opposite ends of this long strip. Spanish America has a certain linguistic and cultural unity, but that is all.

It is necessary to know something of the geology of Latin America to understand its physical, political, and cultural geography. Geologically, the oldest area is the Brazilian plateau, which has been worn down by erosion; Brazil has no high mountains comparable to those of Spanish America. The Brazilian plateau

---

*However, in the last few years there has been a trend among the Spanish-speaking groups in the United States to call themselves "Hispanic Americans."

has an equable climate, far superior to that of the tropical cities of the coast like Rio de Janeiro. In general it is not fertile, and this explains the inadequacy of agriculture in most of Brazil, but it is rich in minerals such as iron and precious and semiprecious stones. Along the Atlantic runs the so-called Coastal Range (Serra do Mar). In reality it is not a mountain range, but the edge of the plateau, which slopes down toward the west. Many rivers have their origin in the coastal range; they flow west and then north to join the Amazon or south to the River Plate. The northern part of Brazil is Amazonia, where a number of rivers come together to form the Amazon, the largest river in the world in terms of the volume of water. In much of Brazil there is a shortage of water, but Amazonia suffers from an excess. Despite their irregularities, the rivers serve as highways, but at the same time their tangled networks block communications and slow down the development of the area.

A geological peculiarity of the American continent is that there is a mountain range all down the Pacific Coast, from Alaska to Patagonia. Once, it was thought that this was all one mountain system, but now we know that it is a whole series of ranges. The Andes proper begin in Venezuela, pass through Colombia, Ecuador, Peru, Bolivia, and Chile, and end in Tierra del Fuego. Geologically, the Andes are quite young, and they are slowly rising. Geologists have long argued about the origin of the Andes, but now it seems certain that they are the product of continental drift. Brazil split off from Africa, moving slowly west, and pushed up the Andes like an immense fold. These mountains, which extend from one end to the other of Spanish America, complicate life in all the countries, from Mexico to Chile. Communications are difficult, and this has impeded the political integration of the various republics. Agriculture is precarious on the mountain slopes, where the soil is poor and, if cultivated, subject to erosion. In general they produce good coffee, but many should be reforested, since the cutting down of the original forests to make way for the coffee plantations has been an ecological disaster.

Much of Latin America suffers from one ecological disadvantage or another. Some areas have vast expanses of desert, others, excessive rainfall. Brazil is expanding westward over old, dry, rocky land. The Amazon valley consists largely of leached soil of dubious fertility. Practically all the western strip of Latin America is subject to earthquakes. In December 1972 a severe earthquake practically destroyed Managua, the capital of Nicaragua.

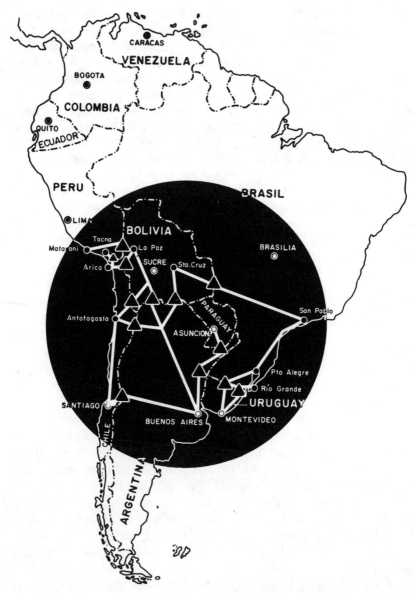

One reason why the European Common Market functions is that the continent has a superb network of railroads. The only area of Latin America that is tied together by railroads is the "Southern Cone," consisting of Argentina, Uruguay, Chile, Bolivia, Paraguay, and the southern sectors of Peru and Brazil. Chile, Bolivia and Peru, Ecuador, Colombia, and in a limited way Venezuela, form the Andean subregion of the Latin American Common Market.

Argentina presents a totally different picture. It is an immense plain stretching east of the Andes from north to south. The soil, especially in the humid pampa around Buenos Aires, is excellent, and since the pampa extends from the tropics to the temperate zone, it produces a great variety of crops. Communications are easy because of the flat terrain, and the British built in Argentina a good system of railroads. The Andean republics are faced with extremely difficult living conditions, but there is no country more blessed by nature than Argentina. It is far from the centers of world conflict, and this has allowed it to follow a more or less isolationist policy. If in recent years Argentina has not prospered, it has been in large measure because of the incapacity and demagoguery of its leaders and the irresponsible attitude of the population. In any case, Argentina has enjoyed a much higher standard of living than the rest of Latin America, and even today it continues to do so.

Uruguay and Paraguay are virtually extensions of Argentina, and the three republics are known as the River Plate Republics. Whereas the vast Amazon network is so unreliable that it has been a barrier to progress, the River Plate has served as a link among the countries of the area, which is now being integrated economically under a project sponsored by the Inter-American Development Bank. The whole river system will be brought under control, something which will be almost impossible with the Amazon.

The Antilles form an archipelago of extraordinary complexity. Indonesia, another tropical archipelago, is much simpler. Politically, the Antilles are a weird mosaic. Cuba, Haiti, and the Dominican Republic are independent republics. Cuba and the Dominican Republic belong culturally to Spanish America, while Haiti, a black republic where Creole (a kind of pidgin French) is spoken, has practically no connection with the rest of Latin America except for its usually negative and sometimes bloody relations with its neighbors, Cuba to the west and the Dominican Republic to the east.

Puerto Rico has a Spanish American culture, but politically it is tied to the United States, and its relations with the rest of Latin America are poor. Latin American countries do not want Puerto Rican immigrants, and in any case Puerto Ricans prefer to go to the U.S. mainland, where they can make more money and where they can enter freely as U.S. citizens.

The former British colonies, which speak English and which only now are beginning to develop relations with the rest of Latin

America, have become free members of the Commonwealth. Three of them (Jamaica, Trinidad and Tobago, and Barbados) have joined the Organization of American States, and only a boundary dispute with Venezuela has prevented Guyana from joining. Thus, they officially become "Latin American." even though they have nothing "Latin American" about them and resent the label.

In the French territories, i.e. the islands of Guadeloupe and Martinique and the South American territory of French Guiana, the situation is just the reverse. Although the population is predominantly black, its culture is French, i.e. Latin. Thus, culturally, they are "Latin American," but politically they are not. Since World War II they have become French departments, like those of metropolitan France, and they have no direct political or diplomatic relations with the countries of Latin America. Since they are not sovereign states, they cannot be members of the Organization of American States. Their status is somewhat similar to that of Puerto Rico.

The Dutch territories, that is to say the Netherlands Antilles in the Caribbean and Surinam on the north coast of South America between Guyana and French Guiana, constitute with the Netherlands (Holland) a tripartite kingdom in which the two American governments have complete autonomy except in the areas of foreign affairs and defense, which are controlled from the Netherlands. They are not sovereign states and do not belong to the Organization of American States. At present, therefore, the governments of Willemstad (capital of the Netherlands Antilles) and Paramaribo (capital of Surinam) do not have diplomatic relations with the Latin American republics. However, in Surinam there is an independence movement, and it is possible that the tripartite kingdom may be modified. Following the serious 1969 disturbances in Willemstad, the Dutch Government said it would give the Netherlands Antilles their independence if they wished it.

A Circumference, Perhaps; A Center, No

Does Latin America have a political center? This is a problem which faces other areas such as Europe, Africa, and Asia. In Europe it seemed at first as though it would be Geneva, then Paris. Now it appears it will be Brussels, although the European Parliament is in Strasbourg. It is a fiction to promote Addis Ababa as the capital of Africa, and no city can claim to be the capital of Asia.

Likewise, Latin America does not have a natural center. The liberator Simón Bolívar thought that Panama would be the natural meeting place for Americans, and he organized there the famous congress of 1826. This made some sense in the days of sea communications, but Panama can no longer claim to be the natural center of the hemisphere. Montevideo is the headquarters of the Latin American Free Trade Association (LAFTA), but it is not centrally located, and this is one of the causes of LAFTA's weakness. The Peruvians claim that Lima is the historic center of Latin, or at least South, America, and many inter-American meetings are held there; but Lima faces the Pacific, while in general Latin America faces the Atlantic. Moreover, Peru has been plagued with racial and social difficulties, making Lima an inappropriate locale for international organizations. Santiago is the most remote of the Latin American capitals, but Chile had a reputation as a stable, democratic country, and for this reason some organizations such as the U.N. Economic Commission for Latin America established their headquarters there, despite the heavy travel expenses involved. However, Chile is now controlled by a Marxist coalition, and it has close ties with the Soviet Union and Cuba. In the light of these developments, the selection of Santiago as the seat of international organizations would seem to have been unfortunate. There has been a suggestion that the Northeast of Brazil would be a good location for the "capital" of Latin America, but the hard fact is that Latin America has no natural center. It is unlikely that Latin America will have one capital. Presumably, the different inter-American organizations will continue to operate in different cities and, even if a united Latin America develops, its organizations likewise will be scattered. Despite Latin American efforts to move the Pan American Union, i.e. the secretariat of the Organization of American States, to Latin America, it has remained in Washington and probably will do so. There is little likelihood of Latin America's developing any similar regional headquarters, so that organizationally it will never have the strength of the inter-American system.

2 • The Population

The Race Mixture

In Latin America, the three races—the white, the native Indian, and the black—all play an important role. All three exist in more or less pure form, and in addition there is a great variety of mixtures. The population of Argentina and Uruguay is more white than that of the United States, since there are practically no blacks; only in the outlying parts of Argentina are there a few Indians. In Guatemala, Ecuador, Peru, and Bolivia there are many pure Indians.* In Haiti and some other Caribbean countries the population is black. The relations between the three racial groups are very complex, and it is hypocritical to claim, as many Latin Americans do, that there is no race prejudice in Latin America. The Mexican intellectual José Vasconcelos spoke of the "cosmic race," a mystic name he gave to the mixture of the three races which he believed was developing in Latin America. He said that Latin America would be the first region of the world to create such a "cosmic race." In his old age Vasconcelos laughed at the idea and dismissed it as a juvenile fantasy.

In reality this mixture is occurring in only a limited way. In some parts of the Caribbean and Brazil "cosmic" types may be seen, but these triple mixtures are not common in the rest of Latin America, and seldom do even two races mix easily. Even in Brazil the black is in an inferior situation, and whites seldom marry blacks. In Brazil there are two big groups: the whites, who are the result of the mixture of the Portuguese with later immi-

*Paraguay is a mestizo country, even though Guaraní has survived as a second official language, and its culture is wrongly supposed to be predominantly Indian.

16

grants, primarily the Italians of São Paulo; and the mulattoes, who were mostly the product of slavery (which lasted in Brazil until 1888). There are few pure blacks, but this is true also of the United States, where the term "black" is used to describe mulattoes, even near-whites who in Brazil would be classified as whites. The Indian population of Brazil is small in comparison with that of the Andean countries, and they do not have a comparable cultural tradition. The pure Indians are disappearing as the Brazilian frontier moves west. Those who survive usually mix with the mulattoes and occasionally with the whites. These mixed breeds are called *caboclos*, and really correspond to the aforementioned "cosmic race," but the term is not a flattering one.

Argentina and Uruguay had a substantial Indian and black population in the last century, but now the population is almost entirely white, a mixture of Spanish and Italian. The blacks and the Indians were virtually eliminated in the civil wars of the last century. Around Buenos Aires and some other cities there are slums inhabited by Indians or mestizos (mixed Indian and white) from Paraguay or Bolivia. They seldom marry Argentinians, and it seems certain that Argentina and Uruguay will continue to be white countries.

In the other countries of Spanish America the mestizos predominate. The Mexican Revolution of 1910 speeded up the process, giving the Indian and his culture a prestige hitherto unknown. In the old days the aristocrats would boast that they were pure white, but now the same people tend to say, "We all have some Indian blood." In the past Chile was classed sometimes with the white, sometimes with the mestizo countries. Since the popular front government assumed power, many of the white upper class have fled. Mestizo or Indian peasants have been awarded or have seized the lands formerly owned by the heirs of the Conquistadores or of the Germans and Yugoslavs who settled the south in the last century. Chile may now be regarded as a mestizo country, if only because "the people" have come into their own.

We are going through a period when there is a taboo against open debates on the race issue; and there are many in Latin America, as well as in the United States, who avoid the subject for fear of being denounced for their race "prejudice." Nevertheless, the racial policies of Latin American governments may be explained in terms of ideologies which are no longer expressed openly. There are two problems, namely quality and quantity.

The Whites

Since the days of the Conquest, Latin America has been controlled by a more or less white, more or less Europeanized, and in recent decades more or less Americanized oligarchy. This oligarchy, or Establishment, has been the butt of furious leftist criticism, but it must be recognized that it had a certain sense of "order and progress," to use the Positivist motto. This was true of the government of Porfirio Díaz and his "scientists" in Mexico (1877-1911), of the Brazilian empire of Pedro II (1840-89) and the Positivist republic which succeeded it, and of the Conservative Party in Argentina. The power elites now range in political coloration across the spectrum from the conservatives in Brazil to the new groups which have seized power in Cuba, Chile, and Peru. Usually, these new groups slowly move, as in Mexico, from the left to the right. Few of them retain the old European cultural ideals. The new elites have modeled themselves after the United States, or more recently the Soviet Union. However, even in the leftist-controlled countries, the governing group is still predominantly white or mestizo, not Indian or black.

In the past century European immigration was regarded as the means of upgrading the population and preparing it for the industrial age. It was thanks to European immigrants that Argentina, Uruguay, and southern Brazil prospered; still today this area has the highest standard of living in Latin America. However, European immigration has virtually ceased. In the past immigrants arrived penniless and struggled to stay alive. Now, they expect to be financed, and most governments are unable or unwilling to pay the cost. In any case Europe no longer has starving masses; it is a prosperous continent to which workers from other areas flock. Some Latin American governments expected immigrants to go to backward regions where their own people did not want to serve. For example, the Bolivian Government admitted German Jewish doctors fleeing from Hitler and obliged them to go to jungle villages where their own doctors refused to work. For all of these reasons Latin America no longer attracts European emigrants. Some Italian emigrants who went to Argentina after World War II revolted when they realized the conditions in which they were expected to live, and they forced the government to send them back to Europe.

This decline in European immigration coincided with a population explosion in Latin America, resulting primarily from improved health conditions and the lack of birth control. The result is that the population owes less to European immigration and more to its own dynamics. At the same time the emigration of the white upper class has become more marked. This process has been going on since colonial times. During the wars of independence many whites fled, somewhat like the North American loyalists moving to Canada during the American Revolution. In the nineteenth century many wealthy whites preferred to live in Europe, usually in France. In the twentieth century many left their countries when a leftist regime came to power, usually by force. Mexico, Bolivia, Cuba, Chile, and Peru have exemplified this. The numbers involved were seldom great, but the result was that the power elites changed in social and even racial origins.

The Indians

The attitude of whites toward the Indians has changed profoundly. At first the theologians, who were the theoreticians of the Spanish Conquest, could not decide if the Indians were humans or animals. They finally concluded that the Indians were humans but had not reached the age of wisdom and, therefore, should be treated as minors. For this reason they were not subject to the Inquisition. To protect these children from heavy labor, a priest, Bartolomé de las Casas, proposed that blacks should be brought from Africa. Thus, slavery began. The Indians had to be protected, and trusts (encomiendas) were created. A Spanish conquistador was entrusted with a large expanse of land together with the Indians living on it. The trustee (encomendero) thereby became the master of the Indians, who were, in fact, his serfs or slaves. In this way the large estates (latifundios) were created and with them the feudalism which has been one of the curses of Latin America. Despite the declarations of the Spanish crown, the result of the Conquest was that the Indians became oppressed, silent, frightened, and resentful.

A change in attitude began with the rise of the philosophy of the goodness of nature. This philosophy became widespread in the eighteenth century and was expounded in its most notorious form by Jean-Jacques Rousseau, who affirmed that civilized man was corrupt while primitive man, "the noble savage," was still endowed with natural goodness. At the same time the "philosophers" of France and the northern countries propagated the "Black Legend," according to which Spain occupied a special place among the nations of Europe because of its tradition of cruelty, intolerance, fanaticism, lack of enlightenment, and rapacity. This

Black Legend produced a series of works on the Spanish conquest of America in which the Spaniards displayed cruelty and rapaciousness in their dealings with the Indians, who were depicted as noble and good. The Spaniard was said to kill ruthlessly in order to satisfy his unquenchable thirst for gold and silver, which the Indians admired simply for their aesthetic qualities. Above all, the works describing the Incas of Peru gave a false interpretation of pre-Columbian civilization. The European philosophers refused to recognize that the Inca empire was totalitarian and that for many Indians the Spanish tyranny was less oppressive than the tyranny of other Indian tribes. In any case the result was that the Indian was depicted in a romantic glow.

The wars of independence broke out in the first part of the nineteenth century. The motives were varied, as they had been in the American Revolution. Official history stresses the fact that the "patriots" objected to Spanish tyranny. In fact the local oligarchy wanted to control its lands, its Indians, and its fortune without the interference of the Spanish Government. The white landowners declared that they were fighting Spain in order to avenge the abuses committed by the Spaniards against the Indians. This claim was incredibly hypocritical, and, despite all the romantic literature, the real status of the Indians changed little. The landowners were the direct heirs of the Conquistadores whom they denounced.

In the second half of the nineteenth century and the early twentieth century, the oppression of the Indians was justified on theoretical grounds. Today, there is an egalitarian movement reminiscent of the French Revolution, but nineteenth-century scientists, imbued with Darwinism, proclaimed that equality goes against the laws of nature, expressed in such phrases as "the survival of the fittest" in the "struggle for existence." During the dictatorship of Porfirio Díaz the "scientists" who governed Mexico believed that the Conquest had proved the Indians to be inferior to the whites and that it was, therefore, scientifically evident that the whites should govern, while the Indians occupied an inferior position. This belief was buttressed by the dominant philosophy of Positivism (see Chapter 6).

The Mexican Revolution, which broke out in 1910, represented a sharp break with that society. The romantic spirit was reborn with its cult of the Indian, a cult which often diverged from historical reality. The murals of Diego Rivera invariably show the Spaniards as cruel monsters and the Indians as noble creatures with a great artistic sense. Rivera never depicted the cruelty which was characteristic of Aztec society and its religion. The Mexican Revolution has had deep repercussions in Spanish America and, although in Ecuador, Peru, and Bolivia there has been no revolution of comparable violence, the recent coups in all three countries reflect the same kind of problem that gave rise to the Mexican explosion. Fidel Castro launched his expedition to Cuba from Mexico, and Che Guevara's Bolivian campaign had its roots in Mexico and Cuba. He failed, but the fact remains that no Spanish American politician would now dare to speak disdainfully of the Indian.

The Indianist movement is not really an attempt to preserve the Indian way of life but rather to integrate him into the national culture. The Indianists speak affectionately of the Indians and admire their historic culture. Throughout the continent there is a movement to preserve and restore the archaeological monuments which testify to the importance of their artistic tradition. Nevertheless, the defenders of the Indian want the Indian to learn to read and write Spanish, even though Quechua or Aymara may be used as a first step toward this end. They want the Indian to become integrated into the national Europeanized society, and only a few romantics speak of restoring primitive Indian society. There is a general recognition that the ancient culture has disappeared forever, even though some Communists claim that in establishing communal property they are returning to the pre-Columbian property system. In the United States some blacks adopt African clothes and hairdos, but no Latin American Indians do anything similar except in folk festivals. In Guatemala and the Andean countries Indians dress in a mixture of native and European costumes, but their clothes are becoming progressively more Western, and the Indianists are not asking that they return to their native dress. Really, very few of the Indianists are Indians. They are whites or mestizos who have become defenders of the Indians. Spanish America is moving racially toward *mestizaje;* culturally, the mixed breeds are adopting Western civilization.

When Brazilians denounce race prejudice in the United States, they should remember that the *bandeirantes* (frontiersmen) of São Paulo made regular incursions into the interior looking for Indian slaves, and they committed innumerable atrocities. The Brazilians spoke with pride of their Service for the Protection of Indians, but in 1968 it was discovered that the Service had been guilty of so many abuses that it was abolished; it has been replaced by another agency. Following widespread newspaper publicity about the abuses, the Brazilian Government set up more

Aztecs surrounding their symbol, an eagle on a nopal cactus (without the usual snake in its beak). (From the Mendoza Collection in the Bodleian Library, Oxford, as reproduced in Lord Kingsborough, *The Antiquities of Mexico*.)

Indian reserves, where Indian life and culture will be protected. At the same time, the government is building an east-west highway to effectively incorporate Amazonia into the national territory, and it is likely that the Indians will virtually disappear within a few decades. Certainly, there is a sharp contrast between Brazil and Spanish America regarding the Indian heritage.

In colonial Spanish America there was an extraordinarily complex racial hierarchy based on all possible combinations of the three races. This was a kind of caste system which conditioned the various groups to know their place in society and to be resigned to it. The racial pattern of Latin America today is a shadow of the colonial system. Slowly the shadow is fading. How the various groups will meet the test of life once they are freed from the burden of the past is a problem which only the most self-assured futurologist would dare to predict.

The Blacks

The case of the blacks is different. For complex reasons, there has been no general movement to idealize the black as the Indian has been idealized. Theologians justified black slavery with arguments which would surprise us. In colonial society there was a very complicated racial scheme, with the whites at the top of the scale, the Indians in the middle, and the blacks at the bottom. Today for various reasons, the blacks have disappeared from almost all Spanish-speaking America, outside the Caribbean area.

The black has been more important in the non-Spanish-speaking areas. As mentioned earlier the *négritude* movement began in Martinique, and on the political rather than the cultural level the black power movement emanating from Harlem has had repercussions throughout the Caribbean. In Haiti, where there are practically no whites, the blacks, led by François Duvalier (President, 1957-71), were fighting not the whites but the mulattoes. In Brazil there is a large black and mulatto population concentrated primarily in the Northeast, but there is little evidence of black-mulatto rivalry, so for convenience we will use the general term "black." There have been few open clashes between blacks and whites such as we have had in the United States, and the white Brazilians speak with a certain affection of the blacks. They claim that they have no race prejudice because of Portuguese racial tolerance and that, therefore, Brazil has a special role to play in Africa. While these claims are to some extent justified, we should remember that Brazil was the last country of America and one of the last in the world to abolish slavery (1888). There are practically no blacks in high society, in the professions, or even in universities. The racial peace of Brazil reminds one of the Old South in the United States, where there was peace because the blacks "knew their place." If and when Brazilian blacks demand social justice and effective equality with whites, a situation could arise similar to that now prevailing in the United States.

Despite all the speeches about racial equality and the much-publicized role of the blacks in Carnival and in the life of the city of Bahia, the fact is that in Latin America the blacks form a group apart, except in the Caribbean and the Northeast of Brazil. Brazil has had a policy of "whitening" the population by encouraging the immigration of Europeans, especially of Portuguese, Italians, and Germans. Emperor Pedro II had an interesting correspondence with the Frenchman Count Gobineau, whose theories on the superiority of the white race were distorted and finally gave rise to the racism of Hitler. Far from encouraging the immigration of blacks, Brazil has forbidden it. The Dominicans stress their Spanish tradition and claim that they are white, but in fact they are predominantly mulatto (admittedly much less black than the neighboring Haitians). One of the few Spanish-speaking republics where there is a fairly high percentage of blacks is Panama, where thousands of Jamaicans came to help build the Canal. They still speak English, and other Panamanians view them with dislike.

This disdain for the black is not only a heritage of the past but is inspired by the spectacle of countries like Haiti and those of black Africa which give little assurance that the blacks are capable of running a modern state. During the Romantic period the black was sometimes surrounded with a heroic aura, but this has almost disappeared. Haiti was the first Latin American state to win its independence (1803), and the name of the liberator, Alexandre Pétion, was respected in the other republics. However, the history of independent Haiti has been tawdry, brutal, and sordid, and the grotesque dictatorship of François Duvalier (Papa Doc) aroused disgust throughout the world. The stories of O. Henry and, more recently, the novel of Graham Greene, *The Comedians* (1966), have made Haiti a byword for a harsh and pathetic dictatorship.

The Communists like to cast themselves in the role of liberators of the black, and Fidel Castro has done this. The black hero Antonio Maceo, known as "the titan of bronze," has been the object of a cult, and some blacks have risen to positions of responsibility in Cuba, but Castro's government is made up almost entirely of whites. Even in the Soviet Union, racial equality is largely a propaganda slogan.

The debate on the racial issue has not ended. The science of racial studies is still in its infancy, and it is impossible to make categorical affirmations. Physically, the black seems adapted to the wet tropics, and he is at home in the Caribbean and northeastern Brazil. The fact that in the United States blacks have moved to cities like New York, Chicago, or Detroit is due to economic and social reasons which are more powerful than ecology. The black is sometimes physically superior despite his privations, or indeed because he has not enjoyed the easy life of the white upper or middle classes. In Brazil, as in the United States, the blacks take up sports wholeheartedly, primarily soccer; sports open doors for them, while so many others are closed. The Brazilian champion soccer player, Pelé, became a national hero and a symbol of black aspirations. Significantly, Pelé married a white school teacher of simple Portuguese family. The problem is whether the black can adapt himself to the technical life of the modern world, where organization and administrative ability are so important. In the United States cities like Cleveland and Newark have elected black mayors; there are few similar cases in Latin America, except in the Caribbean.

The history of slavery is reflected in words. In the United States the word *negro* was borrowed from Spanish. "Pickaninny" came from the Portuguese *pequenina*, a diminutive of *pequena* (small), and "sambo" came from *zambo*, a mixture of black and Indian. English and American historians use the word *asiento* for the black slave trade between Africa and America. This vocabulary indicates that slavery was primarily an Afro-Spanish-Portuguese-American phenomenon which spread to the South of the United States.

In the United States anyone who has a drop of black blood is called "black," even though he is almost white. It would be logical to classify him as "white" or perhaps "mulatto." This sharp line between whites and blacks, which is the fundamental cause of racial antagonism in the United States, does not exist in Latin America. As a result of the complicated racial structure to which we have alluded, there is no clear line between blacks and whites. In some countries, such as the Dominican Republic, many "whites" have a little black blood. If a light-colored mulatto rises in the economic and social scale and behaves like a member of the white middle class, he is regarded as a white.

In Spanish colonial society there were two groups of whites. The "Peninsulars" were born in Spain, regarded themselves as 100 percent white, and occupied the highest rank in the social and administrative hierarchy. Then came the "Creoles"—whites born in America—who occupied inferior positions. It was very difficult for a Creole to become viceroy, governor, archbishop, or even bishop. One of the principal causes of the wars of independence was that the Creoles wished to occupy the high positions hitherto reserved for the Peninsulars. In a famous essay on Simón Bolívar, Karl Marx accused him of being a false revolutionary because he represented the ambitious Creoles and not the people.

The Creoles claimed to be white, and most of them were, although some rich mulattoes succeeded in passing themselves off as Creoles. Each person belonged officially to a racial group, and sometimes a rich mulatto would bribe a government registrar to upgrade his racial classification. It is possible that Simón Bolívar had some black blood. In view of this and in view of the dark complexion of Spaniards and Portuguese, the custom arose in English of designating mulattoes, as well as whites, as Creoles. This happened in New Orleans, but in discussing Latin America we must remember that Creole means a white person born in the New World.

In the United States many blacks talk about returning to the African way of life, although this really means little. In Latin America where the blacks have far more traces of their African heritage, there is no propaganda for such a return. The only real exception is in the British islands of the Caribbean, especially Jamaica, where among the Ras Tafari "blackness" has been stimulated by agents from Harlem. No black leader in Latin America (outside of the Caribbean there are none) has demanded that Swahili be taught in the public schools. The blacks want to enjoy the middle-class life, and they know the importance of being able to read and write English, Spanish, or Portuguese.

However, there is a return to Africa in religious cults, as in the Brazilian *macumba*. This curious phenomenon worries some Brazilians, who fear that their country is being Africanized, abandoning the European culture of which Brazil was so proud. Despite this, black Latin Americans show little interest in Africa. Many black leaders in the United States have gone to Africa to seek their racial origins. Partly for economic reasons very few Latin American blacks have done this, and there are practically no relations between black Latin Americans and black Africans.

Yet Africa is relatively close to Brazil, and there are marked ethnic and cultural similarities.

Some Latin American countries, like Brazil, feel a vague ethnic relationship with the countries of black Africa, and for this reason Brazil claims to have a manifest destiny in Africa. The present military dictatorship in Brazil has allied itself with the Portuguese dictatorship which is defending Portuguese sovereignty in Angola and Mozambique against the attacks coming from the independent black countries. On the other side, Fidel Castro has intervened in Africa in support of the blacks.

There is no black immigration to Latin America, and it is almost certain that Latin American governments would block such immigration, and except for a few Jamaican blacks who go to cut sugar in Cuba, and Caribbean blacks who go to England, the United States, and Canada in search of work, there is no emigration. It is, therefore, absurd for Latin Americans to affirm that the United States is a monster of race prejudice and should follow the Latin American example. The Latin American attitude may be explained in part by the fear of adding another poor, illiterate element to the population, but the simple fact is that Latin America does not wish to be placed on the same level as Africa.

In the United States the black is much more important than the Indian. In Latin America the reverse is true. The black is important in only a few countries, while the Indian plays a continental role. The status of the Indian is complex. At the time of the Spanish Conquest the high Indian cultures were concentrated in areas, such as Mexico and Peru, of intense sunlight and low humidity. The Indian seems physiologically adapted to these conditions. There were Indians in the humid tropical zones and in cold wet regions (such as southern Chile), but they were quite primitive. Apart from the problem of biological adaptation, there were material obstacles to the development of native cultures, such as the density of the tropical forests and the diseases carried by insects, which multiply fantastically in the humid tropics.

The Origin of the Indians

The origin of man is still a mystery, although some anthropologists such as Louis S. B. Leakey affirm that he came from Africa. Some Argentine and Brazilian ethnographers claimed that the native American developed in South America, but this theory has been abandoned. U.S. anthropologists generally accept the thesis of

Ales Hrdlicka that the American Indians entered this continent via the Bering Strait and moved south, each wave being pushed by the following wave, until they reached Tierra del Fuego. There is still disagreement as to the date at which the Indians reached the various regions of the New World. European anthropologists generally accept the Hrdlicka thesis, but they believe, following the French anthropologist Paul Rivet, that some migrations came across the Pacific. The Norwegian explorer Thor Heyerdahl has written a number of works on pre-Columbian relations across the Pacific, and *Kon Tiki* (1948), the story of his journey on a raft across the Pacific, has been translated into sixty-two languages. Although his scientific studies are serious, and the New York Academy of Sciences elected him a fellow in 1960, some U.S. anthropologists have treated him with unjustified disdain.

There have also been many discussions on the origins of pre-Columbian cultures. There are resemblances between Asian and Indo-American life. Do these similarities derive from migration or parallel evolution? How should we assess the civilization of pre-Columbian Indians? They did not know how to smelt iron, and even the civilization of the Incas of Peru was of a megalithic type. They did not use the wheel, a fact which disturbs the Mormons, since the *Book of Mormon* speaks of chariots in pre-Columbian America. As has happened in various areas around the world, the Aztecs knew the principle of the wheel and used it in their toys, but they did not develop it for practical purposes. Claims are made for Indian culture which often seem inspired by patriotic enthusiasm rather than an objective analysis of the evidence. The Mexican Samuel Martí maintains that the Aztecs had a great musical culture which was destroyed by the Spanish Conquistadores, while Angel Garibay has written books to prove that the Aztecs had a developed philosophy. Dreams of a glorious but nonexistent Aztec past have in recent years revived the myth of Aztlán, a kind of Mexican Atlantis very different from the bloody reality of Aztec culture—a weird chapter of intellectual history which only recently has been unraveled.

A similar problem has arisen in connection with the calculations of the population of pre-Columbian America. The Peruvian Manuel Tello, an Indianist (and Indian) anthropologist, claimed that the Inca empire had a population of 80 million, a far higher figure than is usually accepted. The argument is still going on. A group of scholars at the University of California, Berkeley, has studied the evidence of colonial records and concluded that the Spanish Conquest was followed by a sharp drop in the native population, while the Argentinian Angel Rosenblat rejects their calculations, thus denying the allegations that the Conquest had such disastrous consequences. The two schools continue their argument with considerable vehemence. The Indianists usually exaggerate the value of the culture and the numbers of pre-Columbian Indians, while the Hispanophiles, like the Mexican "scientists" and the Positivists, follow the opposite tendency. Each group is trying to justify the historical tradition it supports. The practical problem today is what to do with the Indians so that the republics where they live may escape from their present backwardness.

The Asian Tie

In the same way as the black feels attracted toward Africa, the Indian senses a vague relationship with Asia. We are not speaking of the masses of Indians who are scarcely aware of the identity of the republic in which they live but of the Indianists and those Indians who have had some contact with the Chinese or Japanese groups of Latin America. During World War II, the Japanese used this in their propaganda, and now Communist China is doing the same thing. The difference between the case of the blacks and that of the Indians is that the blacks arrived in fairly recent times (although some probably came before the Spanish Conquest), bringing with them their culture (some blacks who came from Arab-dominated regions of Africa even knew how to write Arabic), whereas the arrival of the Indians in a remote era is an academic theory which has not reached the Indian masses of today.

Despite the propaganda, there is not much sympathy in Latin America for the Asians. As small businessmen, the Chinese have aroused the same resentment as they have in Southeast Asia. In Panama there have been laws against them, and the Mexican Pancho Villa hated them so much that he ordered them executed whenever found. In recent years there has been considerable Japanese immigration, especially to Brazil and Peru, and they are a splendid catalyst. Indeed, the solution for the problems of many Latin American countries might be a mass immigration of Japanese. The Japanese have opened up the west of the state of São Paulo in Brazil and are now opening up Amazonia, which is practically empty. The Brazilians have shown a great reluctance to migrate there, and a plan to people the area with Chinese in the early years of this century was defeated by propaganda against "mongolization." Possibly, native Brazilians will now follow the Japanese into Amazonia, especially since the building of an east-west highway through the valley. The Japanese are now generally accepted and even admired. As yet there has been little intermarriage between Japanese and other groups in Latin America, and in Peru (but not in Brazil) this has aroused a touch of resentment because the Japanese hold themselves aloof. Japanese propaganda in World War II had no success because Japan was allied with the Axis and, by weird racial chemistry, the Japanese had been declared honorary Aryans by the Nazis. (A similar "honor" is accorded today to Japanese businessmen visiting South Africa.)

Chinese Communist propaganda has had far more success, not among the Indians themselves but rather among mestizo intellectuals. Latin American Communists are sharply divided into Muscovites and Pekinese, or Maoists. The Muscovites have preferred an orderly bloodless revolution (even though they are still supporting Castro's activities, just as they are arming guerrilla fighters in Africa), whereas the Maoists have favored violence. Now that Peking is joining the international community, it is probable that it, too, will adopt officially a less violent policy, even though like Moscow it will support revolution where it seems practical.

Both Moscow and Peking are struggling for hegemony of the Third World, and sometimes Latin America, because of its racial composition and backwardness, is classed with Asia and Africa as constituting the Third World. The white upper class resents this, but the growing mestizo groups will join the Third World if they find it convenient, just as they will collaborate with the United States and Europe if it seems to their advantage. There are no reliable figures on the various racial groups in Latin America, but outside of Argentina and Uruguay the whites are certainly in a minority, and the population feels no racial solidarity with the United States or even Europe. Indeed, the publicity given to U.S. race problems creates in Latin America an antipathy which has been used by Fidel Castro and other anti-American propagandists.

Race and Society

The fact is that where there is a white population the countries have prospered; even in Brazil the driving force comes from the south, where the population is almost entirely European in origin.

Where the masses of the population are black or Indian, development has been slow or has even been reversed. The centers of U.S. cities have deteriorated since the blacks took them over, and Haiti, which was one of the most prosperous countries in the world under French colonial domination, is now the most miserable in the continent. There are some special cases. Thanks to oil, Venezuela, like the Arabian oil states, has boomed. Because of a number of factors, including proximity to the United States and an aggressive business class, Mexico has achieved, at least in certain places, an apparent prosperity; and Puerto Rico's tie with the United States has boosted its economy markedly.

As in the United States, racial and economic imbalance has brought population movements in Latin America. Whereas in this country the blacks have moved into the centers of the large northern cities, in Latin America the Indians have built shanty towns around the edges of the capitals. In some cities such as Rio de Janeiro, Caracas, and Lima these shantytowns reach almost into the business districts.

The problem both in the United States and in Latin America is to educate these new urban masses rapidly enough to save the cities. Some sociologists believe this is impossible and that the cities of both the Americas are caught in an irreversible decadence. This is not only a racial phenomenon; cities such as São Paulo, Montevideo, and Buenos Aires, where the population is white, were in the past very impressive, but now they are suffering from some of the diseases which affect large U.S. cities. However, where the urban problem is complicated by a racial problem, the result is disaster.

The East Indians

Other smaller racial groups should be mentioned. In the former British colonies of Trinidad and Guyana there is a large East Indian population, descended from the workers who came when migration throughout the Empire was free. In Surinam, likewise, there is a large East Indian (primarily Indonesian) population, and the latest census shows that they now have a clear majority. These populations are almost nonexistent in the Latin American republics; quite apart from the language barrier, the governments have kept them out. Like the Chinese, the Indians have been primarily small businessmen, and Latin American governments do not want this kind of migrant. Indian intellectuals are welcomed, however. There has been a minor cult of Rabindranath

Tagore, especially in Brazil, which feels a certain kinship with India, since they are the only major countries in the tropics. There is no interest in Indonesian culture, and Brazilians never compare their country with Indonesia, which likewise is tropical and has a population numerically almost equal to that of Brazil. Moreover, Brazil and Indonesia have a cultural unity which India, unfortunately, lacks.

The Jews

The position of the Jews in Latin America is curious. Jews are divided into two main groups, the Sephardic (descendants of the Spanish and Portuguese Jews who went into exile after 1492 rather than be converted to Catholicism) and the Ashkenazic (the Jews from Central and Eastern Europe—primarily Russia, Poland, and Germany). The main task of the Spanish Inquisition was to ferret out heresy, including "Judaism" among the converted Sephardics, and it is believed that thousands of them came to Spanish and Portuguese America to escape the tentacles of the "Holy Office." It is asserted that cities like Medellín in Colombia and São Paulo in Brazil were peopled largely by Sephardic Jews. This is difficult to prove, since now their descendants have mingled with the remainder of the population, and not many Sephardic congregations exist in Latin America. Even anti-Semitic Latin Americans speak with affection of this Sephardic tradition, just as Californians who despise Mexicans like to boast about their state's Spanish tradition.

The position of the Ashkenazic Jews in Latin America is less fortunate. Many migrated to Latin America, especially to Argentina, to escape from pogroms, and there is a Jewish subculture in Argentina. However, at the time of Hitler the flood of refugees, most of whom were hoping to move on from Latin America to the United States (where the quota system was still in effect) provoked a rash of anti-Semitism, especially among those groups which admired fascism. Would-be immigrants had to specify their religion, and often Jews simply did not receive visas unless they bribed the consul heavily. There was also fear of competition from hard-working, competent, aggressive Jews among Latin American businessmen and professionals, who tried to make sure that the Jews went to places where they themselves would refuse to live. A peculiar Jewish colony was Sosúa on the north coast of the Dominican Republic. Dictator Rafael Trujillo killed three birds with one stone: the Jews had to pay heavily for their visas, the Dominican Republic established a progressive community in a backward area, and the Jewish power elite in the United States was grateful to have a kind of Ellis Island for refugees waiting to get into the United States. In Argentina, which was blacklisted in a U.S. Government blue book for its ties with the Axis, a wave of anti-Semitism unique in Latin America made life difficult for the old Ashkenazic colony and provoked protests from U.S. Jewish leaders. In the United States a Jew can rise to be a Justice of the Supreme Court or a Representative to the United Nations, but in Argentina this would be unthinkable. Peronism, i.e. fascist-inspired totalitarianism, is still very strong in Argentina. It claims to defend the shirtless ones, but the Jews wear shirts and ties.

The "Arabs"

In Latin America generally there has been nothing like the anti-Semitism which formerly existed in the United States and Europe. Since black power does not exist in most countries, the new antagonism between blacks and Jews is not in evidence. There is, however, a peculiar form of race prejudice unknown in the United States, directed against the colonies from the Near Eastern countries. Most belong to one Christian sect or another, and they are made up of refugees who fled when Turkey controlled their countries. For this reason they are scornfully referred to as "Turks" or "Arabs," even though most of them came from Lebanon or Syria. As they rise in economic and social status, they are known as "Syrians," "Syrio-Lebanese," and finally "Lebanese." Most of them become demonstratively Catholic, so theoretically there is no religious antagonism, but by their hard work, commercial astuteness, and evident prosperity, they arouse widespread jealousy. Something similar happened to the Jews in the United States and Europe.

Toward the Arab world the Latin American countries have an ambivalent attitude, as have Spain and Portugal. There is a historical and spiritual affinity between both worlds, and there are curious carry-overs of Arab behavior patterns into the Americas. Intellectuals have often noted this, sometimes with pleasure, sometimes with disgust, but in any case Latin American governments do not want Arab immigration.

All these factors come into play in the competition between Israel and the Arab countries for Latin American votes in the United Nations. Israel has carried on a forceful propaganda in Latin America and has sent technical missions to several Latin

American countries. The Arab approach has been more emotional than professional. Yet an analysis of voting patterns in the United Nations shows that the Latin American governments have frequently sided with the Arab states against Israel.

The Customs

The historical and sociological process we have described is reflected in Latin American customs. Native customs and dress survive best in isolated places where there are Indians. Although there are Indian groups who are proud of their past and wish to preserve their way of life, it is obvious that throughout the continent it is disappearing. In many countries native dress can be seen only at folk festivals organized by the government to attract tourists. In Mexico—in Tehuantepec, for example—it is now difficult to see the beautiful native dress outside of fiestas for American tourists and for Europeanized Mexicans who have a romantic nostalgia for a world they never knew. They are similar to the white businessmen of Santa Barbara, California, many of them not born in California, who look down on the local Mexicans but dress up as *charros* (Spanish horsemen) to recreate a California which, in fact, never existed.

In Guatemala one seldom sees the costumes which were common thirty years ago. The products on sale at the famous Indian market of Huancayo in the Peruvian Andes are now scarcely Indian at all. The Bolivian Government has established an international folklore festival, but even in Bolivia the Indians ride bicycles and behave like any other modern proletariat.

It has not been easy for the Indians to abandon their native customs, and in the past there was a fairly sharp line between the mestizos who had adopted Western habits and the Indians who clung to their native customs. In Guatemala there is an interesting word, *ladino* (i.e. "Latin"), to designate those who have broken with the native tradition and have adopted the European way of life. There are villages of Indians and villages of *ladinos*, and there is no love lost between the two groups.

It is hard for a white man to understand the trauma the Indians suffered as a result of the Conquest. The sad, dirty, silent Indians of the Andes look subhuman, but the splendid pre-Columbian *huacos* (pots) in the shape of happy or sad human faces make us realize that even under the Inca dictatorship the Indians had a life rich in human emotions. After four centuries the Andean Indians are still in a state of bewilderment, sadness, and apathy, provoked by the defeat their ancestors suffered at the hands of the Conquistadores.

When we speak of the disappearance of native customs, we must remember that many customs commonly regarded as native are, in fact, Spanish. Sometimes pictures of "Indian" villages of Spanish America show a scene which in reality is totally colonial. The Indian wears a sombrero of Andalusian origin and European-type denim pants. His donkey is the heir of Spanish donkeys. In the background there is the façade of a baroque church which is European in architecture, although the native handiwork is evident in some details. Admittedly, the Peruvian Indians with their llamas and the Indian women spinning with a spindle have kept a large measure of their original culture; but if we examine their life style carefully, we will see that it is largely colonial. For example, the mayors of Andean villages carry as their symbol of office rods introduced by the Spaniards.

In many parts of Spanish America where there are no Indians, there are no Indian customs. In Argentina, for example, gaucho dress is not common now, and in any case it is of colonial, not Indian, origin. The ordinary Argentinian dresses like a European, and Argentinian visitors to the United States are annoyed when they are invited to a party and told to come in their "native costume."

The upper classes in Latin America are proud of their good European manners, and traditional society is characterized by its social refinement. A coat and tie of the best English or French cut sets the cultured man apart from the worker or the peasant. Often American tourists shock Latin Americans by their lack of respect for etiquette. In some restaurants only those wearing coats and ties are admitted. In this era of generalized vulgarity, traditional elegance is excellent and at the same time a little silly. The English way of dressing, with coat and tie, developed in a country where the weather is seldom hot. Wearing a coat and tie in the tropics is uncomfortable and irritating, and we must feel sorry for the priests and nuns who wear heavy clerical garments which provide excellent protection against the cold in a convent in Castile but which in Latin America must be oppressive. In the tropics, Indians dressed more sensibly; they went almost naked.

There is a reaction against the European manner of dress. The Latin American no longer feels the need to imitate Europeans slavishly. Even a conservative sociologist like Gilberto Freyre has pointed out the lack of functional relationship between European dress and the Brazilian climate. Above all, European men's clothes have become the symbol of the oligarchy which is under so much attack. There is a song from the wars of independence reflecting the hatred the American *descamisado* (shirtless one) felt for the Spanish oppressor. In those days the shirt was the symbol of the oligarchy. Perón chose the word *descamisados* to refer to the masses he was inciting against the oligarchy. His "shirtless ones" wore shirts but not jackets. A shirt of some special color (black, brown) was typical of European fascism; workers traditionally wore shirts but not ties.

In Cuba a strange phenomenon has occurred. In the days of the oligarchy, upper- and middle-class men wore white suits and ties. White cloth was cooler than dark, but it was still too hot for the damp tropics. Even the upper class, therefore, began to wear a *guayabera,* a kind of sports shirt. In Communist Cuba, to wear a jacket and tie would be almost an antirevolutionary declaration; but to go in shirtsleeves is not, as in temperate Argentina, a demonstration of leftist ideas. Therefore, the habit developed of wearing battle fatigues to show one's absolute faith in Fidel Castro and his revolution. In a curious parallel with China and the guerrilla fighters of Mao Tse-tung in Yenan, this manner of dress recalled the struggle of Castro's guerrilla fighters who landed in Cuba in the yacht "Granma" and established a mountain camp in the Sierra Maestra. They wore olive green battle fatigues, and this color is now the symbol of Cuba's revolutionary army. For the crossing from Mexico to Cuba in the "Granma," these clothes were practical, but for the ordinary life in the tropics they are too heavy.

It is impossible to talk about Fidel Castro without thinking of his beard and his bearded ones. Since the colonial period, the beard had been the symbol of the oligarchy and of the aristocratic intellectuals. Almost all American Indians have hairless chins and lips, so the beard became the hallmark of the European. Castro reversed the symbolism of the beard and made it the symbol of his lower-class revolution. He may have been inspired by the medieval Spanish hero the Cid, who fought against his oppressors, both Christian and Moorish, as Castro fought against his Cuban and American "oppressors." He himself explained that in the Sierra Maestra beards provided protection against mosquitoes. The beard became the symbol of Castro's revolution, and American activists appear to have picked up from Castro the habit of growing a beard. However, for Castro the beard is the historic symbol of his revolutionaries; he does not want it to be regarded frivolously, or his regime to look like a government of hippies. He has, therefore, insisted that young Cubans should shave; and in any case beards are seldom worn in Communist societies. To eradicate the hippie spirit, Castro has imposed a military discipline in universities and schools. Most U.S. admirers of Fidel would be horrified if they were subjected to the discipline imposed on young Cubans. It is probable that the beard will disappear from Cuba with Castro. In reality, however useful the beard may be in northern countries without central heating, in the tropics it is more absurd than coat and tie.

The rebellion against the dressing habits of the oligarchy comes also from the other side, from the economic climbers: ambitious, practical, modern individuals, would-be capitalists who wish to show that they have broken with the unprogressive past and are forward-looking like U.S. entrepreneurs, whom they imitate with the same enthusiasm with which their grandfathers copied European elegance. These individuals dress like Americans, drink Coca Cola, and make no attempt to carry on the refined and elegant manners of the old oligarchy.

The old oligarchs were men of culture, and many of them had excellent private libraries. The new oligarch does not read. He watches Westerns on television and assumes that this makes him appear progressive. The old oligarchy built beautiful cities like Havana, Rio de Janeiro, and Buenos Aires which emulated their mecca, Paris. The new oligarchy is indifferent to traditional beauty. There are some exceptions: the new oligarchy which controls Mexico through the official party, PRI (Partido Revolucionario Institucional), has shown a splendid sense of urban planning in developing Mexico City and Guadalajara, but that is because in those cities the old oligarchs had left a tradition of beauty. The newly rich industrial oligarchy of Monterrey, without roots in the past, has shown itself as blind to urban beauty as the industrial oligarchy of São Paulo. Despite the famous artistic biennial exposition, the aesthetic ideal of the businessmen of São Paulo is a factory and a piece of industrial machinery. The visitor to Brasília wonders if the ministries of the new capital, built by São Paulo construction firms, are factories or barracks for the military allies of the São Paulo oligarchy. This is a sorry end for the legacy of beauty which Brazil inherited from the Portuguese colonial regime and from the Europeanized oligarchy of the last century.

It is true that those who built cities like Paris thought primarily of visual beauty and not of the infrastructure which makes a city work. They were not deeply concerned with such matters as drinking water, sewers, bathrooms, or with the life of the worker who badly needed adequate housing. The oligarchy did not represent the masses and did not foresee the needs and problems of the future, but then U.S. leaders have shown even less vision about the future of our cities.

There were aspects of traditional life which should disappear, such as the Andean Indians' custom of chewing coca to kill their hunger and to deaden the misery of life. At the same time, traditional life in Latin America had a charm which is fading away. Many small cities had a quiet and sane life. Americans laugh at the custom of taking a siesta, but in the tropics it is sensible to rest during the heat of the day and to resume work in the fresh hours of the late afternoon. The United States has contributed actively to the Americanization of Latin American cities and life, but this would have happened in any case. Unfortunately, the large U.S. cities no longer function, and the same may be said of Latin American cities like São Paulo which think they are so progressive. The old-fashioned, cultured Latin American had a distinct personality. The new Latin American middle class is a poor imitation of the U.S. middle class. The Guatemalan Indian used to wear his colorful costume; now he wears jeans. Shall all of these developments be considered as progress?

The Population Explosion

The study of the composition of the Latin American population has led us to no definite conclusions as to the results of the ethnic mixture in Latin America. Closely related to the qualitative is the urgent quantitative issue of the numerical increase, of the now-notorious population explosion. Of all the areas of the world, Latin America is the one where the population problem presents the most contradictory aspects. It is the region with the highest net population growth, and this is especially marked in Central America and the Caribbean. It is probable, then, that the Caribbean will be the epicenter of social disturbances, which will continue regardless of whether Castro stays in power in Cuba.

No one thought seriously about the population explosion until World War II. Everyone believed that Latin America was an empty continent that had to be filled. The white race was thought to be the most apt to develop the continent, and, as we have seen, European immigration was stimulated, with good results, especially in the "Southern Cone" and the south of Brazil. A certain density of population was necessary to justify and make possible the building of highways, railroads, telegraphic communications, and so on—what modern economists call "the infrastructure" of a nation. Today, a government regards the infrastructure as its responsibility; in the nineteenth century the infrastructure was usually developed by private companies, often foreign, and by the immigrants themselves.

It was not foreseen that immigration and development would bring serious problems, just as it was not foreseen in the United States that the importation of black slaves would later result, not in agricultural progress, but in terrible social tensions. The population of Latin America began to grow at an excessive rate, due in large measure to the introduction of sanitation and the reduction of child mortality, a humanitarian development which the United States helped generously. This reduction in child mortality brought a sharp increase in the number of children and, thereby, the need for schools. Even with the help of the United States, Latin American nations could not build enough schools or pay the miserable salaries Latin American teachers have to live on. The conditions in the countryside were such that even the peasants did not wish to stay there. In addition, the introduction of modern machinery reduced the need for agricultural workers, although in general Latin American agriculture is far less mechanized than that of the United States, and in mountainous regions mechanization is often impossible. In any case, millions of children were left without schools or possibilities of employment. The peasants and their families poured into the large cities under the illusion that they would find work there and enjoy the wellbeing which was absent in the country. Unfortunately, as black Americans know too well, there is little demand for unskilled labor in cities. In a modern technical society there is no place for an illiterate peasant. The peasants, therefore, sought refuge in cancerous shantytowns and lived there in subhuman conditions.

This process of degeneration of the large cities went on unchecked for some time. Lewis Mumford warned Americans of the approaching disaster as early as the 1920s, but practically no one listened to him. Only after World War II, when there were violent disorders in the black districts of the major cities, did Americans realize that something had to be done. Urban renewal programs were started. In Latin America the problem likewise grew steadily worse, but no one understood its seriousness until Fidel Castro's victory in 1959 established the first Communist government in the Americas. The other American nations were frightened when

THE POPULATION EXPLOSION

	1920	1930	1940	1950	1960	1970	1980	1990	2000
Argentina	8,861	11,896	14,169	17,085	20,850	24,352	28,218	31,909	35,274
Bolivia	1,918	2,153	2,508	3,013	3,696	4,658	6,006	7,782	10,081
Brazil	27,404	33,568	41,233	52,326	70,327	93,245	124,000	164,374	215,510
Chile	3,783	4,424	5,147	6,058	7,683	9,717	11,461	13,734	16,272
Colombia	6,057	7,350	9,077	11,629	15,877	22,160	31,366	43,130	56,731
Costa Rica	421	499	619	849	1,249	1,736	2,281	2,945	3,682
Cuba	2,950	3,838	4,566	5,520	6,819	8,341	10,075	12,053	14,337
Dominican Republic	1,140	1,400	1,759	2,303	3,129	4,348	6,197	8,866	12,539
Ecuador	1,898	2,160	2,586	3,225	4,323	6,028	8,440	11,774	16,149
El Salvador	1,168	1,443	1,633	1,922	2,512	3,441	4,904	7,122	10,372
Guatemala	1,450	1,771	2,201	3,024	3,965	5,282	7,018	9,357	12,355
Haiti	2,124	2,422	2,825	3,380	4,138	5,229	6,838	9,144	12,347
Honduras	783	948	1,119	1,389	1,849	2,583	3,661	5,182	7,205
Mexico	14,500	16,589	19,815	26,640	36,046	50,718	71,387	99,669	135,089
Nicaragua	639	742	893	1,133	1,501	2,021	2,818	3,951	5,460
Panama	429	502	595	765	1,021	1,406	1,938	2,669	3,633
Paraguay	699	880	1,111	1,337	1,740	2,419	3,456	4,860	6,619
Peru	4,862	5,651	6,681	7,968	10,024	13,586	18,527	25,143	33,491
Uruguay	1,391	1,704	1,947	2,198	2,542	2,889	3,251	3,642	3,999
Venezuela	2,408	2,950	3,710	5,330	7,741	10,755	14,979	19,952	26,100
Latin America Total	**84,885**	**102,889**	**124,194**	**157,094**	**207,032**	**274,914**	**366,821**	**487,258**	**637,245**
Bahamas	55	61	70	79	113	162	216	272	330
Barbados	155	159	179	211	233	254	263	236	212
British Honduras	44	51	56	67	91	126	170	218	261
French Guiana	26	30	30	25	32	41	58	86	123
Guadeloupe	150	160	185	206	273	359	443	532	612
Guyana	295	309	344	423	564	745	995	1,309	1,646
Jamaica	855	1,009	1,212	1,385	1,629	1,996	2,382	2,754	3,102
Martinique	165	175	200	222	285	355	419	483	540
Netherlands Antilles	55	72	107	162	192	222	266	314	362
Panama Canal Zone	20	25	31	42	35	39	47	58	71
Puerto Rico	1,312	1,552	1,880	2,218	2,362	2,842	3,200	3,540	3,878
Surinam	130	170	193	215	290	392	543	749	982
Trinidad and Tobago	389	405	510	632	831	1,067	1,255	1,411	1,555
Windward and Leeward Islands	280	301	352	381	448	524	584	636	696
Total	**88,854**	**107,408**	**129,589**	**163,411**	**214,465**	**284,126**	**377,765**	**499,969**	**651,737**

Source: Economic Commission for Latin America.

This table, summarizing the population growth of Latin America since 1920, covers the whole of Latin America but separates the twenty Latin American republics from the other territories, giving a total for the republics and then a grand total for the area. Obviously, the projections for the future are uncertain. The striking fact is that by the year 2000 Brazil will supposedly have a population of 215 million, out of a total of nearly 652 million for the whole area. Mexico will have 135 million, but there is no indication that Mexico can support such a population with a decent standard of living. It is for this reason that, after rejecting the whole concept of population control out of hand, the Mexican authorities have suddenly come to realize that the country faces a crisis. Colombia will have 57 million, and, given the rugged nature of much of the country, it too will face an almost insoluble problem, although it hopes to open up the tropical lowlands in the southeast of the country. Argentina, the one country where there is obviously space for more population, since no other country has so much habitable land, will have 35 million. One major technical problem is how much of Latin America's land may be made habitable. For example, Herman Kahn suggested "conquering" the Amazon area by building several large lakes which would hold the enormous water flow, preventing flooding and permitting irrigation in the dry season. Brazilians greeted Kahn's suggestion with anger. Whether the plan of the present government to open up the area for population simply by building an east-west highway through it will succeed is dubious. Ecologists warn that the climate of the whole area and indeed of the world may change. The Brazilian Government claims that the country is so big that the environment can take more blows than in more crowded countries; the ecologists must not hold up "progress."

---

they realized that in all Latin America, both in the countryside and in the cities, there was an extremely dangerous situation which could bring about a Communist revolution. The official U.S. reaction was clear; Latin American governments must be helped to improve their police and their armies so that they could suppress riots and maintain the capitalist order. In addition social reform programs had to be introduced: more schools, more U.S.-style labor unions, more industrialization to create jobs (and also to provide a market for U.S. investments). The Latin American Free Trade Association was created to broaden the market for industry and thereby permit what economists call "economies of scale," i.e. factories big enough to produce at a low unit cost. Since all these measures were not sufficient to solve the problems arising from the population explosion, birth control had to be introduced, as had been done in India and Japan, where the population explosion had likewise created serious problems. At first the U.S. government avoided the issue, but finally under President Lyndon B. Johnson, it began to speak clearly on this sensitive matter. Private organizations could act more frankly, and U.S. foundations, especially Ford, Rockefeller and Tinker, promoted the study of the problem by Latin American scientists. Clearly, birth control could not be imposed from the outside. It could be introduced only by Latin Americans themselves—scientists, intellectuals, and government officials.

The reaction in Latin America was varied. Some supposedly educated Latin Americans still do not understand the population problem. They say that the Indians and the blacks are happy in their misery. Or, as one upper-class Catholic woman in Mexico once said when the misery of the poor was brought out, "They will have their reward in heaven." Since Latin American culture is still more aesthetic than scientific and since the social sciences still have not taken root deeply in Latin America, there is much more indifference to population problems there than in the United States.

Many Latin Americans still believe that there is a direct and simple relation between the number of inhabitants of a country and its importance. There are still Brazilians who say with pride that one day their country, which now has 100 million inhabitants, will have 500 million. They believe that this would make Brazil more important than the United States or the Soviet Union, whereas in reality it would make Brazil the India of the New World. It is curious that the Brazilians who are interested in India do not realize this. There are already more Latin Americans than North Americans, and anti-U.S. intellectuals, when the population explosion is mentioned, say arrogantly, "Some day we shall be twice as numerous as the gringos!" This may well happen, but it does not bode well for the relations between the two Americas. They would be like those between China and the Soviet Union— different cultures, with the more populous country complaining bitterly that the less populous but more powerful country had seized some of its territories in the nineteenth century.

Moreover, Latin Americans still judge the importance of cities by the number of their inhabitants. In the developed countries we no longer engage in the sterile argument over the population of London, New York, or Tokyo to decide which is the largest and, therefore, the most important and most modern city. We know today that large cities are a disaster. Some urban specialists say that no city should have more than 250,000 inhabitants. Of the three aforementioned cities, Tokyo now has the greatest population and also the most problems. In Latin America there is still a belief in the alleged relationship between the population of a city and its importance, and the numerical comparison between Mexico City and Buenos Aires still gives rise to debate. The inhabitants of São Paulo are proud that their city is the largest in Brazil, perhaps as big as Buenos Aires, but they do not see how it has deteriorated, while the small cities of the interior retain their charm and health.

In a way the problem is more serious in Latin America than in the United States. It is generally thought that Latin America is an essentially agricultural area, and indeed half of the population is still rural, but with the migration to the cities it has in parts become very urbanized. The extreme case is Uruguay, where half of the population lives in Montevideo. In Argentina a quarter of the population lives in greater Buenos Aires. In a few places such as Mexico City the government has exercised some control and imposed urban planning. In others, as in São Paulo and Rio de Janeiro, there has been unbridled land speculation, as in the United States, and the result has been an inhuman, ugly development. To some extent Rio de Janeiro is saved by its landscape, but the famous Copacabana district is now a concrete jungle without charm. Old timers recall the gracious Rio before the boom and regret that it has disappered. The most popular Brazilian poem has as its refrain "My land has palm trees where the sabiá sings," the sabiá being a tropical bird. Today there are few palm trees in Rio de Janeiro and even fewer in São Paulo, and a sabiá would be incensed at the thought of living in either of the two Brazilian metropolises. Unfortunately, the anguish Americans feel when they think of their urban problems is not shared by many Latin Americans. Each year the smog gets worse, but few seem worried. At the Stockholm U.N. conference on environmental problems in 1972 the attitude of most Latin American delegates was that they could not afford environmental controls which would hold up their industrialization and that Latin America still had vast empty spaces so a little smog would do no serious harm. Environmental controls were fine for the United States but not for them. Industrial power means much more to them than the quality of life.

There is a group of Latin American scientists and intellectuals who are aware of the danger of the population explosion, but there is powerful resistance from two sides. Apart from the ignorance, the indifference, and the optimism of which we have spoken, the two centers of opposition are at ideological extremes: the Roman Catholic Church and the Communist Party. Birth control presents doctrinal problems for both.

THE LARGEST CITIES OF LATIN AMERICA, 1970

Countries	Cities	Population in Thousands	Percentage of National Population
Argentina	Buenos Aires	8,400	34.5
	Rosario	803	3.3
	Córdoba	791	3.2
	Mendoza	573	2.3
	La Plata	556	2.2
Bolivia	La Paz	564	12.1
	Cochabamba	123	2.6
	Oruro	112	2.4
	Santa Cruz	97	2.0
	Potosí	82	1.8
Brazil	São Paulo	7,849	8.4
	Rio de Janeiro	6,821	7.3
	Recife	1,626	1.7
	Belo Horizonte	1,436	1.5
	Pôrto Alegre	1,410	1.5
Chile	Santiago	2,781	28.4
	Valparaíso	314	3.2
	Concepción	183	1.9
	Viña del Mar	169	1.7
	Antofagasta	128	1.3
Colombia	Bogotá	2,551	11.5
	Medellín	1,012	4.6
	Cali	872	3.9
	Barranquilla	695	3.1
	Cartagena	307	1.4
Costa Rica	San José	440	24.5
	Alajuela	24	1.3
	Punta Arenas	24	1.3
	Limón	24	1.3
Cuba	Havana	1,963	23.5
	Santiago de Cuba	276	3.3
	Camagüey	185	2.2
	Guantánamo	149	1.8
	Santa Clara	144	1.7
Dominican Republic	Santo Domingo	671	15.4
	Santiago de los Caballeros	155	3.6
Ecuador	Guayaquil	766	12.7
	Quito	532	8.8
	Cuenca	80	1.3
	Ambato	71	1.2
	Manta	60	1.0

This table shows the relationship of the largest cities in each country of Latin America to the total population of the country. In general the population is concentrated in the capitals. Only Brazil has many large centers: São Paulo (8 million), Rio de Janeiro (7 million), Recife, Belo Horizonte, and Pôrto Alegre (about 1.5 million each). The largest city in Latin America is still Buenos Aires (8.5 million), although Mexico City

Countries	Cities	Population in Thousands	Percentage of National Population
El Salvador	San Salvador	370	10.8
	Santa Ana	97	2.8
	San Miguel	55	1.6
Guatemala	Guatemala City	772	14.9
	Quetzaltenango	59	1.1
	Escuintla	33	0.6
	Puerto Barrios	29	0.6
Haiti	Port-au-Prince	283	5.4
	Cap Haïtien	50	1.0
Honduras	Tegucigalpa	223	8.6
	San Pedro Sula	117	4.5
	La Ceiba	35	1.4
Mexico	Mexico City	8,360	16.5
	Guadalajara	1,135	2.2
	Monterrey	920	1.8
	Puebla	450	0.9
	Ciudad Juárez	403	0.8
Nicaragua	Managua*	353	17.5
	León	53	2.6
	Granada	34	1.7
Panama	Panama City	412	29.3
	Colón	68	4.8
	David	35	2.5
Paraguay	Asunción	464	19.2
	Encarnación	22	0.9
	Concepción	21	0.9
Peru	Lima-Callao	2,815	20.7
	Arequipa	172	1.3
	Trujillo	141	1.0
	Chiclayo	135	1.0
	Cuzco	113	0.8
Uruguay	Montevideo	1,415	49.0
	Salto	72	2.5
	Paysandú	64	2.2
Venezuela	Caracas	2,277	21.2
	Maracaibo	695	6.5
	Barquisimeto	328	3.0
	Valencia	280	2.6
	Maracay	245	2.3

*Managua was evacuated following a severe earthquake in December 1972.

Source: Economic Commission for Latin America.

is almost as large. The country where the population of the capital is the highest percentage of the national population is Uruguay; Montevideo, with nearly 1.5 million inhabitants, has almost half the total population of the country. In El Salvador, the most densely populated country in the Americas, only 10 percent live in the capital; the population is fairly evenly spread out in the small country.

While tolerating prostitution and extramarital love affairs (although, of course, it approves of neither), the Catholic Church has been fiercely opposed to divorce and birth control. Throughout the world the problem of birth control has created a crisis in the Church. Catholic women generally approve of it; where there are public birth control clinics, women frequent them because they are tired of the burden of large families. This was evident in Puerto Rico, where, during the administration of Rexford Guy Tugwell (the last U.S. Governor), birth control was introduced. As in the United States, many young priests accept birth control, but the conservative clergy do not, and they accuse Protestants, U.S. missionaries among others, of promoting birth control among Latin Americans.

The encyclical of Pope Paul VI, *De humanae vitae,* in which he condemned artificial birth control, exploded like a bomb in the Catholic world and provoked a schism in the Church. Shortly after the publication of the encyclical in 1968, the Pope visited Bogotá to address a eucharistic congress. The reaction among intellectuals, especially among those conscious of the population problem in Latin America, was negative. The Colombian Minister of Foreign Affairs resigned, on the eve of the Pope's visit, to express his disagreement. The reaction of conservative elements was the opposite. The military dictatorships of Brazil and Argentina, which sought the support of the Church, openly expressed their approval of the Pope's encyclical. There is no doubt that the encyclical, which went against the recommendations of the ecumenical councils which had taken place in the Vatican shortly before, was a serious blow for the birth control programs in Colombia and elsewhere. However, it seems likely that science will win over dogma. When he assumed office in 1970, President Luis Echeverría of Mexico spoke scornfully of birth control programs in an obvious effort to win Catholic support. In 1972, realizing that Mexico simply cannot feed and educate its teeming children, he made cautious pronouncements in favor of family planning, although he avoided the word "control" and said that such programs were voluntary. Hitherto, some progressive clergy had, despite the Vatican's ban, talked of birth control. Now some Mexican Church leaders began to do so openly.

The opposition of the Communists has likewise created a doctrinal schism. Communist opposition is based on the writings of Karl Marx and is aggravated by Communist hostility to the United States and to the capitalist system it represents. They say: "There can be no excess of population since vast areas of Latin America are virtually empty. The population explosion is not a bad thing in itself; it is simply that the capitalist system is incapable of channeling it. The system must be changed; under communism there would be no problem. Birth control is an invention of capitalism, which can find no other solution to the demographic problem. It is a Yankee trick to prevent the growth of the Latin American population. It is an invention of the whites, who wish to keep down the number of blacks."

The Communists fail to explain how communism would solve the population explosion. They may believe that a total agrarian reform, like that of Castro's Cuba, would put an end to the rural misery which drives peasants off the land to the cities. They may think that in a society controlled by a Communist dictatorship it would be possible to force the masses to leave the cities and settle in the empty spaces like Amazonia. Perhaps, seeing the development of Siberia, where the Soviet Government has built whole cities and peopled them in an authoritarian way, they think that something similar could be done in Latin America. They fail to realize that even the Soviet knout has failed to achieve effective settlement of much of Siberia and that, where the stick has failed, the Soviets are feverishly waving carrots. Perhaps the Latin American Communists believe that a communist educational program would put an end to illiteracy, and with it the problem of the untrained and unusable proletarian, and direct students into those areas where manpower is needed.

Karl Marx did indeed say that birth control would not be necessary in a communist society. This has created a problem for Communists, since the facts are simply not so. We know that if the population continues to grow at the present rate there will eventually be a square yard of land or less per inhabitant. It is an illusion to think that mankind could then feed itself from the sea. In any case, only an idiot would want to create a world in which each inhabitant would have to live on a yard of ground. Some Soviet scientists have tried to save Marxist doctrine by saying that the solution would be to shoot people into space, and recently this weird idea has appeared in the United States. It is appropriate that the word "lunacy" means moonstruck. In fact, the Soviet bloc countries, where adverse factors have kept down the population, have not been too successful in housing their present populations.

The Communist Party, then, faces a dilemma. In the Soviet Union, in China, and in Cuba official pronouncements have been contradictory. The party faces the same dilemma as the Catholic

Church. In the past the party denounced as traitors to the cause any Marxists who spoke favorably of birth control. Some years ago the president of the University of Shanghai was dismissed for having said that China faced a population crisis. Regarding his people as cannon fodder, Mao Tse-tung said that China could lose 200 million people in a nuclear war and survive, but that neither the Soviet Union nor the United States could do so. The Chinese Government now realizes that it faces a population problem and is actively promoting birth control. Fidel Castro spoke of birth control as an imperialist invention. The massive emigration of Cubans provided a safety valve for a time, but now that is ended, and Castro is faced with the harsh reality of population pressures.

Human fertility is an extremely complex problem, and the Soviet bloc countries have had a relatively low birth rate; moreover, the Soviet Union is eager to have more people to occupy the border areas China would like to recover. In Eastern Europe, therefore, the problem has not loomed so large, although there, too, there have been contradictory pronouncements.

Like politics, birth control makes strange bedfellows. Of all the major world religions, Catholicism is the only one which stubbornly opposes birth control, so debates about it have a bitterness absent in countries where Protestantism, Islam, Hinduism, or Confucianism predominate. Therefore, birth control is a more divisive issue in Latin America than in any other part of the world. It is probable that, without admitting that they have abandoned their prior viewpoints, both Catholics and Marxists will recognize the need for birth control, although the argument between capitalists and communists as to the best way of developing an evermore densely populated Latin America will continue.

There is an enormous divergence of opinion about Latin America's capacity to absorb more population. On the one hand are the Latin American visionaries who see the growth of great populations in the empty spaces of Amazonia, on the eastern slopes of the Andes, in Patagonia, in the valleys of the Orinoco and Magdalena rivers, in southeastern Mexico. On the other side are the sober foreign specialists who stress the immense obstacles to the peopling of these regions. Nationalist politicians and intellectuals believe that more population broadens the market for industry, forgetting that poor people cannot buy. Their assertions that the national territory must be occupied effectively is answered by the conservationists who charge that this occupation is destroying the equilibrium of nature. President Garrastazu Medici of Brazil has pushed the development and peopling of the Amazon valley, but foreign ecologists say that this endangers the source of much of the world's rainfall. Perhaps the ecologists are crying "wolf!" because they like wolves, whereas the developmentalists prefer people. Whether wolves are really necessary to humans is highly dubious, but the argument goes on.

It is sometimes asserted that, when a country industrializes and its standard of living rises, the birth rate will fall automatically, and industrialization should be promoted to solve the population problem. This argument may be just another way of avoiding the issue and promoting indiscriminate industrialization. The Latin American experience does not entirely bear out this thesis. In urbanized Argentina and Uruguay families are small, but there has been no marked decline in the birth rate in Mexico or southern Brazil, despite considerable industrialization. The problem of the population explosion in Latin America is extremely sensitive, but it should not be avoided.

3 • History and Great Men

The study of Latin American history is complex and can easily become boring if one gets lost in a mass of details. Each of the republics has its history, with numerous presidents and constitutions. It is somewhat as though we had to study the history of the United States not in terms of the nation but in terms of all the individual states. Educated Latin Americans are often very well informed on the history of their own country but ignorant of that of the neighboring republics. Latin American history had some unity during the colonial period when the Spanish and Portuguese empires still functioned, but this unity was shattered with independence. The question has often been asked: Does Latin America exist? We may also ask: Does Latin American history exist?

Pre-Columbian Civilizations

Pre-Columbian Indians had no writing, so technically they did not have history, but prehistory. For our knowledge of what went on before the Conquest, we are dependent on archaeology, the interpretation of some Aztec and Mayan codices, the accounts of Spanish chroniclers of the sixteenth century based on oral traditions, and the interpretation which modern scholars have given to vague and confused data. Since these scholars are often emotionally involved and less than impartial, many contradictory theories contain more passion than science. We discuss elsewhere the argument between hispanophiles and others about the population of pre-Columbian America. We might also mention the debates about Mayan chronology. The interpretation of Mayan hieroglyphics triggered a fight among U.S. and other archaeologists so bitter that the author of one of the theories, Herbert J. Spinden, director of the Brooklyn Museum, died embittered, only to be vindicated scientifically after his death. The Soviet scientists of "academy town," the computer center near Novosibirsk in Siberia, have published a three-volume work giving a new chronological interpretation of Mayan hieroglyphics on the basis of computer studies, but specialists are skeptical of the results. Since there are only a handful of such specialists, most Latin Americanists cannot voice an opinion.

These academic squabbles would have little importance if they did not reflect ideological, nationalistic, or political beliefs. The Argentinian and Brazilian anthropologists who claimed that American man was a native of their respective countries were motivated by nationalism. Something similar is involved in the arguments about the antiquity of American man and the problem of pre-Columbian relations across the Pacific. Especially notorious are the arguments about Columbus. Some Spanish nationalists and their friends have gone to great trouble in a vain attempt to prove that Columbus was not an Italian but a Spaniard: a Spanish Jew, a Galician, a Minorcan—practically every region in Spain claims him as its son. However much they may squabble on this point, Latin Americans and Spaniards are almost unanimous in their condemnation of scholars who belittle Columbus' exploit by stressing northern explorations.

A curious case concerns the interpretation of the destruction of the Mayan empire in Yucatán. Although Indianist painters like Diego Rivera take delight in depicting the cruelties committed by the Spanish Conquistadores against the Indians, and even though the destruction of the Aztec empire and its capital, Tenochtitlán (on the site of modern Mexico City), was the barbaric work of Hernán Cortés and his soldiers, the Spaniards cannot be blamed for the destruction of Chichén Itzá and the other cities of the Mayan empire in Yucatán and Guatemala. Admittedly, Bishop Diego de Landa ordered the destruction of the relics of Mayan civilization because he regarded them as pagan and, therefore, the work of the devil, but the fact is that the Mayan cities had been abandoned before the Spanish Conquest. Many theories have been put forward to explain this phenomenon. Perhaps the most interesting is that of a Russian scholar, who claims that it was the result of popular riots against the priests, who monopolized science and had enormous power in Mayan society. This theory appears reasonable, but it should be noted that it dovetails with the anticlericalism which is an essential part of Marxist-Leninist dogma.

The first Inca, Manco Capac, and his wife, Mama Oello, both children of the Sun, gather the savages together and create Inca civilization. (From Jorge Juan and Antonio de Ulloa, *Voyage to South America*.)

The great Inca civilization of South America, with its capital in Cuzco, Peru, has been idealized by the Indianists, and indeed by many European believers in the primitive goodness of man, as a just society worthy of emulation. More objective scholars view it as an oppressive form of socialism, rigid toward its own subjects, and overbearing toward conquered people. The Spanish Conquistador Francisco Pizarro, who is for the Indianists a monster like Cortés of Mexico, is idealized by the Roman Catholic conservatives, as is Cortés.

The Mapuche or Araucanian Indians of Chile were a primitive, ruthless lot, but the Chileans have idealized them as freedom fighters, since they resisted the Spaniards so valiantly. The Colombians admire the gold work of the Chibcha Indians, but there is little idealization of Chibcha society. There are one or two novels idealizing the primitive Indians of Brazil, but this is not a significant part of the Brazilian outlook. The pampa Indians of Argentina were savage, and the attitude that the only good Indian is a dead Indian, more common in South America than we have been led to believe, found its most marked expression in Argentina, which prides itself on being European.

The Colonial Period

The three centuries of Spanish colonial rule, that is to say the sixteenth, seventeenth, and eighteenth, were a period during which Spanish America lived in isolation except for the twice-yearly arrival in Cartagena (Colombia), Portobelo (Panama), and Veracruz (Mexico) of the fleet which came from Seville, or later from Cadiz. The Spaniards fought skirmishes with the English, the French, the Dutch, and later the North Americans, who rejected the Spanish claim that God had given the Spanish king a divine right to half of the globe, including all of the Americas except for a small slice of the east coast of South America which God in his good wisdom had assigned to the Portuguese. The Catholic monarchs, Isabel I of Castile and Ferdinand V of Aragon, had persuaded Pope Alexander VI, who was a Spaniard, to issue a bull conveying this gift of God to them personally; technically, Spanish America did not belong to Spain, but to the kings, who passed it on from father to son. Catholic King Francis I of France rejected the Spanish Pope's affirmations about the will of God. The linguistic and cultural confusion which characterizes the Caribbean today is the result of the struggle between Spain and the other European powers for control of the area, which was then the key to the New World.

In the early nineteenth century, the independence leaders claimed at first that they were defending the divine right of the King of Spain against the usurpation by Napoleon, but they soon cast off this pretense and said they were restoring the rights of the Indians which had been usurped by the Spanish Crown and the Conquistadores to whom it entrusted the enslavement of the continent.

There was occasional excitement in the Spanish colonies: the arrival and departure of Spanish ships, skirmishes with the ships of other powers (which, nevertheless, were able to carry on a trade which the Spaniards regarded as contraband, since they had proclaimed a Spanish monopoly on commerce with the Indies), and occasional riots of Creoles or Indians. Above all, there was a prolonged peace, scarcely interrupted by a series of administrative reforms which have little interest for us. The primary concern of the Spaniards was the gold and silver they extracted from the mines of New Spain (Mexico) and Upper Peru (Bolivia).

The Spaniards saw in the gold and silver which they greedily took from America a source of prosperity which would allow them to live in luxury and ease. Moreover, the mere accumulation of gold and silver was regarded as wealth. The "royal fifth" (the fifth of all the gold and silver exported from America) was the principal revenue of the Spanish Crown. But all this was an illusion. As Adam Smith pointed out in his *The Wealth of Nations* (1776), wealth and prosperity derive not from gold and silver mines but from work and trade. The Spanish colonies in America were similar to the oil-producing countries today, i.e. the Middle Eastern countries and Venezuela. Heaven knows what will happen to these countries when the oil runs out, unless they learn the lesson of the Spanish empire. Venezuela talks about "sowing oil," that is, transforming the country economically and industrially while the "black gold" lasts.

One result of the much-criticized Spanish exploration of America was the slow and almost invisible creation of contemporary Spanish America. The Spanish American republics are the direct heirs of the administrative divisions of the colonies. During the independence period, the liberators accepted the principle of *Uti possedetis,* i.e. each republic had the right to the territory controlled by the colonial division of which the republic was heir. For this reason, in the boundary disputes which have been the curse of Spanish America since the independence period (a notorious case is the endless dispute between Ecuador and Peru), each government has recourse to colonial documents to prove that the disputed territory was under the jurisdiction of the colony of which the republic is the successor. The republics had a gestation of three centuries and were not born spontaneously at the beginning of the nineteenth century.

It is commonly said that the English came to the New World to devote themselves to agriculture and to settle permanently, while the Spaniards came only to exploit the mines and to return to Spain as *indianos*. There is some truth in this, but we must also recognize that Spain created in the New World beautiful cities in which the most noteworthy monuments were the churches, usually baroque in style. North American Protestantism did not permit as much ostentation in Christian worship. While Anglo-American cities grew rather haphazardly, the Council of the Indies, the royal organ entrusted with the administration of America, laid down plans for the building of Spanish American cities, which still have an orderly appearance deriving from the urbanistic spirit of the Spanish monarchy.

The Spanish empire had its foci in the two regions where there was an abundance of gold and silver, namely New Spain and Peru. Mexico City and Lima were the capitals of the two viceroyalties into which the Indies were divided until the eighteenth century, when two new viceroyalties were created: New Granada, with Bogotá as its capital, and the River Plate, with Buenos Aires as its capital. In addition to the viceroyalties there were lesser administrative divisions, the captaincies general and the audiencias. Today the wealth of Latin America is not in its gold and silver; and where the mines are exhausted there are today cities which have remained as colonial jewels simply because there was not enough money (in Spanish *plata* means both silver and money) to modernize them. U.S. tourists know the old mining cities of Mexico, such as Taxco, Guanajuato, and Zacatecas, but of the Andean cities they know only Cuzco, and they go there to see not the colonial buildings but the Inca ruins of places like Machu Picchu. They should also visit colonial cities like Ayacucho, Juli, Pomata, and Sucre.

Sucre, which few tourists visit because it is difficult to reach, is one of the most charming cities of Spanish America. Today it bears the name of Bolívar's companion, but in colonial times it was known as Charcas or Chuquisaca (Indian names) or La Plata, an appropriate name since it was near the great silver mine of

1.Pont de Liane, ou Bejuques. 2 Tarabite pour passer les Animaux 3.Tarabite pour passer les Hommes.

Crossing an Andean torrent in Peru. (From Jorge Juan and Antonio de Ulloa, *Voyage to South America.*)

Potosí. Potosí is also an interesting colonial city, but since it is at an altitude of 13,612 feet, the mine owners preferred to live at a lower altitude, in the temperate climate of La Plata. The "city of four names" was the seat of the audiencia of which modern Bolivia is the heir. The tourist who, with great difficulty, reaches Sucre is surprised to see impressive baroque churches and colonial palaces in a town from which the white aristocracy has virtually disappeared, leaving only a mass of picturesque but illiterate Indians.

Despite the censorship, which forbade the importation of "subversive" books, cultured Latin Americans were aware of the liberal movement which had inspired first the American Revolution and then the French Revolution. Like France, Spain entered the American Revolutionary War not out of a love of freedom but to obtain revenge for the defeat inflicted on them by the British in the war with the French and the Indians, known in Europe as the Seven Years' War (1756-63). The Spanish statesman Count Aranda realized that Spain was making a mistake in encouraging the independence of the British colonies in America because the Spanish colonies would inevitably follow their example. This is precisely what happened.

The Wars of Independence

The final collapse of the Spanish empire was brought about by the chaos caused by the Napoleonic wars in Spain. Napoleon persuaded Charles IV and his son Ferdinand (who later became Ferdinand VII) to abdicate the throne in exchange for chateaux and pensions in France. The two pathetic men accepted, and then Napoleon put his brother Joseph on the throne of Spain. The Spanish people regarded him as an imposter, and the Spanish national holiday, the Second of May, commemorates the popular uprising in Madrid against the French occupation army in 1808. The rebellion was crushed brutally, but the Spaniards continued their struggle. The liberals took refuge in Cadiz, where a parliament *(cortes)* met in the name of Ferdinand and drew up the constitution of 1812.

The Spanish colonies did not know to which king they owed loyalty. The French King Joseph I claimed to be the legitimate King of Spain and of Spanish America, but few Spanish Americans acknowledged his claim. Some colonies accepted the invitation extended by the free Spanish government in Cadiz to send deputies to the constituent assembly. However, the general reaction in the colonies was to take advantage of the prevailing confusion to set up independent governments, although they camouflaged this by saying, with different degrees of sincerity, that they were acting in the name of King Ferdinand VII. Spain had no control over its Spanish colonies because the Spanish fleet, which ensured communications between Spain and America, had been destroyed in the Battle of Trafalgar (1805), the last and greatest victory of Admiral Nelson.

After the defeat of Napoleon, Ferdinand returned as King of Spain, but, instead of showing gratitude to the liberals for their support and sacrifices, he pursued and exiled or jailed them. The constitution was abolished, and the very word "constitution" became anathema. Ferdinand was unwilling to come to terms with the liberal Spanish American leaders, and he attempted to restore absolute rule in the New World. It was said that after their return to power, the Bourbons had learned nothing and forgotten nothing.

Ferdinand VII failed in his attempt to restore the old order in Spanish America. The forerunner of the wars of independence was the Venezuelan Francisco de Miranda. He led the first liberation movement, but another Venezuelan, Simón Bolívar, denounced him as a coward and betrayed him to the Spanish authorities. Bolívar freed Venezuela and then marched triumphantly through Colombia, Ecuador, Peru, and Bolivia, which since then have been known as the Bolivarian republics. The very name of Bolivia recalls the final stage of Bolívar's campaign. In Argentina, the other great focus of the South American independence movement, José de San Martín marched his army across the Andes to free Chile, where he helped the Chilean national hero, Bernardo O'Higgins, to become president. He then advanced on Lima, which was the main stronghold of the Spaniards in South America. After a famous interview with Bolívar in the Ecuadorean port of Guayaquil, San Martín abandoned the independence struggle, leaving Bolívar to liquidate the Spanish armies which were still fighting in Peru. There were a few minor battles later in Bolivia, but the victory of the young Venezuelan Antonio José Sucre in Ayacucho (1824) is generally regarded as marking the final defeat of Spain in South America.

The struggle in Mexico was more confused because the two great liberators, Miguel Hidalgo and José María Morelos, failed. The Spaniards captured and executed them. Mexican independence came about in a very odd way. Agustín de Iturbide, irresponsible and ambitious, named himself Emperor Agustin I and proclaimed the independence of Mexico. He was exiled by the Mexicans, who regarded him as a tyrant, and when he tried to return to power, he was arrested and executed. Mexicans are a little embarrassed that they owe their independence to a man for whom they feel no admiration. They prefer to speak to Hidalgo and Morelos, whom they regard as the heroes of Mexican independence, despite their failure.

Central America won its independence as part of the empire of Iturbide, but when he fell, the former Captaincy General of Guatemala proclaimed itself a sovereign state with the name "United Provinces of Central America." It later broke up into five republics: Guatemala, El Salvador, Honduras, Nicaragua, and Costa Rica.

The Nineteenth Century

As a result of the wars of independence, Spanish America divided into eighteen republics. Cuba, which won its independence only in 1898, is a special case. After its defeat in the war with the United States, Spain lost Cuba, Puerto Rico (which was annexed by the United States), and the Philippines (which gained their independence only after World War II). Each of the Spanish American republics has its history, its presidents, and its revolutions; it is possible to mention here only a few of the highlights.

The war between the United States and Mexico (1846-48) ended with the defeat of Mexico and its resultant loss of Texas, New Mexico, Arizona, and California. For the first time the Spanish Americans realized that the "Colossus of the North" was a threat to them. Although Mexico has had to accept the loss of half the territory it claimed, that loss is still a source of bitterness. The trauma provoked by this defeat was followed by a conservative nationalism which brought about the empire of Maximilian (1864-67), an Austrian prince supported by Napoleon III. A liberal reaction inspired the republic of Benito Juárez (1867-72), who, with the help of the United States, defeated and executed Maximilian in Querétaro. He then carried on the work of the "Reforma" (Reformation) to put an end to the power of the Roman Catholic Church.

Porfirio Díaz began as a liberal soldier in Juárez's army, but after becoming President of Mexico he set up a dictatorship (1877-1910) with the support of the Catholic Church and U.S. businessmen. Mexico was generally regarded as a showcase of the benefits of capitalism, which ensures peace, well-being, and progress, when the Revolution of 1910 broke out. It was led by Francisco Madero, who held the Presidency briefly (1910-11) but was assassinated by supporters of Porfirio Díaz. The Mexican Revolution was the most important event in the history of the Spanish American republics until the revolution of Fidel Castro. A new political order finally was established in Mexico, but in theory the revolution continues, and the government party calls itself the Institutional Revolutionary Party (PRI).

In South America after the wars of independence there were no developments of international importance comparable to those in Mexico. In the War of the Pacific (1879-83) Chile defeated Peru and Bolivia. Since then, Chile has occupied the coast formerly belonging to Bolivia, and the bitter and unceasing complaints of Bolivia have led to a kind of permanent break of peaceful relations between the governments of La Paz and Santiago.

The War of the Triple Alliance (1865-70), in which Paraguay was defeated by Argentina, Brazil, and Uruguay, was primarily the result of the ambitions of dictator Francisco Solano López, who wanted Paraguay to win an important place in South America while the republics were still in a state of flux. There had been a separatist revolution in southern Brazil, and the revolts of the provinces of Argentina against Buenos Aires threatened the very existence of that republic. In these circumstances Paraguay had a chance to become the key nation in the south of the continent. Asunción was an older city than Buenos Aires, which it regarded as an upstart, much as Mexico looked down on the United States as a newcomer. Both Mexico and Asunción miscalculated the strength of their aggressive neighbors, and both were defeated. The defeat of Paraguay was bloody. It is said that all the able-bodied men of the nation died, and travelers who visited the country after the war reported that only women and children remained.

Bolivia and Paraguay have been sad, backward countries, the only landlocked countries of the continent. There was a senseless war between the two republics, the so-called War of the Chaco (1932-35), to see who owned the vast and nearly empty region known as the Chaco. Paraguay won the war because the Bolivian Indians who came down from the highlands could not stand the heat of the tropical plains, but, strangely, this war has left no bitterness between the two peoples. Both know that they have a common fate—they are caught between two powerful neighbors, Argentina and Brazil. The Bolivians blame the stupidity of their President for the Chaco war. The Paraguayans believe that the real cause was the rivalry between two great oil companies which thought there was oil in the Chaco. One supported Paraguay, the other Bolivia. This attitude reflects a distressing tendency among Latin Americans to blame the United States and the other great powers for their misfortunes.

Geographical Shifts in Power and Wealth

The cases of Argentina and Venezuela deserve special attention. Until the nineteenth century the most important areas of Spanish America were Mexico and Peru, where the great gold and silver mines were located. The Spaniards showed little interest in the Argentinian pampas or the plains of Venezuela. Neither Buenos Aires nor Caracas were important cities in the colonial period. The Viceroyalty of the River Plate was founded in 1776 for strategic and military reasons. Caracas was merely the seat of a captaincy general, while Bogotá was the capital of a viceroyalty.

A fundamental change occurred in the second half of the nineteenth century. The region of America between the two tropics lost its importance because the gold and silver mines became exhausted and because the market for many tropical products such as indigo and cochineal disappeared with the invention of synthetic products in Europe; indigo and cochineal were no longer used to dye cloth blue or red. Until the nineteenth century, the northern region of North America and the southern region of South America, i.e. the misnamed temperate zones, had little interest for Europe, which was not yet suffering from the excess of population which stimulated the great emigration of the last century. Europe still did not have to import large quantities of meat and cereals. In any case, meat from America could not be imported until the invention of refrigerated shipping toward the end of the nineteenth century. Cattle had to be transported live across the Atlantic, which was a difficult and infrequent journey. In a famous remark about the "acres of snow of Canada," Voltaire expressed his disdain for the land which France had lost; he did not see the importance it would have later. The great cities of the United States—New York, Boston, Philadelphia, and Washington —could not compare with Mexico City at the beginning of the nineteenth century.

At the other end of the continent something similar occurred. Buenos Aires was a small, wretched town until the last decades of the nineteenth century. Although there are differences between the Argentinian pampa and the Venezuelan *llanos* (plains), the two regions were devoted primarily to the raising of cattle— not the English shorthorn variety, which was introduced into the pampas toward the end of the nineteenth century and which produces fine meat, but the Spanish longhorn, which gives little meat and was raised chiefly for its leather. The pampas and the Venezuelan plains produced a human type similar to the Texas cowboy —the *gaucho* and the *llanero*. There is an authoritarian tradition in Texas, and the *gaucho* and the *llanero* likewise created a society predisposed to dictatorship.

The Tradition of Dictatorship

With the exception of Uruguay, Chile, and Costa Rica, open or disguised dictatorship seems endemic in Spanish America, and even in Uruguay and Chile the democratic structure seems less stable than in the past. The absence or failure of democracy in Latin America has been explained or judged in different ways. Some say it is part of the Spanish inheritance. The liberals who scorn the Spanish tradition regret the phenomenon and say that Spanish America should follow the example of the advanced democratic countries. The conservative admirers of the Spanish heritage feel an ill-disguised contempt for democracy. They believe that an authoritarian system of government is part of the Spanish American tradition, that Anglo-Saxon-style democracy is not suited to the Spaniard or the Spanish American, and that the existence of dictators such as Francisco Franco is understandable, natural, and healthy.

It is curious that the word caudillo, which is used in English to designate the petty dictators of Spanish America, often has a favorable connotation in the Spanish American republics. In Spain General Franco took the title "caudillo"; the prototype of the caudillo, and that indeed was the title he used, was the national hero of medieval Spain, the Cid Campeador, who led the fight against the Moorish invaders.

Some historians say that modern dictatorships were born at the beginning of the nineteenth century, when the liberators became dictators. Some liberators, even Simón Bolívar himself, openly proclaimed themselves dictators, whereas the contemporary dictator prefers to avoid this term, which has become odious. The defenders of dictatorship claim that it is a kind of authoritarian democracy. In a book entitled *Democratic Caesarism* Laureano Vallenilla Lanz defended Venezuelan dictatorships. Some explain the military dictatorships of Spanish America by the fact that after the wars of independence the armies created by the liberators were the only forces capable of governing the new republics.

In general writers and teachers are liberals because, not having any administrative responsibilities, they think it is easy to change things. Since the nineteenth century the liberal viewpoint has predominated in history books; according to it, the evils of Spanish America stem from an unholy alliance of the army, the oligarchy, the Roman Catholic Church, and large foreign corporations. Naturally, these groups have had their defenders, and there are writers who praise the historic role of the Church and of dictators. They were not numerous until totalitarian movements flourished in the present century. Some attack democracy from the right, others from the left. Both groups say that history must be rewritten, freeing it from the liberal straitjacket. This movement to rewrite history and give it a new interpretation is called "historic revisionism." The term is applied primarily to those who defend the authoritarian tradition in Spanish America. For example, there is a school of Paraguayan historians who believe that the history of their country was distorted by the famous Argentinian statesman and writer Bartolomé Mitre. The spokesman for this group has been a historian with a very un-Paraguayan name, Juan Emiliano O'Leary. He defends the dictatorship which ruled Paraguay in the nineteenth century: José Gaspar Rodríguez Francia (1814-40), Carlos Antonio López (1841-62), and Francisco Solano López (1862-70).

There is also a historic revisionism of the left, which claims that the liberal movement of the last century was a camouflage for the economic ambitions of business and the middle classes. It parallels the interpretation of the U.S. constitution by Charles Beard. These revisionists derive their inspiration from Karl Marx, who in a famous essay denounced Simón Bolívar as a false revolutionary whose sonorous phrases on independence and liberty hid the interests of his class. In the Soviet Union now many books are appearing about Latin America with a Marxist interpretation. Sometimes rightist and leftist revisionism meet.

The most noteworthy case of historic revisionism concerns the Argentinian dictator Juan Manuel de Rosas. A caudillo of the pampa, he was regarded as the prototype of the Creole. He changed his name from Rozas to Rosas to make it sound more Latin American. He ruled Argentina from 1829 until his exile in 1852. The liberals who created modern Argentina, such as Presidents Bartolomé Mitre (1862-68) and Domingo Faustino Sarmiento (1868-74), regarded Rosas as a monster whose exile was a victory for the liberals.

The theme of Sarmiento's book *Facundo, or Civilization and Barbarism* (1845) was that men like Rosas and Facundo (Facundo was another caudillo of Rosas' time) represented the barbarism of the pampa as opposed to the civilization of Buenos Aires. Rosas rose to power as a champion of the countryside against Buenos Aires, which wished to impose its will, embodied in a centralist or unitarian constitution, throughout the republic. Calling himself a federalist, Rosas insulted the unitarians in the grossest terms. He belied his promises completely after he seized power and established a totally centralist dictatorship.

The defenders of Rosas say that he reflected the primitive Argentina of his period and that a modern liberal politician would have been incapable of governing the country; Rosas understood his people, just as some later Latin American dictators have done. It is possible to justify the role of Rosas at that particular historical moment. For the liberals who shipped him off to exile in England, he represented the past. When Sarmiento wrote *Facundo*, he wished to show that Argentina had to abandon the barbarity of the past and follow the example of U.S. and European civilization.

Unfortunately, Argentinian nationalists regard Sarmiento as a traitor to the Argentinian tradition, as someone who sold out to the "Colossus of the North." They claim to continue the tradition of Rosas, although what they really want is simply authoritarian nationalism.

In his old age the liberator José de San Martín praised Rosas, and the modern dictator Juan Domingo Perón claimed to be the heir of San Martín and Rosas. Peronista propagandists demanded that the remains of Rosas be brought back in triumph to Argentina, but they still lie in Southampton, England, because Perón was overthrown by a group of conservative generals in 1955 and exiled to Spain. These generals claimed to be acting in the name of democracy, but in fact they established a dictatorship without the popular base of Perón's regime. They have said nothing about Rosas, although probably in their hearts they too regard themselves as the heirs of San Martín and Rosas.

In addition to Argentina, the other focus of violent dictatorship in South America has been Venezuela, once a cradle of liberty. Francisco de Miranda, Simón Bolívar, Andrés Bello, Antonio José Sucre, and the other leaders of the independence movement in the Bolivarian countries were mostly Venezuelans. It is a strange phenomenon that a backward city like colonial Caracas should have produced a group of leaders devoted to the ideas and ideals of liberty. The enemies of Bolívar and of the Venezuelan heroes in the other republics liberated by them say that they were motivated not by a love of freedom but by a desire to rule in the new republics, where they acted as though they were monarchs. For this reason there was a reaction against them and almost all, including Bolívar and Sucre, were rejected by the peoples they had liberated. Bolívar died in 1830 on his way to exile, believing that his life had been a total failure. The fact is that Bolívar and his friends did not even represent Venezuela, but rather a certain group in Caracas. They were rejected by the Venezuelans themselves, who proclaimed their country's secession from the Gran Colombia (Colombia, Venezuela, and Ecuador) created by Bolívar. A typical *llanero*, José Antonio Páez, seized power, and after him the history of Venezuela was an almost uninterrupted series of dictatorships similar to that of Rosas. Until this century Venezuela was a primitive country and played a minor role in the world; for this reason the terrible dictatorship (1908-35) of Juan Vicente Gómez had few repercussions outside of Venezuela.

When the Argentinian economy developed at the end of the last century and transformed the country into the most important Spanish American nation, Argentinian dictatorships began to have an international impact. Something similar happened in Venezuela when the discovery of oil deposits in Lake Maracaibo transformed that country into a rich and progressive state. The dictatorial tradition continued during the regime of Marcos Pérez Jiménez, who was a great friend of Perón. He was overthrown in the series of democratic victories which followed the fall of Perón in Argentina. Modern Venezuelan democracy is the work of Rómulo Betancourt, who succeeded in finishing his presidential term (1959-63) despite attempts on his life. When he left the presidency, his party, Acción Democrática, split into two factions, and thus lost power to the Christian Democrats, headed by Rafael Caldera. Pressure from the left has forced the Christian Democrats to take an aggressive nationalistic line, and the future of democracy in Venezuela is not clear.

U.S. "Manifest Destiny" in Latin America

U.S. imperialism in the Caribbean was manifest in 1898 and 1903. Americans claim that the United States intervened in the war between Cuba and Spain to put an end to Spanish imperialism in the New World, but the Cubans assert that the real motive was U.S. desire to control the Cuban economy. When President

Theodore Roosevelt boasted that in 1903 "I took Panama," he confirmed the Cuban interpretation of U.S. intentions in the Caribbean.

After the 1898 war, the United States wanted to assure its naval supremacy in the Caribbean. Despite Cuban independence, the United States maintained control of the island through the Platt Amendment, which gave Washington the right to intervene in Cuba, and through Cuba's ceding to the United States a base at Guantánamo, near Santiago. These two things limited Cuba's sovereignty and created a deep resentment among the people. As part of the Good Neighbor Policy, President Franklin D. Roosevelt revoked the Platt Amendment, but the United States has not been willing to return Guantánamo to Cuba. When Fidel Castro visited Moscow in 1972, the Cuban and Soviet Governments issued a joint statement demanding that the base be returned to Cuba.

After its victory over Spain, the United States was left in possession of Puerto Rico, and it controlled Cuba. It completed its domination of the Caribbean with the creation in 1903 of the Republic of Panama, which had hitherto been a part of Colombia. The United States helped Panama to achieve its independence from Colombia, and in return received the strip of land in which it built the Canal.

U.S. victories in the Caribbean did not bring democracy. On the contrary, the Caribbean islands have been notorious for their dictatorships. We have already spoken of François Duvalier of Haiti, who proclaimed himself "Life President" and who, on his death in 1971, was succeeded in a similar capacity by his pathetic nineteen-year-old son Jean-Claude. However, because of the linguistic and cultural barrier between Haiti and Spanish America, this dictatorship has had little impact elsewhere. Far more important in the Spanish American context are the dictatorships of Cuba and the Dominican Republic. For many years, the two islands were under the control of dictators allied with a network of such dictatorships in Spanish America: Perón in Argentina, Stroessner in Paraguay, Odría in Peru, Pérez Jiménez in Venezuela, and Somoza in Nicaragua. The strongman of Cuba was Fulgencio Batista, that of the Dominican Republic, Rafael Leonidas Trujillo. Somoza, Batista, and Trujillo were all products of the U.S. occupation of their republics. Even after the occupation ended, the three countries were really U.S. protectorates, like Guatemala and Honduras and other Central American and Caribbean dictatorships.

The presidents of these *republiquetas,* to use the Brazilian expression, were puppets of Washington, which supported them and gave them arms and so-called technical aid so that they could control their populations by force. In response to Washington's generosity, Caribbean dictators created very favorable conditions for U.S. investments. In the case of Cuba, there was the attraction of Havana, a beautiful and pleasant city where gambling and prostitution flourished, as well as businesses often controlled by U.S. gangsters. The United States proclaimed its democratic principles and fought against Hitler and Mussolini, but in its backyard it protected third-class dictators.

The result in Central America and the Caribbean was a wave of indignation against the dictators and their U.S. protectors. In Guatemala liberal elements took advantage of the democratic surge which swept the world after the defeat of the Axis and overthrew the dictatorship of Jorge Ubico. Juan José Arévalo set up a liberal government, but when his successor, Jacobo Arbenz, wished to introduce radical reforms which affected the United Fruit Company, U.S. Secretary of State John Foster Dulles denounced him for accepting Communist military support, and the CIA organized an invasion which threw out the Arbenz regime. Since then, Guatemala has had a precarious political life and has been the scene of a bloody struggle between rightist and leftist armed gangs.

In Nicaragua it has not been possible to put an end to the Somoza dynasty. Anastasio Somoza was killed by a student in 1956, but he was succeeded as strongman by his son. Traditionally, the enemies of the misnamed Liberal Party have been the Conservatives, but in reality the two parties represent two groups within the oligarchy, each allied with foreign, and especially U.S., interests. To the disgust of members of both parties, the two groups made a deal in 1972 to put through a constitutional reform which will allow the Somozas to stay in power.

Cuba and Castro

However interesting Guatemala and Nicaragua may be, the key points in the Caribbean have been Cuba and the Dominican Republic. Because of Fidel Castro, Cuba has attracted the attention of the entire world. After World War II, Cuba had a brief moment of democracy, which it failed to establish solidly. Batista seized power again in 1952 and swept aside democratic procedures. Until then Batista had enjoyed considerable support among the masses, but, when he betrayed the new democratic order, almost all groups turned against him. His most daring enemies were the students of the University of Havana, who stormed the presidential palace and nearly succeeded in assassinating him.

The repression was fierce, and then a group of students led by Fidel Castro attempted a similar coup in Santiago, at the eastern end of the island. They burst into the Moncada barracks on July 26, 1953, and this date gave its name to Fidel Castro's movement, 26 de Julio. Once more the students failed, and again there was violent repression. Castro was taken prisoner and while in jail wrote his own defense entitled "History Will Absolve Me." This later became the classic speech of the Cuban Revolution and was reprinted in thousands of copies. In it Castro declared that he was struggling for the democratic principles which Batista had betrayed. Soon Castro himself was to betray them. It seems probable that he lost his faith in democracy later, after he came under Communist influence, but some observers argue that he was already a crypto-Communist, preaching democracy while waiting for the appropriate moment to declare his real beliefs.

The government condemned Castro to imprisonment on the Isle of Pines, but he was later paroled and exiled to Mexico. There he met with a group of Cuban revolutionaries and began to prepare the invasion of Cuba. Again, he planned to start his revolution in Oriente Province, far from Havana and the traditional cradle of Cuban revolutionary movements. He bought an old launch with a U.S. name, "Granma," and, after a stormy crossing, his guerrilla fighters landed on the Oriente coast. Batista's troops tried to cut him off, and a bloody skirmish ensued. A handful of revolutionaries (the story is that there were twelve, like the Apostles) succeeded in escaping to the Sierra Maestra, and there, in mountainous and isolated country, they began the campaign which ended with Castro's victorious entry into Havana on January 1, 1959.

At first the Batista government refused to pay much attention to Castro's band and spread the rumor that he was dead. Although the story was generally accepted, Herbert Matthews of the *New York Times* did not believe it, and he carried out a spectacular journalistic coup. Dressed as a U.S. tourist who was going fishing, he crossed the Batista lines and went up into the Sierra Maestra. There he interviewed Fidel Castro and returned to the United States with the sensational news that Castro was still alive. Thus was born the Castro legend, and the Batista regime was discredited. Almost all Cubans were tired of the bloody and corrupt dictatorship, and Batista's soldiers were unwilling to fight. At the same time as Castro's revolutionaries were moving toward Havana from the east, in the capital the underground carried on a relentless campaign against Batista's machine. Caught between two revolutionary groups, his government collapsed and he fled the country.

Castro's army entered Havana in the first days of 1959, and immediately a struggle for power began between the two groups of revolutionaries. The Havana revolutionaries included men of a certain education, many of whom were intellectuals and professional leaders. Castro's army was made up primarily of uneducated peasants—the famous *barbudos* (bearded ones). Castro began to persecute the members of the Havana underground who opposed him when he seized power. Many Batista followers were charged with crimes against the people and were ordered shot after a series of circus trials which were the object of much adverse publicity in the United States.

Many of the revolutionaries who did not accept Castro's authority fled to the United States, Mexico, Spain, and other European countries. Obviously, among those who fled were also many followers of Batista, many members of the oligarchy and the money-crazy middle class, and many scoundrels who took advantage of the situation to emigrate to the United States, which is the dream of many Latin Americans. In any case, Cuba lost a large number of its best-trained people. Castro denounced his enemies as *gusanos* (worms) he was glad to be rid of, but the loss of professional skills, so badly needed in Cuba, was severe. As a result of Castro's seizing total power, the hope of establishing a democratic regime in Cuba disappeared. Perhaps it was an illusion to hope to set up a viable democracy in an island which ever since the Spanish Conquest had lived more or less continually under an oppressive government.

In the United States, Castro's revolution had been widely applauded, but public opinion turned against him not only because he shot, imprisoned, or exiled his enemies and critics, real or alleged, but because the vast U.S. interests in Cuba were also the victims of his revolution. In reality, few Americans take any serious interest in the internal problems of Latin American republics. For them Havana was merely a pleasant city where they could have a good time. Now it was no longer attractive. Castro wanted to suppress prostitution, gambling, and other abuses. Havana, which previously had been so elegant, was now a proletarian, joyless city. Washington made a clumsy effort to come to terms with Castro, but it failed, and early in 1962 the two countries broke relations.

Then Castro began to move openly toward communism. Unless he was indeed a crypto-Communist, this may have been his reaction to the hostility of the United States and Cuban democrats. Castro is a vain and difficult individual, and he took offense at a series of alleged affronts, among them the refusal of the United States to grant his extravagant requests. Castro avenged himself by joining the Soviet bloc. His relations with the Soviet Union have been far from easy, even though the Soviets support him to the tune of over $1 million a day. However, Castro visited Moscow in 1972 for the first time in many years, and the disagreements were patched up. Cuba formally joined COMECON, the Soviet economic bloc.

Castro is an intelligent man, interested in ideas, but he goes from one political doctrine to another like a bee going from flower to flower. He apparently read Communist books while he was in the Sierra Maestra and was convinced by their criticism of capitalism and of "bourgeois" democracy. There was in Cuba at the time a group of Communists led by Carlos Rafael Rodríguez who played a very shrewd game. At first Castro despised them because they had worked with Batista and had not helped the cause of his revolution. They succeeded, nevertheless, in winning him over and in converting him to communism.

When Castro moved into the Communist camp, the CIA had the unfortunate idea that it could repeat in 1961 what it had done in Guatemala in 1954 when it organized the invasion by Castillo Armas which overthrew the pro-Communist regime of Arbenz. Taking advantage of the presence in the United States, and especially in Florida, of a large number of Cuban refugees eager to invade their island, the CIA set up in Guatemala a camp to train an invasion army. This tragicomic episode was an unqualified failure. The CIA did not know how to handle the various groups of Cubans squabbling among themselves, and it made the mistake of entrusting the leadership of the expedition to followers of Batista, who were detested by almost all the other revolutionary groups. In the United States the government tried to keep the plan a secret, but in Guatemala it provoked arguments in the government, in the press, and on television. Obviously, Castro knew about it, and when the American public realized that it had been kept in ignorance, there was a general outcry.

President John F. Kennedy not only kept the American public in the dark, he did not even inform the Cabinet, the Senate, or

Adlai Stevenson, the U.S. representative in the United Nations, who publicly denied the rumors that were circulating about an invasion. When the invasion came, Stevenson, realizing that Kennedy had fooled him, was indignant because he had, in all innocence, given the world the impression that he was a liar. Kennedy also failed to provide the air cover which the refugees said he had promised them.

The invasion fleet sailed from Nicaragua, a country controlled by the Somozas, who have been allies of the United States and enemies of Castro, and it landed at the Bay of Pigs, on the southern coast of Cuba. It was a colossal mistake on the part of the CIA to assume that the Cuban masses were hostile to Castro and that they would seize the opportunity to rise against him. In general they supported Castro, who imprisoned thousands of suspects as a precautionary measure on the eve of the invasion.

The United States and the CIA were victims of their own propaganda and of the propaganda of the refugees. It was impossible to repeat the exploit of "Granma," even with all the equipment the United States had given the invaders. The "Bay of Pigs"* is a swampy area, inappropriate for an invasion from the sea. The invaders got lost in the swamps, and most of them were killed or captured by Castro's soldiers. The invasion was counterproductive because it consolidated the regime of Castro, who now appeared as the defender of his nation against Yankee imperialism. For a long time Castro had been accusing the United States of preparing a coup to overthrow him. These denunciations were commonly laughed off as products of Castro's imagination and paranoia. Now no one was laughing.

The honeymoon between Castro and the Soviet Union was soon beclouded. Since both the Soviet and the Communist press are strictly controlled, as is the press in all Communist countries, neither spoke with any candor on this subject, so the information we have is fragmentary. The Soviet Union was delighted to have near the coast of the United States a military base similar to the U.S. bases where missiles are directed against the Soviet Union. When President Kennedy, still smarting from the Bay of Pigs disaster, found out about the Soviet installations, he threatened to take all necessary action if the Soviet Union did not withdraw its missiles from Cuba. This led to the famous "eyeball to eyeball" confrontation between Kennedy and Khrushchev. Fortunately, the Soviet leader decided to avoid war; the spectacle of Soviet

---

*Bahía de Cochinos is mistranslated, since *cochinos* here refers not to pigs but to a tropical fish.

vessels removing missiles from Cuba was humiliating for the Soviet Union and for Cuba.

Castro, who had played a pathetic role in the confrontation between the two superpowers, accused the Soviet Government of having betrayed him. The Soviets had decided that they could defeat the United States peacefully and that historic determinism would lead to the collapse of the capitalist system and of the capitalist nations. This was one of the reasons for the break between the Soviet Union and China, which preached the need for violent revolution throughout the world. Since then China has, in fact, adopted the Soviet policy of peaceful coexistence with the United States, as a result of the visits of Henry Kissinger and President Nixon to Peking, even though the deep doctrinaire hatred of the United States as a capitalist country remains unchanged in both cases.

Fidel Castro has shown no interest in peaceful coexistence with the United States or with the anti-Communist governments of the Organization of American States, which had expelled him. He waited to take vengeance by using guerrilla fighters to overthrow the governments which had condemned him. He could not break openly with the Soviet Union, which was giving him technical assistance and subsidizing him generously.

When Salvador Allende was elected President of Chile and led that country down the "socialist" road, the Soviet Union did not wish to have another Cuba on its hands and preferred not to see Chile isolated and dependent entirely on the USSR. Moscow was indeed eager to make commercial deals with any Latin American government, even a military dictatorship like Brazil. Castro regarded this pragmatic behavior of the Soviets as treason to Communist ideals, and he continued to support guerrilla fighters in Guatemala, Venezuela, Colombia, and Bolivia.

These guerrilla fighters enjoyed great popularity among university youths who believed that traditional Latin American society was utterly rotten, that Western democracy was a farce which would not help the peoples of Latin America to escape from their misery, and that the only solution was the violent overthrow of governments by guerrilla action. Most of the guerrilla fighters were unscrupulous adventurers, but there were a few idealistic intellectuals. Among them was the Colombian priest Camilo Torres, a professor of sociology at the National University of Bogotá, who left the Roman Catholic Church and the university to fight with a guerrilla band. Government troops killed him, and he became a national, even an international, hero.

The most famous guerrilla fighter was Ernesto Guevara, who, being an Argentinian, was nicknamed "Che," this being the typical form of greeting in Argentina. "Che" Guevara, a physician by profession, became a revolutionary early in life. He went to Guatemala, where Juan José Arévalo, a teacher who had lived for years in Argentina, had become President after the fall of the dictator Ubico. When the United States overthrew the regime of Arévalo's successor Arbenz, "Che" Guevara was among the losers. Castro's revolution gave him the opportunity to avenge himself. He became one of Fidel's chief advisers, and, after the Cuban revolution triumphed, he held a series of important posts. He was the key man in the agrarian reform which abolished the large estates, and he served as president of the National Bank of Cuba.

Suddenly he disappeared. Castro refused to state where he was, except to say that he had left Cuba on an important mission. Fidel was undoubtedly glad to be rid of a leader whose popularity rivaled his own, but the rumor that he had liquidated "Che" proved to be untrue. "Che" had left Cuba to revolutionize the world. Cuban revolutionaries began to figure in the liberation armies of black Africa, and later it became known that Guevara had been in the Congo. However, Africa was only of secondary interest to Castro and Guevara. Their aim was a Castro-sponsored revolution in Latin America. Castro had said that the Andes would be the Sierra Maestra of South America, and, as an Argentinian, Guevara was especially interested in that part of the hemisphere. Castro and Guevara mistakenly believed that Bolivia was ripe for revolution and that they could start guerrilla warfare in the eastern lowlands of that country with the support of the peasants. However, the Bolivian peasant is not like the Cuban, and the center of unrest in Bolivia has traditionally been in the tin mines, where the miners are organized and know how to handle dynamite. Castro and Guevara failed to win the support of the miners. The Bolivian army had firm control of the mining area, and "Che" fought with the Bolivian Communist leaders because of personal rivalries and because the Bolivian Communist Party followed the orders of Moscow, which opposed Castro's "adventures." The Bolivian army, which had been trained in guerrilla warfare by the U.S. Green Berets, pursued Guevara's band and captured him. He was apparently shot after his capture by a Bolivian soldier. Thus was born the legend of "Che" Guevara, which is still alive today. For some years after this, Castro's relations with the Soviet Union were cool, but when Castro visited Moscow in 1972 in appearance at least the breach was healed.

Trujillo and the Dominican Republic

After Cuba, the most important stronghold of despotism in the Antilles has been the Dominican Republic. The Dominican dictator Rafael Leonidas Trujillo became the archetype of the petty Latin American dictator in the service of the United States and U.S. economic interests. We must recognize that in some ways he achieved positive results. When the capital, Santo Domingo, was virtually destroyed by a hurricane, he rebuilt it better than it had been before and renamed it Ciudad Trujillo. After the fall of the dictator, the old name of Santo Domingo was restored.

Whereas Somoza was a jolly and only relatively cruel person, Trujillo was bloody. The Dominican Republic had been under the tyranny of black Haiti until 1844, and ever since then the Dominicans have viewed the Haitians with fear and hatred. Trujillo was disturbed by the number of Haitians who entered the Dominican Republic illegally to work in the sugar fields. Suddenly he ordered them to be killed. It is not known how many were massacred. The figures go as high as 30,000. Trujillo was likewise implacable toward his personal enemies. He regarded President Betancourt, who had overthrown his friend Pérez Jiménez and had set up a democratic government in Venezuela, as a danger for the Dominican dictatorship. Trujillo tried to kill him by engineering a dynamite explosion at a spot in Caracas where Betancourt was driving by. Although badly wounded, the President survived.

A notorious case was that of Jesús Galíndez, a Basque nationalist who emigrated to the Dominican Republic after the defeat of the Spanish republic. He became the tutor of the dictator's children, but realizing what was going on under the dictatorship, he fled to New York, where he became a lecturer at Columbia University. He wrote his doctoral dissertation on *The Era of Trujillo*, describing the Trujillo dictatorship in prosaic terms. Trujillo was furious and gave orders that he be killed. It seems that Trujillo's agents kidnapped Galíndez, took him to Ciudad Trujillo, and threw him into the sea, where hungry sharks were waiting for him.

Since the death of Trujillo, the Dominican Republic has naturally been a center of unrest. There is constant tension between the military, who wish to return to some kind of dictatorship, and the leftists, who want a regime similar to that of Fidel Castro. The great fear of the U.S. Government has been that the Dominican Republic might join the Castro camp and give the enemies of the United States another valuable base in the Caribbean.

In 1965, thinking that a Castro coup was imminent, the United States sent warships to the Dominican Republic, and the capital was occupied by U.S. troops. It seemed as though the Caribbean was returning to the period of U.S. interventions. Washington claimed it was acting in response to a request for help from the existing legal government and tried to disguise its intervention as an international expedition. It gave the expeditionary force the name "Inter-American Peace Force" (although the Organization of American States had, at best, a passive role), and a Brazilian general was named to head it. However, no one was fooled by the inter-American disguise, and the U.S. Government was widely criticized for its action, which was compared to the Soviet occupation of Hungary in 1956 or of Czechoslovakia in 1968.

In all of these cases the United States and the Soviet Union alleged that they were obliged to intervene. The U.S. Government proclaimed that the aim of its intervention was to protect the lives of U.S. citizens, to avoid a civil war, and to pave the way for democratic elections. The inter-American force was withdrawn in 1967, but Dominicans realize that there is always a danger of U.S. intervention if Washington deems it necessary.

Puerto Rico

Although it is U.S. territory, Puerto Rico is part of Spanish America and deserves mention. Until 1898, like Cuba, it was a Spanish possession, and the Spanish tradition is still strong in the island. Dictator Franco's "Hispanic" propaganda has had considerable success, and now the Puerto Ricans in New York like to be called "Hispanic Americans." The nationalist movement in Puerto Rico is a weird mixture of Marxism and the Falangista ideas which Franco Spain's official party, the Falange, took from Mussolini's fascism.

After the 1898 war the United States simply hung on to the island for strategic reasons. It was a decision of dubious wisdom, for since then Puerto Rico has been a headache for Washington. At first the United States attempted to assimilate the island by imposing the use of English and discouraging everything connected with the Spanish tradition. Yet the Puerto Ricans were not given U.S. citizenship, and they felt lost and humiliated. The resentment against the United States led to the formation of two anti-U.S. movements: the nationalists wished to use violence to obtain independence, while the "Independentistas" preferred more peaceful methods. The resentment of Puerto Ricans was somewhat assuaged when they were given U.S. citizenship.

As part of his Good Neighbor Policy, President Roosevelt tried to find a new formula for the island, and he sent Rexford Guy Tugwell there as the last U.S. Governor of the island. Cooperating loosely with the Puerto Rican leader Luis Muñoz Marín, the U.S. Government prepared a new status for the island, which was transformed into a Commonwealth, or an "Associated Free State" (Estado Libre Asociado). In reality it is neither a commonwealth, nor free, nor a state.

Some concessions were made to the island. It was given complete freedom to develop its own culture, and the attempt to impose English as the language of the island was abandoned. The governor of the island is elected by popular vote, and, naturally, he is a Puerto Rican. Muñoz Marín occupied this post until 1964, and, even after the defeat of his party, the Puerto Rican Popular Democratic Party, he has remained a significant figure in island politics. Puerto Rico has a considerable degree of autonomy in its internal affairs, and its flag flies at the same level as the U.S. flag, giving an impression of sovereignty and equality.

Yet all this is an illusion. In the British "Commonwealth" the members such as Canada or Australia are completely sovereign nations, with the same rights as any other sovereign nation. Puerto Rico lacks most of the important attributes of sovereignty. It does not have control of its foreign policy, its defense, or its currency. Officially, Puerto Rico has no foreign policy; its young men serve in the armed forces of the United States, and its currency is the dollar. In fact, in spite of all that has been said, Puerto Rico is still a territory. It does not even have effective representation in Washington. The Puerto Rican commissioner in Washington may speak in Congress, but he has no vote, and no one pays much attention to him.

Washington would like to believe that the Puerto Rican problem has been solved. While he was in power, Muñoz Marín, as the creator of the Associated Free State, regarded the new statute as flexible but definitive. Muñoz Marín's party lost the elections of 1968 as the result of an internal division, and the Statehood Party won power. The new governor, Luis A. Ferré, produced figures during the campaign which were alleged to show that statehood would benefit Puerto Rico. These figures were illusory, and the island does not wish to lose the financial advantages it derives from its present status. As a result, Ferré made no positive move toward statehood during his administration. In 1972 the Popular Democratic Party won the elections, and the statehood issue seemed to fade away when Ferré left the governorship.

The number of nationalists grows ever smaller. During the presidency of Harry Truman, they staged a shoot-out in Congress, but no one was killed, and only a few wounded. They tried to kill Truman himself, but they succeeded in killing only one of his bodyguards. There are more supporters of the independence movement, especially among the university students whose heroes are Fidel Castro and "Che" Guevara. However, these two leaders are losing their charisma, and only a minority of the Puerto Rican population wishes to break its links with the United States. The "Independentistas" claim, without any proof, that they have more supporters than is indicated by the number of votes they receive in elections.

In reality, the relationship between the United States and Puerto Rico is a marriage of convenience. The Puerto Ricans are not happy; on the contrary, they complain bitterly about the treatment they receive. Sociological studies have shown that they occupy a lower place on the social scale in New York than the blacks, even though they are generally white or near-white. Despite this, the Puerto Ricans flock to New York because the island is overpopulated and there is a shortage of work there. As U.S. citizens, they can come to the mainland freely, although many return when they have earned a certain amount of money. If Puerto Rico were independent, they would be subject to the usual immigration laws. Puerto Ricans have the advantage of U.S. citizenship without one of its main disadvantages: they do not pay income tax. Moreover, U.S. tourists, U.S.-owned industry, and U.S. bases are important sources of revenue for the island.

What advantages does this marriage offer to the United States? In this age of nuclear missiles, naval bases may be less important than before, but the United States, alone among the nations of the world, still has a strategy based on a worldwide network of bases. In view of the Soviet naval expansion throughout the world, these bases have acquired a new importance, and Puerto Rico can offset the Soviet naval presence in Cuba.

For U.S. corporations, Puerto Rico provides abundant low-cost labor. Puerto Rico claims that U.S. industries have been attracted to the island by "Operation Bootstrap," which offers U.S. investors substantial tax advantages. However, "Operation Bootstrap" would have had little success were it not for the manpower, which is cheaper than on the mainland. It is sometimes said that in view of the mechanization and automation of industry, labor costs are no longer of decisive importance. This may be true of some industries, but in most cases labor costs are an important factor in determining prices, and in our competitive society, prices are a matter of life and death for industrial concerns. Industries still locate factories where there is abundant, good, and cheap manpower. When pressure from labor unions raised wages in the North of the United States, industries began to move to the South, where the unions were weaker and the wages lower. When the unions gained strength in the South, industries moved to Puerto Rico, where wages are even lower and from where manufactured products can enter the U.S. mainland without any tariff barriers. In recent years labor unions, especially the Teamsters, have attempted to gain control of the island's workers. If as a result of union activity wages rose to the mainland level, a large part of the island's industry would collapse, because the shipping costs between the island and the mainland are still a factor. Puerto Ricans realize this, and the fear of losing the island's industries creates an uneasy peace in labor relations.

It is difficult to understand the motivation of the statehood leaders such as Ferré. They are businessmen accustomed to making cold calculations. They may have believed that the statehood plank would attract votes, since it is rather humiliating for Puerto Rico to be the only important territory which has not achieved statehood. When Hawaii and Alaska became states, there was a surge of feeling in favor of statehood, but this seems to have abated. Ferré was appealing to the voters also when in the 1968 campaign he said he would raise wages to the mainland level. He did not do it, and he presumably knew he could not do it.

The Discovery of Brazil

Brazil is a world apart from Spanish America. Despite numerous similarities, Brazilian history has a different rhythm from that of Spanish America. In Brazil there were no native civilizations comparable to those of Spanish America, and the conquest of Brazil was not carried out by dramatic, bloodthirsty Conquistadores, although their Portuguese counterparts, the *bandeirantes,* were less than gentle. The discovery of Brazil is still the subject of debate. The official version is that in 1493 the Spanish Pope Alexander VI divided the world between Spain and Portugal, marking as the dividing line the meridian which passes 100 leagues to the west of the Azores. This division would have left all the American continent in the hands of the Spaniards. By the Treaty of Tordesillas (1494) the dividing line was moved west to 370 leagues west of the Cape Verde Islands. The Portuguese claimed that they needed more space for their navigations to India, since a sailing ship rounding Africa has to go far to the west and then sail east toward the Cape of Good Hope. The Spaniards accepted this change in the dividing line, which, when extended to the Pacific, left the Philippines in the Spanish hemisphere. The Spaniards did not know that South America, and more precisely what would become Brazil, extended much further to the east than the Caribbean and that a slice of South America was now in the Portuguese hemisphere. The Portuguese claimed they did not know this either and that Brazil was discovered by accident when the wind pushed Pedro Alvares Cabral, on his way to India, westward to the coast of South America. Portugal thus discovered Brazil "by accident" in 1500.

Some historians reject this "theory of the accident" and propose instead the "theory of the secret," according to which the discovery of Brazil was no accident. The Portuguese, who were splendid navigators, knew of the existence of Brazil but kept it a secret, since in those days navigational discoveries were protected with a secrecy similar to that now surrounding discoveries in the field of nuclear weapons. When the Portuguese requested that the dividing line be moved west, they knew of the existence of Brazil but did not wish to reveal this secret to the Spaniards. At the opportune time Portugal announced that Cabral had discovered Brazil "by accident." Specialists argue heatedly about the two hypotheses. Since the interpretation of the relevant documents is extremely difficult, it would be unwise to express unqualified support for either thesis.

Now Portugal was legally entitled to the land east of a line which passed roughly through the mouth of the Amazon and the site of the city of São Paulo. This narrow strip of territory was to be transformed into the immense nation which became Brazil by a series of undramatic westward moves. In the international law of the period as codified by Hugo Grotius, effective occupation was a decisive criterion of sovereignty. Already the *uti possedetis* principle was operative. A notable westward expansion of Portuguese occupation took place during the period 1580-1640, the so-called "Babylonian captivity," when Portugal was under the Spanish Crown and there was no legal impediment to the migration of Portuguese into Spanish territory. When Portugal recovered its independence in 1640, Spain could not undo what had happened; it had to recognize Portuguese occupation of an immense area west of the dividing line, including most of the Amazon valley, which the Spaniards had explored but which they had not occupied. Admittedly, the Portuguese occupation was very spotty, but when Spain and Portugal signed the Treaty of Madrid in 1750, establishing the limits between Spanish and Portuguese America, the boundaries of Brazil were almost the same as those of today.

The conquest of Brazil was not an epic like that of Spanish America. There was in Brazil no Cortés, no Pizarro. At first Brazil attracted few Portuguese because the precious metals which had triggered the conquest of Spanish America had not yet been discovered. Portuguese attention was focused on India, which provided the spices that were worth a fortune in Europe. At first almost the only export of Brazil was a red dye obtained from a tree popularly known as *brasil,* because its color suggested a *brasa* (hot coal). The official name the Portuguese had given to the territory was "Land of the Holy Cross," but it was soon forgotten, and "Brazil" remained as the name of the country.

The Economic Cycles of Brazilian History

Economically, Brazil has passed through a number of "cycles," i.e. it has depended in world trade on one product after another which has become exhausted or ceased to be important. The result has been an unstable economy. When one cycle began, the corresponding region of Brazil entered a period of prosperity, but when that cycle ended, it decayed. Brazil has been dependent on the caprices of first the European and later the U.S. market. Like other Latin Americans, Brazilians said that they had won their political independence but they still had colonial economies.

The brazil-wood cycle ended fairly quickly. It was followed by the sugar cane cycle in the Northeast, especially in the region of Recife, where there developed a traditional society described by Gilberto Freyre in books such as *The Masters and the Slaves* (1933). This society led a feudal life like that of the Old South of the United States; this is why after the Civil War a number of Southerners migrated to Brazil. It is hard to see why Freyre maintains that the Portuguese were excellent colonizers in the tropics. The masters of the plantations he describes were lazy, vulgar, generally uneducated, and took advantage of black men and, especially, black women.

The eighteenth century was the period of the gold cycle. Precious metals were discovered in Brazil much later than in Spanish America. As the name indicates, Minas Gerais ("general mines") was the province from which the Portuguese extracted gold and precious stones. As in Spanish America, the mother country profited most from this wealth. The Portuguese Government surrounded the area with barriers to prevent the smuggling out of gold and jewels without paying the Crown the "royal fifth." Since Rio de Janeiro was the principal export point for this wealth, the capital was moved there from Bahia in 1763. Colonial Bahia has remained almost intact, and it is the most historical city in Brazil. Only Ouro Prêto, the colonial capital of Minas Gerais, can compare with it.

The Brazilians complained that the wealth of their country flowed to Portugal and that Brazil derived little profit from it. Father Antonio Vieira said the clouds formed in Brazil but the rain dropped in Portugal. Nevertheless, we must recognize that Portugal left in Brazil a noteworthy legacy of baroque art. Both in Portugal and in Brazil there was in the eighteenth century a remarkable flowering of baroque. Significant in this regard are the cities of Ouro Prêto, São João del Rei, Tiradentes (formerly São José del Rei), and Congonhas. The great artist of Minas Gerais in this period was "o Aleijadinho," a mulatto born in Ouro Prêto in 1738. His name was Francisco Antônio Lisboa, but he is known by his nickname "o Aleijadinho" (the little crippled one) because leprosy had crippled his hands. Despite this handicap, he executed remarkable works of sculpture and architecture. His masterpieces are the famous statues of the prophets in front of the church at Congonhas (1800).

The Independence of Brazil

Ouro Prêto was also a center of intellectual and political activity. The national hero of Brazil is "Tiradentes" (toothpuller). The real name of this army officer was Francisco Joaquim José da Silva Xavier, but he is always known by the nickname given him because he was a dentist. Tired of the abuses of the Portuguese Government and inspired by the American and French Revolutions, he organized in 1789 a conspiracy to proclaim the independence of Brazil. The plot was discovered, "Tiradentes" and some of his companions were executed, and the rest were exiled to Africa. Brazil, like Mexico, has no real liberator and, therefore, must idealize one who, like Hidalgo and Morelos, failed. Despite his failure, "Tiradentes" is the symbol of Brazilian independence.

Brazil finally achieved its independence undramatically. There were no epic and bloody campaigns like those of Bolívar, San Martín, and other Spanish American liberators. "Happy the peoples who have no history," we are told, and in this regard Brazil is a happy nation. The dramas of Cortés, Pizarro, Bolívar, and San Martín have no parallels in Brazil, but the history of Spanish America would have been happier if it had solved its problems less dramatically. While Spanish America was exhausting itself in theatrics, Brazil was quietly expanding its boundaries, absorbing more and more territory until it became the most important nation of Latin America.

The independence of Brazil was the result of the Napoleonic invasion of the Iberian Peninsula. The British Government advised the Spanish and Portuguese governments to take refuge in their American domains. The Spanish monarchy could not carry out the plan, and, as we have seen, Carlos IV and Fernando VII chose to abdicate, leaving the throne of Spain to Napoleon's brother, Joseph Bonaparte. The Portuguese monarchy succeeded in escaping to the New World, rather like the European monarchies fleeing from Hitler to escape to England during World War II. Protected by the British fleet, the court of João VI moved in 1808 from Lisbon to Rio de Janeiro, which for some years was the capital of the Portuguese Empire.

After the defeat of Napoleon the Portuguese demanded that the royal family return to Lisbon. The court was living happily in Rio de Janeiro and had no great desire to return to Portugal, where a bitter struggle between liberals and conservatives was in progress. João VI finally decided to return, but he left his son Pedro in Brazil. He advised him that, should the situation in Portugal become impossible, he proclaim the independence of Brazil. The Portuguese Government did not approve of Pedro's remaining in Brazil and demanded that he too should return to Lisbon. Pedro replied with a negative which is famous in the history of Brazil: "Fico!" ("I am staying here in Brazil.") When the Lisbon government insisted, Pedro proclaimed the independence of Brazil in 1822 and took the title of Emperor Pedro I.

The Brazilian Empire

Pedro was really somewhat like Iturbide of Mexico. He was not very popular, and the so-called First Empire ended badly; Pedro I abdicated in 1831. This is now glossed over, and the remains of Pedro I were returned with great ceremony from Portugal to Brazil in 1972 and paraded solemnly through all the major cities before reinterment. Pedro II came to the throne in 1831, and his reign, the Second Empire, lasted until 1889, when he was overthrown by a typically peaceful Brazilian revolution; he died in Europe in 1891.

Pedro II was very different from his pleasure-loving father. Serious and scholarly, he led a sober life; whereas his father had been arbitrary and more or less absolutist, Pedro II was a constitutional monarch, and his government was modeled after the British parliamentary system. It was said with admiration and irony that Pedro II was the only really republican leader in all of Latin America.

Brazilian society was very conservative, and this may be explained by the fact that slavery lasted longer in Brazil than in the rest of America. In reality, behind the façade of parliamentarianism, power was in the hands of the landowners described by Gilberto Freyre, and they had no interest in seeing slavery come to an end. British liberals wanted to abolish slavery everywhere in the world, and Joaquim Nabuco, who was in close contact with the British abolitionists, was the hero of the emancipation movement in Brazil. In 1888, during the absence of her father, Pedro II, Princess Isabel gave in to pressure from the emancipation leaders and signed a decree ending slavery. The angry landowners withdrew their support, and the empire collapsed. The imperial family sailed for Europe, and in 1889 the republic was proclaimed.

Brazilians had an affectionate regard for the emperor and were sorry to see him go. The republic did not bring effective democracy; it was military, authoritarian, and positivist. Since 1889, Brazil has had few periods of effective democracy. Although under Pedro II the government was controlled by the oligarchy, it was more democratic, or certainly more representative and parliamentary, than most of the later governments.

The peaceful transition from the colony to the empire and from the empire to the republic was one of the main reasons why Brazil remained united while Spanish America split up into eighteen republics. The contrast between the unity of Brazil and the disunity of Spanish America is striking. There are various reasons. The Portuguese are temperamentally different from the Spaniards. The Portuguese are less nervous, more silent, more persistent; the Spaniards are more violent, more dramatic, and more diffuse.

We should not forget that, despite its vast area, the principal cities of Brazil were and are on the coast. The main exception is São Paulo, which is only a short distance from the ocean and is closely connected with its port, Santos. Pôrto Alegre is on a lagoon with direct access to the sea, and ocean-going vessels can sail up the Amazon as far as Manaus. It is only in the last few years that, thanks primarily to aviation, a few important inland cities like Belo Horizonte and Brasília have developed. Brazilian cities were traditionally linked by the sea and the Amazon during the centuries when maritime communications were easier than land communications. By way of contrast, many of the most important cities of Spanish America are in the interior, in places which before aviation were difficult to reach, and communications among them were very slow or nonexistent. In Brazil there were two separatist movements, one in the south and one in the north, but they were easily put down. In Spanish America it was difficult to send an army to the centers of insurrection. Junín and Ayacucho, the last great battle in the wars of Bolívar, were fought at an altitude of about 13,000 feet.

Nevertheless, the decisive factor in the preservation of Brazilian unity was the continuation of the Portuguese monarchy transformed into a Brazilian empire. People who have grown up in a republic or even in a modern monarchy have no idea of the ancient symbolic value of monarchy. Although the cult of the emperor in Brazil could not be compared with the ancient cult of the emperor in Japan, the imperial crown was a symbol which unified Brazilians. Had Brazil become a republic upon winning its independence, as did the nations of Spanish America, it is doubtful if the national unity would have been preserved. Brazilians had no doubts about the legitimacy of their emperor. The Spanish Americans were faced with a quite different predicament: there were three supposed kings—Charles IV, Fernando VII, and José Bonaparte—and the Spanish Americans did not know which had the legitimate claim.

Brazil. The Republic

In the Brazilian republic the legitimacy of the government came into question, and many coups have been staged on the pretext that the government was not legitimate. The most noteworthy case was that of Getúlio Vargas, whose 1930 revolution gave Brazil its best-known dictatorship. The motives and pretexts for the coup were numerous. It is sufficient to say that, with a group of fellow *gaúchos* (inhabitants of Rio Grande do Sul), Vargas carried out a revolution which really had little ideological content. He had no fixed political principles, and he changed his views many times to suit the circumstances. He was an astute and not very violent individual, a benevolent dictator.

Vargas' pretext for revolting was that the government had usurped power. Then, the *Paulistas,* who lost, returned the charge and staged a revolution in 1932. This was the only time when Vargas acted with ruthless violence. He won the civil war and established a centralized and authoritarian government. The supreme authority in each state was an *interventor* named by Vargas. He held a ceremony at which the flags of the various states were burned to demonstrate that sovereignty resided in the nation. To bring both capital and labor under control, he introduced a corporative system similar to that prevailing in Italy and Portugal. Under this system the administration of an industry was in the hands of a tripartite committee representing the owners, the workers, and the government, whose representative had a decisive role. The New State proclaimed by Vargas in 1937 was clearly fascist in inspiration. This was the time when Italian and German fascism, which the American aviator Charles Lindbergh said was the wave of the future, seemed certain to triumph. During World War II, after the initial victories of Italy and Germany, Vargas believed the Axis would win, and he made speeches hailing their victory.

When England continued to fight and the United States entered the struggle, Vargas realized that he had made a mistake, and he astutely changed sides. He was also very clever in the way he made the Allies pay a high price for his switch. The United States wanted to stamp out fascism and nazism in Latin America. Argentina was the principal focus of these movements, and the result was a bitter struggle between Washington and Buenos Aires. Washington wanted to isolate the Argentine Government, and it therefore had a special interest in winning the support of Brazil. Moreover, the United States needed landing fields in the north of Brazil for its planes going to Africa; in those days bombers did not have enough range to cross the Atlantic directly. Vargas promised to collaborate with the United States in exchange for a series of favors, the most important being the building of a steel plant at Volta Redonda; it is now the largest in Latin America.

When the democracies were victorious in Europe, the survival in Latin America of dictators protected by the United States seemed to be an anachronism. Vargas gave up power in 1945. He was followed by a democratic but colorless regime. Despite his totalitarian record, Brazilians generally liked Vargas. He was commonly known by his first name, Getúlio, and he had been called "the father of the people." Vargas wished to rehabilitate himself in the eyes of history and prove that he could gain power democratically. He did so, winning the elections of 1950, but his administration ended sadly. He committed suicide in 1954, leaving a mysterious note in which he accused, among others, "foreign forces" of having driven him to this end. The suicide of Vargas has never been cleared up, and the note he left was a mystery which no one could or would explain. Brazilians believed that Getúlio was accusing U.S. corporations, and this made him a national martyr. After his death, his followers divided into two major parties, the PSD (Social Democratic Party) and the PTB (Brazilian Labor Party). His conservative enemies formed the principal opposition party, the UDN (National Democratic Union).

The administration of Juscelino Kubitschek (1956-60) was noteworthy because he brought about the old dream of moving the national capital from Rio de Janeiro to the interior. The new capital was called Brasília. It is located in the highlands, and its climate is much better than that of Rio de Janeiro. It is more or less on the dividing line between the valley of the Paraná (i.e. the rivers which go south) and the valley of the Amazon (i.e. the rivers which go north). Until a few years ago the vast interior of Brazil was practically empty. The creation of Brasília was an essential step in the "Westward March," the aim of which was to transform a country which was really no more than a string of coastal cities into a nation which would effectively occupy its territory. The government had to get away from the congestion of Rio de Janeiro, where it could not operate efficiently. Moreover, it was correctly assumed that the presence of the new capital would attract large numbers of people to the interior and stimulate development there.

The building of Brasília was the target of much criticism. It was charged, with reason, that the costs were exorbitant. At first all the materials had to be taken in by plane. Only later were highways built to São Paulo, Rio de Janeiro, and Belem. The railroad came last. A branch line was built connecting the new capital with the national railroad network, which is admittedly very deficient, with different gauges preventing an effective integration of the system. Little by little the various ministries and other activities moved to Brasília, and by 1972 it was the de facto as well as the de jure capital.

Brasília represents an important step forward in the history of Brazil. It was an essential move in the occupation of the interior highlands and of the Amazon valley, which is just beginning. From its new capital, Brazil dominates all of South America. The other republics are like a necklace strung around the neck of Brazil.

Many countries have built new capitals: Madrid, Ottawa, Canberra, New Delhi, Ankara, and Islamabad are the best-known examples. Brazil is the only country which has built many new state capitals, among them Belo Horizonte in Minas Gerais and Goiânia in Goiás. The old capitals, Ouro Prêto and Goiás Velho, have become museum cities. São Paulo has announced that it will build a new capital near Campinas.

The building of Brasília and the enormous expense it incurred was one of the main causes of an inflation which almost wrecked the Brazilian economy. President Kubitschek was widely accused of corruption. He was succeeded by a rather odd language teacher, Jânio Quadros, who was elected because he gave the impression of being scrupulously honest; he took a broom as his symbol. He was greeted as a national savior, but he was unequal to the job and resigned after being in power for less than a year. His vice-president, João Goulart, took over. Although he was wealthy himself, he seemed to be paving the way for a Cuba-type revolution, and there was a national scandal when he decorated "Che" Guevara. He deliberately undermined military discipline, and the army reacted by overthrowing him; he fled to Uruguay.

Since then, Brazil has lived under a military dictatorship. General Humberto Castelo Branco was succeeded in the Presidency by General Artur da Costa e Silva. The military government abolished the old parties and created two new ones, the government party and the opposition party. However, these synthetic parties have no real life, and no one took this democratic façade very seriously. After repeatedly saying that they were preparing the country for democracy, the military made it clear in 1972 that this goal is still in the invisible distance. Businessmen and U.S. interests were generally happy, since the military government slowed down inflation and proved itself to be efficient. There was much discontent because of the Draconian measures taken by the government; many politicians of the old regime lost their political rights and a number of them went into exile. Student revolts were suppressed ruthlessly, and the government succeeded in crushing guerrilla activities. In 1969 the military junta closed Congress, alleging that some deputies had insulted the army. Brazil thus became a dictatorship as total as that of Argentina. However, whereas the Argentine military, having lost support by their ineptness, were trying to establish a democratic order, the Brazilian military won more and more support by their efficiency and the prosperity the country enjoyed under their administration. The people seemed generally content, and talk among U.S. intellectuals of a forthcoming violent revolution in Brazil appeared to have little basis in fact. Perhaps the military dictatorship reflects the realities of Luso-Brazilian culture. The Mexican Revolution of 1910 and the fate of many Latin American military dictatorships should remind us that law, order, and prosperity are fragile and even illusory. But then so is Latin American democracy. The technical battle continues between the forces of law and order and the forces of unrest and revolt.

4 • The Economy

It is impossible to understand a civilization without knowing its economic basis. The economy of Latin America is fairly complex because of the differences among the various countries. At the same time, all the countries have had more or less parallel economic histories. All have gone through the pre-Columbian period, the colonial period, the independence period, and now the period of industrialization, or at least modernization.

The Pre-Columbian Economy

The pre-Columbian economy is not well known, although even today remains of it survive in isolated areas. There were primitive tribes which pursued primarily hunting and fishing, while in the regions of the great cultures, above all Mexico and Peru, a fairly advanced agriculture had developed. The traveler going by train from Lima to Huancayo in Peru is surprised to see thousands of terraces built by pre-Columbian farmers. Almost all of these terraces are now abandoned, a mark of the catastrophic decadence provoked by the Spanish Conquest.

In other areas, such as Yucatán, agriculture was more primitive. The Indians burned an area of forest, and the ashes provided fertilizer. The plough was unknown in pre-Columbian America; the Indians simply made a hole with a stick and put a seed in it. After two or three harvests the soil was exhausted, so the Indians moved to another part of the forest, and the process was repeated. Obviously, such a nomadic agriculture did not permit the development of a stable civilization.

At the same time, we must admire the tenacious and inventive work of the Indians, especially those of Peru and Middle America, in selecting wild plants and transforming them into cultivated crops; the basis of agriculture is the artificial creation of plants by a process of selection. The plants which the Indians gave the world (such as maize, the potato, the tomato, and cacao) are the result of a long creative process. It is interesting to follow the development of maize from primitive *teozintle* to its modern varieties. This process is still going on. In Mexico the Rockefeller Foundation maintains an international maize center, which is developing new strains which give more and better food. The international campaign the Rockefeller Foundation is carrying on is part of a worldwide fight against hunger in the less developed areas of the world.

The Indians made no comparable effort to domesticate animals. The horse, the cow, the sheep, the pig, and the goat were domesticated in the Old World and introduced into the New World by the Spaniards. The absence of a similar development in America was doubtless due to the fact that in this continent there were few wild animals which could be domesticated. For complex reasons of geology and climate, the fauna of the New World was very different from that of the Old. The Peruvian Indians had domesticated the llama, which is related to the alpaca and the vicuña, and which corresponds zoologically not to the sheep of the Old World, as the Spaniards thought, but to the camel. The Peruvian Indians used the llama as a beast of burden, and they still do, but dried llama meat, known in Quechua as "charque" (hence, the English word "jerked," as in "jerked beef") is seldom eaten nowadays. The custom of eating dried meat (beef, not llama) was adopted by the gauchos of Argentina. Mexican Indians fattened and ate a peculiar kind of dog, but apart from this almost the only meat the Indians ate came from hunting. Unfortunately, in what is now Latin America there was not the large game characteristic of Africa and other parts of the Old World. The Carib Indians ate human flesh (the word "cannibal" derives from "Carib"), but this habit was not widespread among the other Indians of America. The coastal Indians fished, but in general the Indian diet was lacking in proteins. There was no milk or cheese, and only in a few places were there some strange hens which laid blue eggs. Maize, which was the basic food in much of the area, has a limited food value, and some specialists wish that instead of maize the Latin American diet had another base, such as, for example, wheat (long a primary crop in Argentina and Uruguay, it is now increasingly common in southern Brazil and Mexico). However, it is difficult to change the food habits of a continent.

Although the principal occupation of pre-Columbian Indians was agriculture, we must not give the impression that their economy stopped there. Textile-making had a noteworthy development, especially in Peru; the mantles of Paracas, a ceremonial center on the coast, are remarkable. Technically, Indians were still in the Bronze Age, since they had not learned how to smelt iron. They did not use the wheel, which in the history of the Old World goes back to earliest times. Since the Indians, not having iron, had neither iron weapons nor iron armor, and likewise had neither firearms nor chariots, they gave the Spanish Conquistadores the impression of being very primitive, but we must remember that, without iron tools, they carved stone and built, especially in Middle America, buildings of classic beauty.

The native economy was based on barter, although in Mexico cacao grains were used as a kind of currency. Gold and silver, which aroused the greed of the Spaniards, were for the Indians symbols of beauty and prestige. It was for this reason that the Incas acquired the reputation of being nobler in their economic attitudes than the Europeans, but we may suppose that in the market places the Indians bargained as they do today. This means that they were not disinterested idealists, but simply had not yet reached the point, characteristic of Western civilization, of regarding gold and silver as the measures of the economic value of objects.

In general the Indians did not have the system of private personal property which is a characteristic of our Western society. There was a sense of communal property, and some writers speak of native communism. Some historians maintain that the imposition of the European capitalist system represented a violent break with the native tradition and that today communism finds a favorable atmosphere in regions where the native predominates, because it represents a return to the primitive economic condition of the continent.

The airplane has completely changed the communications picture in Latin America. Today it is fairly easy to go from one capital to another. Before World War II it was almost impossible. A journey to Tegucigalpa, the capital of Honduras, was a veritable epic. To reach Bogotá, the capital of Colombia, took almost a week from the port of Barranquilla. Most of the journey was up the Magdalena River; the last stretch was made by road, or later by train. The return trip, down the Magdalena River, was somewhat faster. During the pre-Columbian period communications were almost impossible or nonexistent, except in a few areas.

Archaeologists speak of the commercial relations between the great centers of pre-Columbian culture: Mexico, Central America, Colombia, and Peru. These relations doubtless existed, but they were not intense and they cannot be compared with the commercial interchange today. Perhaps we should make an exception for the Inca empire. As always in pre-Columbian history, there is a lack of precise data and an abundance of conflicting theories. Even though the Inca capital, Cuzco, was in the high Andes, the Inca empire controlled the coast from Ecuador to Chile, and a system of paths (not roads) linked the various parts of the empire. With the use of rafts, the Incas apparently developed a communications network across the Pacific. Easter Island was in some ways a dependency of the Inca empire. There is evidence of commerce across the Pacific between Oceania and South America, but here again we should not exaggerate the volume of this exchange, in view of the enormous size of the Pacific. Moreover, there was in pre-Columbian America a great linguistic confusion, even though in the Inca empire Quechua was imposed as the official language and Tupí-Guaraní was spoken through much of Brazil. When, with the Conquest, Spanish and Portuguese became the dominant languages, they facilitated communications between regions which spoke mutually incomprehensible languages.

The Colonial Economy

The Conquest transformed the economy of the New World. Before then the Indian worked to satisfy his personal needs. Now America belonged to the mercantile system in which the colonies of each European nation were supposed to complement the economy of the mother country, for which the colony was to produce the raw materials, receiving in exchange manufactured products. There was no free trade. All the trade of Spanish America had to pass through Spain.

In America, Spain and Portugal sought above all precious metals and also tropical products such as sugar, cacao, indigo, and cochineal. According to the mercantile theory, the colonies should not produce anything which could compete with the mother country. Consequently, Spanish and Portuguese America should not grow grape vines (for wine), olive trees, or anything which Spain and Portugal could produce. This prohibition was absurd, since, when they introduced into the New World plants and animals from Europe, the peninsular governments were going against the letter of mercantilism. The Spanish Government decided from time to time to enforce mercantilist laws rigidly; it ordered olive trees and vineyards to be torn-up and did everything possible to close down industries (textile mills, etc.) which competed with those of the homeland.

It also blocked commerce among the various colonies and forbade direct trade with other European countries such as England. It was virtually impossible to stop this trade, and the result was large-scale smuggling which was carried on openly and almost proudly, rather like the Boston Tea Party, which was also a challenge to the metropolitan government. American tradesmen detested the impediments imposed by Spain and Portugal. The rich Creoles wanted free trade; the Spanish Government saw the danger, and at the end of the eighteenth century it abolished almost all the prohibitions deriving from the mercantile system, but it was now too late. It is fair to say that the principal motive for the wars of independence was not the desire to speak and think freely but the desire to trade freely.

The Modern Economy

When the Spanish and Portuguese empires collapsed, the new governments had to seek the economic aid of Great Britain, which poured an immense amount of capital into South America, where British capital was predominant until World War II. England was forced to sell its investments to pay for the cost of the struggle against Hitler, and since then U.S. capital has predominated, although West German and Japanese investments have become substantial. How should we judge the role of foreign capital in Latin America? In general Latin Americans refuse to recognize what they owe to it. Without British capital Latin America would be much more backward than it is today. Some Argentinians criticize the building of their railroads by the British, but the fact is that British capital gave Argentina an excellent rail system, which began to deteriorate when the Argentine Government imposed impossible controls on such things as tariffs and labor conditions. When, under Perón, the Argentine Government took over the railroads, the results were disastrous.

Latin Americans try to make it appear that the British derived enormous profits from their investments. Some of these investments were indeed profitable, but many were a complete loss. It has been calculated that the average interest paid by British investments in Latin America was lower than the average interest paid by investments in England itself. When Latin Americans

OIL DOES NOT LUBRICATE INTER-AMERICAN RELATIONS

Source: Pravda

The Soviet's long-term aim is to gain control of the world's oil resources and thereby of the West and its industrial machinery, not to mention Japan. In Soviet caricatures of Western corporations as robber-barons, U.S. and other oil companies are singled out for special attention. Even under Acción Democrática, Venezuela was the Latin American country where U.S. oil companies enjoyed the best relations. Now the Christian Democrat government has embarked on a campaign to eliminate foreign oil concessions. Soviet commentators attempt to portray the Venezuelan Government as a passive victim, whereas in reality it is, to the Soviet's delight, doing its best to tie the oil companies up in knots.

begin trade negotiations, they do it with the idea of obtaining the best possible conditions, yet they expect foreigners to invest in Latin America in unfavorable conditions. Capital goes abroad, especially to areas like Latin America which are prone to revolutions, civil war, inflation, and confiscation or expropriation, only if it will yield a better return than at home. It is a lamentable fact that, while Latin Americans complain about foreign investments in their own countries, they themselves prefer to invest their money in the United States or in secret Swiss bank accounts. If all the money which Latin Americans have invested abroad, often in defiance of the laws of their own countries, were repatriated, the capitalization problems of Latin America would be greatly alleviated.

At present the country which has the greatest investments in Latin America is the United States, and U.S. capital is the target of attacks from both the left and the right. The arguments about U.S. capital have become what Spaniards call "a conversation among deaf people." Oil companies, especially the affiliates of the Standard Oil Company of New Jersey, have been the object of harsh criticisms. Even Venezuela, which boomed thanks to foreign oil companies which found a favorable atmosphere there, has turned against the Standard affiliate, Creole; now the attacks are coming not only from the left but from the right and from the moderate Christian Democratic government. The Standard affiliate in Peru was nationalized after a long and bitter fight, and now the Venezuelan Government is determined to terminate the Creole concessions. Latin American governments turn the nationalization policy on and off as it suits them. Admittedly, the oil companies have been clumsy and have allied themselves with any dictator prepared to give them a concession. But it must be understood that petroleum exploration is a costly and risky business; often wells prove to be dry, and the investment is lost. Risk capital expects high returns. In general Latin American countries do not have the capital and the technical capacity for oil exploration and development. Costs are much lower in the Middle East, and Latin American governments change their policies when they realize that they are unable to meet the competition. Having expropriated foreign oil companies with resounding denunciations, they proceed to invite the same or other companies in again. Perón came to power with a promise to nationalize foreign oil companies. When he invited them back, the Argentinian people felt they had been deceived, and this was one of the principal causes for his fall. The Peruvian and other governments have acted in similar fashion.

The Organization of Petroleum Exporting Countries (OPEC) tries to present a common front against the consuming countries (Western Europe, the United States, and Japan) but there is competition from new sources not controlled by OPEC (Alaska, the North Sea, Canada) and from atomic energy. Yet the situation is more critical than most people in the West realize, and the Soviet Union, which wants to sell its own petroleum products and to weaken the West, is doing all it can to encourage the producing countries to nationalize foreign-owned oil companies. If the Soviet plan succeeds, the entire world would be virtually at the mercy of the Soviet Union.

The nationalists would reply that under state ownership the Soviet Union has become a leading oil producer and that their governments can follow this example without being controlled by Moscow. The expropriation of foreign oil companies in Latin America, indeed throughout the world, was triggered by the example of Mexico, where President Lázaro Cárdenas expropriated British and American oil interests in 1938. They were taken over by a national monopoly, Petróleos Mexicanos (PEMEX), which has served as a model for similar government oil monopolies in other Latin American countries. Cárdenas was a leftist nationalist, in many ways a precursor of Fidel Castro, for whom he had shown considerable sympathy. The expropriation of the oil companies was for him a Mexican victory over Yankee imperialism. Almost as a warning, the Mexican Government built, at the entrance to Lomas de Chapultepec, the most elegant district of Mexico City where many Americans live, an impressive monument commemorating the expropriation of the oil companies. This is part of the patriotic mythology of Mexico; it is impossible to discuss it candidly. In reality the oil production of Mexico has declined considerably. When foreigners attribute this to the incompetence of PEMEX, Mexicans reply that it is because the oil fields are becoming exhausted. The expropriation aroused strong resentment in the United States. It was submitted to the International Court of Justice in The Hague, and Mexico paid the required indemnity. The U.S. Government declared it was satisfied, since it does not oppose expropriations provided they are accompanied by adequate, prompt, and effective payment of indemnity (i.e. in cash, not in bonds which may become worthless). PEMEX has cordial relations with U.S. business, and the Bank of America has given it substantial loans. The U.S. oil companies are still not happy because of the repercussions the expropriation is still having around the world. For example, Iran, which is now contemplating the expropriation of foreign oil interests, is studying the Mexican case with great interest.

The trend throughout the world is for mineral resources, including petroleum, to be taken out of foreign control, either by leaving the foreign companies with only minority participation (what President Frei called "Chileanization") or by outright expropriation (the policy followed by Allende). If the government refuses international arbitration, a U.S. company is reduced to making the best deal it can, as did the Cerro Corporation, or trying to obtain redress by international litigation, the method adopted by the Kennecott Corporation. Latin America has a bad record in this regard, and U. S. businessmen commonly say they would sooner deal with the Soviet Union, which has a scrupulous respect for contracts.

For many Latin Americans the monster of U.S. economic imperialism is the United Fruit Company. There is a whole literature attacking the company, including the novels of the Guatemalan writer Miguel Angel Asturias, who won the Nobel Prize for Literature in 1967. The United Fruit Company was indeed clumsy and ruthless in its early days and was happy to make a deal with any Central American dictator who would give it a concession—hence, the expression "banana republics." However, since World War II the United Fruit Company has not acted as though it controlled these republics, and in many ways its behavior has been exemplary. The charges made against it could much more properly be made against the local landowners. The United Fruit Company pays better wages and provides better working conditions than they. All Central Americans criticize the company, and all want to work for it. It has been a powerful stimulus to Central American agriculture, not only by setting an example in using modern methods but also by the magnificent work of the Pan American Agriculture School it founded in Zamorano, Honduras, which trains agricultural experts for many Latin American countries.

Central Americans forget that growing, exporting, and selling bananas require capital, an international organization, modern technology, and administrative experience. The campaign against the United Fruit Company was so harsh in Central America that, to offset it, the administration of President John F. Kennedy accused the company of being a monopoly and forced it to sell its subsidiary, the International Railways of Central America (IRCA). In 1968 IRCA was declared bankrupt; the Guatemalan Government took it over and created a state monopoly entitled Ferrocarriles de Guatemala (Guatemala Railroads). It is hard to say if

EXPORTS OF MANUFACTURED PRODUCTS

	1960	1969	1970	Percentages of total 1960	1970
Latin America	238	1,124	1,499	100.0	100.0
Argentina	30	220	246	12.6	16.4
Bolivia	—	—	1	—	0.1
Brazil	21	223	421	8.8	28.1
Chile	26	38	53	10.9	3.5
Colombia	7	60	79	2.9	5.3
Costa Rica	—	36	43	—	2.9
Dominican Republic	5	5	6	2.1	0.4
Ecuador	1	3	2	0.4	0.1
El Salvador	6	64	66	2.5	4.4
Guatemala	4	65	81	1.7	5.4
Honduras	1	13	14	0.4	0.9
Mexico	92	302	371	38.7	24.7
Nicaragua	2	19	28	0.8	1.9
Panama	—	2	1	—	0.1
Paraguay	4	5	5	1.7	0.3
Peru	6	11	15	2.5	1.0
Uruguay	9	28	36	3.8	2.4
Venezuela	24	30	31	10.1	2.1

Source: Economic Commission for Latin America.

The figures represent millions of dollars. In assessing the growth of these exports, the rise in prices should be considered, but the growth is sufficient to indicate that Latin America is no longer almost exclusively an exporter of raw materials and agricultural products. The striking feature is the rise of Brazil from fifth to first place. Despite the talk about Mexican industrialization, Brazil easily surpasses Mexico, which once led by a wide margin. Brazil now exports almost twice as much as Argentina, which used to lead Brazil in manufactured exports. While some critics of economic growth question how much the Brazilian people have profited from this, the figures clearly reflect the growing role of Brazil in world trade.

the Kennedy administration was justified in breaking up the two companies, but a basic problem is that companies like the United Fruit Company are so big that they frighten Latin Americans. The main factors behind expropriation, however, are nationalism and the simple desire to take over U.S. facilities and jobs.

The bitterness of Latin Americans may be explained by three centuries of colonial rule. The same phenomenon is occurring in a milder form in other parts of the world. Until recently the United States pointed to Canada as a country which welcomed U.S. investments and benefited from them, but now Canada is showing concern that so much of its industry is owned by U. S. interests.

With their colonial habit of attributing their woes to "imperialist" countries, Latin American economists claim that the terms of international trade are loaded against them. They repeat uncritically the thesis put forward by the Argentinian Raúl Prebisch that the difficulties of areas like Latin America spring from the disparity between the falling prices of raw materials and the rising prices of industrial goods. This thesis is questionable. Those who remember the depression of the early thirties know that such depressions hit industrial societies harder than agricultural ones, which continue to live off the land. Moreover, it is absurd to suggest that the terms of trade are dictated by a wicked capitalist conspiracy against Latin America.

Be that as it may, Latin American countries believe that the only way to escape from economic colonialism is by industrialization, and this course is urged by ambitious Latin Americans eager to become heads of industry. The most striking case is that of São Paulo, Brazil, which claims to be the fastest-growing city in the world. Unfortunately, even when the industrialization is successful, there is so little planning that the environmental crimes of the nineteenth century are being repeated, leaving a legacy of ugly, dirty, and depressing cities.

Sometimes this forced industrialization distorts the national economy almost beyond repair. Argentina was a prosperous, stable country when it promoted its agriculture, but after Perón tried to industrialize it with the proceeds of taxes on agriculture, the country fell into an economic and social chaos from which it seems incapable of recovering.

Another difficulty is that many industries are beyond the capacity of the majority of Latin American countries. They require capital, technology, and a large market. The automobile industry is a case in point. If there were a large free-trade area, Latin Americans could enjoy the advantages of inexpensive small cars, but the attempts to create such an area by organizing groups such as the Latin American Free Trade Association or the Central American Common Market have had very limited success. Latin American countries have placed heavy tariffs on, or even blocked, the importing of automobiles to stimulate local production, and the result is that cars cost three or four times as much as they do in Europe. Is it socially wise for a country to produce its own automobiles if this restricts their purchase to the affluent? Some countries such as Brazil, Argentina, and Mexico may offer a large enough market for mass production by a limited number of factories, but the others do not. The problem becomes more acute as factories grow bigger to permit economies of scale. Some argue that even uneconomic industries provide jobs for the growing population, but many industries are capital intensive rather than labor intensive.

One of the aims of industrialization is to cut down the balance of payments deficit which affects so many Latin American countries. Many governments forbid the importation of goods which can be produced locally. One result is an increase in the cost of living, inflation, and social unrest. This has been a major problem for Argentina, Uruguay, and Chile. In the Caribbean countries, which have been more closely tied to the United States and where there has not been a wild rush to industrialize, there has been less inflation than in South America, where Venezuela, with its oil wealth and its strong economy, is the only country which has had a stable currency. (Paraguay is a special case.) Some countries (Guatemala, Panama, and the Dominican Republic) have a currency on a par with the U.S. dollar, others (El Salvador, Honduras, Nicaragua, Costa Rica) pegged to it. In theory the Cuban peso is on a par with the dollar also, but since there is no trade between the two countries, this parity is fictitious. The Cuban peso is really worth much less than a dollar, but Cuba's trade with countries such as Japan, Spain, England, and France has been conducted on a governmental level, so the official rate means little on the open market. In 1972 Cuba became a full member of the Soviet bloc COMECON, and its currency now follows the same patterns as that of other COMECON countries. However, because of the physical isolation of Cuba both from the COMECON and the capitalist countries, a black market such as flourishes in Eastern Europe has not developed.

The business and banking world believes that international prosperity is impossible without a more or less stable relationship among world currencies, and the International Monetary Fund

(IMF), which reflects this criterion, has put pressure on Latin American governments to stabilize their currencies. This would involve fiscal discipline, including the reduction of government expenses even for such items as social benefits. In Uruguay, for example, the number of recipients of government pensions was enormous, since workers could retire at age forty-five or fifty. This policy was so expensive that in 1968, faced with economic chaos, the government took extreme measures. The crisis shocked Uruguay, which had the reputation of being the most democratic country of Latin America, and it was one of the causes of the violence which has tormented it since then.

The measures recommended by the IMF are unpopular in Latin America. To obtain a loan from the World Bank, a Latin American government has to follow these recommendations. The IMF and the World Bank are twin institutions located in Washington. Although they are international organizations, they are closely linked with the U.S. Government, not only because of their location but because the United States is the principal stockholder in both institutions.

The Currencies and Banking

To get some idea of the inflation in Latin America, we should remember that at the beginning of the century Latin American currencies were on a par with the dollar. The general name of the currency unit in Spanish America was the peso, and the symbol $ is still commonly used.* The present names of the Latin American currencies reflect national pride: the quetzal, a forest bird which dies in captivity, is the symbol of Guatemalan liberty; the guaraní is the name of the Paraguayan Indians; the sol (sun) was the god of the Indians of Peru; Lempira was the Indian hero who fought against the Spaniards in Honduras; the balboa (Panama), the colón (Columbus—El Salvador), and the córdoba (Nicaragua) recall the discovery and Conquest; the Ecuadorian sucre bears the name of the national liberator, as does the Venezuelan bolívar. The Brazilian cruzeiro is an abbreviation of "Cruzeiro do Sul"—the Southern Cross, a constellation which can be seen only from the Southern Hemisphere and is the symbol of Brazil; it is the central

---

*It represents the two Columns of Hercules, i.e. the Straits of Gibraltar, with a band on which was written *Plus ultra* (Go further), a proud affirmation by the Conquistadores, who were defying the ancient veto against sailing west of Gibraltar: *Ne plus ultra*.

feature of the Brazilian flag. The Haitian gourde is an old French word for the Spanish American peso.

Often the new names indicate a vertical devaluation. In 1962 the Bolivian currency was devalued, and a new peso was created equivalent to 1,000 old bolivianos. In Brazil in 1942 the cruzeiro replaced the milreis (1,000 reis). In 1966 a "new cruzeiro" was created, equal to 1,000 cruzeiros! This wild inflation has been slowed down to a reasonable rate by the present Brazilian military government. In 1970 Argentina changed its currency, the new peso being worth 100 old pesos. The name remained unchanged, but the symbol was changed from M$N to $A. However, while the Brazilian government has succeeded in bringing the cruzeiro under control, in this as in most other things the junta in Argentina has shown much less competence, and the inflation continues unchecked; in 1972 Argentina was said to have the highest rate of inflation in the world. This inflationary whirl has not affected the currencies pegged to the dollar: the Dominican peso, the Haitian gourde, the Guatemalan quetzal, the Salvadorean colón, the Honduran lempira, the Nicaraguan córdoba, the Costa Rican colón, and the Panamanian balboa. Because of its close trade relations with the United States, Mexico has found it wise to maintain a stable peso.

The dissatisfaction among Latin Americans with the strict loan provisions of the World Bank led to the creation in 1959 of the Inter-American Development Bank (IDB), which gives loans under easier conditions. This is one of the regional banks which the United States supports, somewhat unwillingly; in 1968 the U.S. Congress voted a resolution opposing the creation of more regional banks. The United States believes that regional banks undermine the authority of the World Bank and the financial discipline imposed by the IMF. Unlike the Organization of American States, where all votes are theoretically equal, in the IDB as in the World Bank votes are weighted according to each government's contribution; since the United States in both cases is by far the heaviest contributor, it has effectively a veto power. The creation of the IDB was welcomed in Latin America, but then Latin American governments began to complain that the United States was blocking loans which it deemed unwise. The Latin Americans claimed that the United States was using the IDB as a political instrument, but the reality is that many Latin American governments attempt to get the U. S. Government to give them money without any strings; when the United States refuses to do this, they protest that they have been insulted. The first president of the IDB, the Chilean economist Felipe Herrera, is a close friend of the Chilean President, Salvador Allende, and he was criticized in Washington for using the IDB to promote Latin American personal and political interests. Following his resignation to return to Chile in order to work with Allende, the U.S. Government insisted on a careful reassessment of the IDB's activities.

To complete the picture, we should mention the Agency for International Development (AID). It carried on in Latin America the work begun by Nelson Rockefeller as Coordinator of Inter-American Affairs. This office was created because the State Department was regarded as slow and unwieldy. President Franklin D. Roosevelt, who proclaimed the Good Neighbor Policy, thought an independent, well-funded agency would be more effective in providing technical assistance to Latin American governments and thus winning their support in the struggle against the Axis. The Coordinator's Office was indeed able to make a real impact, but its activities aroused bitter resentment in the State Department, which regarded it as an upstart and succeeded in bringing it under its control. It was merged with the worldwide Point Four program, named after the fourth point in a presidential message of President Harry Truman. In one of the reorganizations typical of Washington bureaucracy, the agency received its present name, AID.

In Latin America AID works in conjunction with the State Department, but its activities have slowly changed. The technical assistance program, which in effect gives funds to Latin America, has been moved to a small semi-independent organization called the Inter-American Foundation. AID itself has become basically a loan agency rather like the World Bank and the IBD. There is supposed to be a gentlemen's agreement among the three, dividing their spheres of activity, but there are complaints that this agreement is not respected. AID also sponsors OPIC (Overseas Private Investment Corporation), which insures U.S. corporations against expropriation, always a threat in Latin America. The expropriations of U.S. corporations by the Allende administration in Chile placed a heavy strain on OPIC's resources.

The Peruvian Case

The case of Peru is interesting and may be a warning of what to expect in Venezuela. Even more than Venezuela, Peru was the Latin American country where U.S. capital received the warmest welcome. U.S. corporations developed vast complexes there, especially the Cerro de Pasco Corporation, which exploited the copper mine of the same name in the Andes, and W. R. Grace Company, which owned some of the most important sugar plantations on the coast. All this went sour because of fishing, oil, and the new attitude of the Peruvian military. The Pacific Ocean along the coast of Peru is rich in fish, especially anchovy and tuna; Peru is the leading fishing nation in the world today, although in 1972, because of weather changes, the fish suddenly became scarce. U.S. fishing boats, most of them from San Diego, fish in international waters of the Pacific coast of South America. Ecuador, Peru, and Chile proclaimed their sovereignty over a 200-mile-wide strip of coastal waters, far beyond the traditionally recognized 3-mile limit, which has been extended to 12 miles for certain purposes. The United States refused to recognize the 200-mile claim, but now a number of Latin American countries, including Brazil, have made the same claim, so there is an international stalemate on the issue.

The United States has succeeded in working out an agreement with Brazil but not with the Pacific coast countries. U. S. fishing boats caught fishing there are seized, the crews sometimes jailed, and heavy fines imposed. Ecuador has been the most aggressive in this regard, but there were also some incidents with Peru, resulting in U.S. Senate protests and demands that economic aid to Peru be cut off.

On top of this came the long fight over the La Brea and Pariñas oil fields, near Talara in the north of Peru, which were exploited by an affiliate of Standard Oil of New Jersey. The Peruvian Government wanted to expropriate the oil fields but hesitated to endanger its AID funds. The Peruvian air force demanded that the United States provide it with supersonic planes but was refused on the grounds that the horrible poverty of the Peruvian masses made supersonic war planes an unnecessary luxury. The Peruvian air force then tried to buy supersonic planes in England, but the United States blocked this by invoking a U.S.-British arms agreement. De Gaulle, always eager to embarrass the "Anglo-Saxon" powers, happily sold French Mirage planes to the Peruvian air force; the planes had won worldwide admiration because they had facilitated Israel's victory in the Six-Day War. In retaliation the U.S. Senate carried out its threat and cut off aid to Peru, which responded by confiscating the La Brea and Pariñas oil fields. The military seized the opportunity and took advantage of the wave of emotion in Peru to throw out the civilian President, whom it accused of excessive complacency toward the United States. A military dictatorship replaced him.

Frequently in the past, military coups have been carried out with the tacit approval of the United States, which often can get along better with a military dictatorship than with a liberal regime, but now the roles were reversed. The Peruvian armed forces decided that the old policy of allying themselves with the oligarchy, the Church, and foreign corporations was bankrupt, and that they should follow what used to be called a "Nasserite" policy and is now sometimes referred to as the "Peruvian way," i.e. using the armed forces to bring about national socialism and overthrow the groups with which they had previously been allied. The same reversal took place in Egypt when the army overthrew King Farouk. The Peruvian military junta has been opportunistic. It has expropriated or made life intolerable for some of the old established U.S. corporations, while inviting other U.S. companies to help develop the new oil fields in the Oriente. It has reestablished relations with Castro's Cuba and accepted Soviet aid to modernize its fishing industry. In general the Communists are delighted with the Peruvian junta, while the old cordiality in U.S.-Peruvian relations is gone. Even the Ecuadorian junta believes the Peruvian junta has gone too far.

The Land, Agriculture, and the Peasants

In their obsession to escape from what they call economic colonialism, Latin Americans are fascinated by economic development and industrialization. They wish to build a modern façade to hide the poverty of the masses, both urban and rural. Mexico does not wish to be considered a land of braceros. Latin American leaders are aware of the injustices of which the peasants are victims, and practically every country has an agrarian reform program. Sometimes, as in the case of Argentina, Uruguay, and Brazil under the present military government, and most of the Central American countries, its existence is at best nominal; in others, such as Cuba, Chile, Bolivia, and Peru, it has been ruthless and even violent.

In general, agrarian reform programs have not achieved the important aim of increasing food production to reduce the hunger of the masses. Yet a mythology has grown up around agrarian reform, and the large landowners have been vilified as parasites, with the result that an intelligent discussion of agrarian problems is impossible. A Mexican who points out that the division of large estates into *ejidos* has been a failure and that the only way to have an adequate national food supply is through large-scale exploitation, such as large estates permitted, is liable to be denounced as an enemy of the Mexican Revolution and even of the

Mexican nation. In the United States, which has the world's most productive agricultural system, many family farms are disappearing as large-scale corporations take over. There are few Latin American politicians who dare to propose openly that their country follow the U.S. example.

Only in Argentina has there been a kind of reverse taboo. Little was said about agrarian reform; Perón talked about expropriating large landowners, but he did it only to one of his political enemies. The aim of the Peronista government was to make the wealthy landlords pay for the industrial development of the country and with it the improvement of the lot of the working classes. The rest of the continent has been attracted toward the Mexican example, and talks about distributing land and creating a class of small landowners. However, there has been no real imitation of the Mexican *ejido,* that is to say the common ownership of lands with a prohibition to sell it. The Mexican system was supposed to avoid a rural exodus and land speculation. It has done neither, nor has it provided Mexico with an adequate supply of food. The most impressive agriculture in Mexico is along the West Coast, where there has been a California-style development: large-scale agriculture has been made possible by a number of legal devices to circumvent the agrarian law.

The politicians in Latin America want to appear as the friends of the peasants and to be photographed handing out land titles to them. When the landlords are powerful enough to fight expropriation, the politicians have tried to kill two birds with one stone by giving the peasants lots in government lands which are in remote areas the government wants opened up. This has been tried in Amazonia, in eastern Bolivia, in Venezuela, and in Colombia. However, this system has failed almost as badly as the *ejido.* Peasants do not like to move to remote areas. The Mexican Government tried to open up the Papaloapan area with peasants from northern Mexico, and the Bolivian Government tried to send highland Indians down into the fertile eastern plains of the country. In both cases the peasants resisted the move. There have been a few successes, as in the Río Balsas area of Mexico. In addition to peasant resistance, there is the need for the government to build roads and provide equipment to make the new areas economically viable.

The countries influenced by the Soviet example propose to destroy the landowning class. They want to pay only nominal compensation because they have neither the funds nor the desire to do otherwise. In any case, if they gave the expropriated landowners market value for their property, it would simply turn them into urban capitalists, another group which is the object of Communist odium. The aim is virtual confiscation and the creation of large-scale government farms or cooperatives. Only where leftist governments have the brute force necessary to carry out expropriation or where the army is unwilling or unable to prevent land seizures has such expropriation been carried out. The countries where this has happened are Mexico, Cuba, Bolivia, Chile, and Peru. Attempts were made in Guatemala under Arbenz and in Brazil under Goulart, but in both countries a military coup reversed the course of history. In Cuba the case was complicated by the fact that after 1898 many of the large estates were acquired by Americans, so there was a double motive to attack them. Fernando Ortiz wrote a famous book, *Cuban Counterpoint*, contrasting the democratic life of the small tobacco grower and the impersonal life of the large sugar plantations. The U.S. plantation owners brought efficiency to Cuban agriculture, and the striking rise of sugar production there led to the wild prosperity of the "dance of the millions," which was reflected in the grandiose capitol building and the opulence and ostentation of Havana. This prosperity ended in the crash of 1929.

To create stable market conditions, the United States introduced the quota system for sugar imports. Each of the sugar-producing countries was given a quota, that of Cuba being the largest. Moreover, sugar brought in under these quotas received a pegged price higher that the fluctuating world price. The whole system is very complex; it responds to conflicting sugar interests, the rivalry of U.S. sugar beet growers and foreign sugar plantations, the need to assure the United States a steady sugar supply at a stable price, and the U.S. Government's desire to guarantee certain friendly nations an adequate source of dollars. Thanks to this system, Cuba enjoyed a general prosperity. Even among the peasants the standard of living was higher than in almost any other rural area of Latin America. Peasant misery was not the cause of the Castro revolution, which was brought about by many factors, one being simply the psychological distance between the peasants and the plantation owners, many of whom lived in the United States or Havana. Castro based his revolutionary movement on the peasantry, and, when he gained control of Havana, he shot, jailed, or forced into exile the leaders of the urban revolutionary groups.

From the beginning of his revolution in the Sierra Maestra, Castro stressed agrarian reform. He attached so much importance to it that he created the National Institute of Agrarian Reform

(INRA), which in the first years of his administration was virtually the government of Cuba, being on a higher level than the various ministries. The mystique of agrarian reform slowly faded as it became clear that it was not the magic formula to solve all the island's problems. Castro is eclectic and unmethodical in his thinking, and he has changed the direction of agrarian reform several times. Only in a negative sense was its meaning clear— the expropriation of the large landowners and of foreign companies.

At first, in the Sierra Maestra, Castro staged dramatic ceremonies in which he handed the peasants title to a small piece of land. There are still some Cuban peasants who own land; a maximum of 67 hectares (about 165 acres) is permitted. However, Castro soon realized that his attempt to vary Cuban agriculture and to create vast numbers of small farms was no solution to the island's problems, since it had to export large quantities of sugar to pay for essential imports, and only large plantations could supply the sugar mills with sufficient cane. His Communist advisers made this clear to him, and they recommended the creation, as in the Soviet Union, of large state farms or cooperatives.

Castro, like Perón, wanted to bring about a forced industrialization. At the beginning of his government he had confiscated foreign-owned oil refineries and made the wild statement that there was abundant oil in Cuba but that the foreign oil companies had prevented its discovery. (This irresponsible accusation is part of the anti-U.S. arsenal in Latin America.) He said that he would find the oil and that it would provide a basis for Cuban industrialization. With the help of Soviet technicians, he looked for this El Dorado, but when it did not appear, the dream of large-scale industrialization faded.

The Soviet Union has tried to impose on its satellites a mercantile system in which the metropolis (the Soviet Union) would provide industrial products and the satellites, agricultural products and raw materials. So Cuba found itself back where it started: an island dependent on the monoculture of sugar. The master and the market were now the Soviet Government rather than the U.S. and Cuban capitalists. Despite some advances in education and a greater class pride, the peasants were not conspicuously better off—in some ways their lot was worse—while Havana, which had prospered on the money derived from agriculture and tourism, had lost both supports and deteriorated into a drab city with a far lower standard of living than before.

It was no longer capitalist competition but harsh work quotas which determined the production aims of sugar plantations. Instead of the old dance of the millions of dollars, Castro instituted the mystique of the ten million tons. He failed in his effort to meet this quota, which clearly had been set too high. In the Soviet system quotas are set which the workers then surpass, and this supposedly boosts their morale. The failure of Cuba to achieve the mystical ten million tons deflated the peasants' morale, and the impending miracles of agricultural production have practically disappeared from the Cuban press. But large sectors of the population are still pressed into the sugarcane harvest. At first Castro attempted to force all industrial and office workers to take part, but when it became clear that many city workers had no taste or ability for cane cutting and that industrial production was suffering, only those workers who had shown one summer that they were good cane-cutters were sent into the fields during the next harvest. Cane-cutting is one of the most exhausting forms of agricultural labor, and wherever it is done by hand there is unrest. In Hawaii cane-cutting is done by machine, but in Cuba the first attempts to use Soviet-built machines for this purpose failed. The machines are being redesigned. If they work, the harvest will be greatly simplified, but this will throw many peasants out of work. Moreover, Cuba, which is already being supported by the Soviet Union at the rate of over $1 million a day, would be faced with a major expenditure for the machines. In any case, a comparison of Soviet and U.S. agriculture shows that the Soviet system does not result in great improvements in production, so the outlook for Cuban agriculture is not spectacular. Ironically, revolutionary Cuba is now the most striking example of a one-crop colonial economy.

The Argentinian situation suddenly became worse in 1972 with the shooting of a number of political terrorists trying to escape from a southern jail. The once-quiet cities of Córdoba, Mendoza, and Santa Fé were the scenes of violent riots. Industrialization has certainly not brought them peace. There were few reports of rural unrest except for the sugar-growing area of Tucumán, but it is hard to believe that the violence in the Chilean countryside has had no impact in Argentina. Certainly, the old Argentina, stable and prosperous thanks to its agriculture, in a tumultuous and primitive continent over which it claimed to have a natural hegemony, has gone forever.

In Chile the U.S. economic presence manifested itself in the ownership of the large copper mines, which were the target for the most spectacular expropriations. Chile has traditionally been incapable of feeding its people and has imported foodstuffs from Argentina, but there was no problem of monoculture, as in Cuba. The stress derived from the gap separating the landowners from the farmhands and the landless peasants. President Allende had a rather cautious plan to expropriate the large estates, but, with an extreme leftist group inciting them, the farmhands and peasants seized many estates, and Allende lost control of the situation. Many landowners fled the country in fear, and agricultural production declined. This led to a worsening of the food situation, although the Allende government attempted to fix the prices of all basic necessities. Housewives' discontent with food shortages was expressed in a much-publicized demonstration in which they beat upon pots and pans.

Bolivia, whose economy had been based on tin, failed to solve its problems by nationalizing the big mines. It was compelled to ask for foreign help to keep its national tin company, COMIBOL, operating. The economic center of the country was moving to the agricultural area of Santa Cruz, where the large landowners who had overthrown the leftist regime in La Paz, were setting up a system similar to that of neighboring Brazil. The rural unrest on which "Che" Guevara had tried to capitalize seemed to be under control.

In Peru land reform took a peculiar twist in that the army abandoned its traditional alliance with the landowners and set out to destroy them as a class. The large family estates in the Andean highlands and the newer coastal sugar plantations (the largest owned by W. R. Grace and Company) were expropriated and turned into state farms or cooperatives. Production dropped, but, as with most authoritarian, especially leftist, governments, it is difficult to obtain precise, reliable, and detailed figures.

In Brazil the old agricultural order has survived and, indeed, is booming. Some observers wonder if Brazil does not present a new model for national development. In addition to the two cycles discussed earlier (brazilwood and mining) Brazil has gone through three other cycles: sugar, rubber, and coffee. It is an over-simplification to reduce Brazilian history to a succession of cycles and to assume that the sugar cycle is over. It continues, even though it ceased in the nineteenth century to be the mainstay of the Brazilian economy, which was in the process of becoming more varied. The sugar plantations of the colonial Northeast are indeed gone, but modern sugar plantations, especially in the state of São Paulo, are booming, and Brazil may now be producing more sugar than Cuba.

The coffee cycle still continues, although the importance of coffee in the Brazilian economy steadily diminishes. The coffee bush is a native of Africa and spread widely through Latin America during the nineteenth century. From the Guianas it went to Central America, where it transformed the whole economy, and to Brazil, where the same thing happened. During the nineteenth and the first half of the twentieth century, the coffee area of Brazil moved slowly south. Coffee exhausts the soil, and new coffee plantations were developed in virgin soils, so that the center of production moved south to the state of São Paulo and then on to Paraná. In the second half of the nineteenth and the first decades of the twentieth century, São Paulo was the center of coffee production, and since then it has been the state with the biggest population and the greatest wealth.

Since slavery no longer existed and the blacks did not wish to work in the coffee plantations, Italian immigration was encouraged. The dominant element in the population of São Paulo is the Italian ethnic group. Campinas, in the interior of the state of São Paulo, was the center of the coffee zone, but now the principal crop of the area is sugar. The capital produced by coffee was invested in industry, and the city of São Paulo was transformed into a great industrial center, the most important of Latin America. This development would not have come about without the enterprising spirit of the *Paulistas,* Italian man-power, and the hydroelectric plant built by a Canadian corporation using water from immense artificial lakes near the crest of the coastal range.

Today the great coffee plantations are in the north of the state of Paraná. The landscape presents a spectacular sight: millions of coffee bushes cross the rolling land in straight lines exposed to the full sun. It is a very different scene from the coffee plantations in the rest of Latin America, where the coffee bushes grow under shade trees and can scarcely be seen. In the coffee area of the state of Paraná, new cities like Londrina have arisen. Coffee-growing cannot move any further south because it has reached the limits of frost, which coffee bushes cannot tolerate. Sometimes a freeze coming from the south invades the coffee zone, and destroys the crop. In exceptionally cold winters millions of bushes die.

Despite the attempts to diversify Brazilian agriculture and despite the industrialization of São Paulo, Brazil still depends heavily on its coffee exports. It is the greatest coffee-producing country in the world. This dependence on coffee exports causes serious instability in the nation's economy because of the fluctuations of the price of coffee in the United States, its most important market. When the cost of a pound of coffee declines in U.S. markets, there are serious repercussions in the economy of Brazil and indeed of all the coffee-producing countries.

This problem has played an important part in the internal politics of Brazil, which can be understood only if we take the international price of coffee into consideration. During the depression, when Getúlio Vargas was dictator (1930-45), the price of coffee collapsed, and a price-support system was introduced. The government bought and destroyed millions of bags of coffee. It still has a monopoly on the export of coffee. The plantation owner sells his coffee to the government, which exports it according to the market possibilities. Representatives of the producing and the consuming countries meet and fix a quota for each country, so as to keep the world price within agreed limits. This system has worked fairly well; without it, the economy of Brazil might slip into chaos.

Brazilian coffee is the so-called "robust" type and is not the best in the world. Highland coffees fetch a higher price, and Costa Rica, Guatemala, and Colombia argue as to which produces the best coffee. Brazilian coffee is important for its volume. Moreover, for making instant coffee, Brazilian coffee is as good as the others. The old monopoly of Brazilian coffee on the world market has almost ended. Africa is now producing large quantities of coffee and at prices lower than Brazil's. Latin Americans claim that African coffee is not very good, but it is certainly quite adequate for instant coffee. A recurrent nightmare of Brazil is that the United States will invent synthetic coffee.

The Future of Inter-American Economic Relations

What are the prospects for inter-American economic relations? Despite all the troubles, inter-American trade is growing. The difficulties have involved largely U.S. ownership of mines. Such ownership has been concentrated in the Andean countries, which, following the Mexican example, have been expropriating foreign mining and oil companies and replacing the old concessions with service contracts. While the Latin American Free Trade Association and the Central American Common Market have been casualties of international politics, the Andean regional trade organization (Colombia, Ecuador, Peru, Bolivia, and Chile), which established its headquarters in Lima, showed a surprising willingness to cooperate in a common market; foreign ownership of factories, mines, and land will be allowed only on a temporary basis.

THE GROWTH OF LATIN AMERICAN EXPORTS, 1961-1970

| | 1961-1965 | | 1966-1970 | | 1970 | |
	Latin America	World	Latin America	World	Latin America	World
Argentina	191.3	1,289.6	323.4	1,562.3	369.1	1,773.2
Bolivia	3.7	96.9	13.8	180.2	16.3	211.1
Brazil	120.1	1,410.1	222.6	2,065.4	309.2	2,738.9
Chile	52.8	579.1	102.5	1,001.3	160.6	1,253.3
Colombia	15.9	486.4	53.6	581.1	94.8	722.9
Costa Rica	10.5	96.4	40.9	174.9	54.5	230.6
Cuba	4.7	617.5	—	—	—	—
Dominican Republic	1.2	157.3	0.8	170.6	1.4	213.6
Ecuador	9.8	118.8	15.8	168.8	17.3	201.5
El Salvador	29.4	155.2	74.7	208.5	74.2	228.9
Guatemala	18.9	143.9	75.2	241.9	106.0	290.2
Haiti	—	39.3	—	—	—	—
Honduras	15.2	90.7	26.4	163.6	25.2	169.6
Mexico	50.6	984.9	102.8	1,271.5	122.1	1,370.1
Nicaragua	6.2	108.0	28.9	156.0	48.3	178.6
Panama	1.4	47.2	16.9	94.5	39.8	106.6
Paraguay	12.4	42.3	18.2	52.2	24.5	64.1
Peru	56.0	582.2	55.4	863.7	66.4	1,048.3
Uruguay	13.0	172.7	24.3	191.1	29.3	232.7
Venezuela	187.9	2,632.0	246.8	2,997.7	247.6	3,204.9
Total	**796.3**	**9,193.7**	**1,443.0**	**12,145.3**	**1,806.6**	**14,239.1**

Source: Economic Commission for Latin America. Figures in millions of dollars.

These figures, from the Economic Commission for Latin America, show the growth of each country's trade with Latin America and with the world as a whole. During 1961 to 1970 the Central American Common Market was functioning well; this explains why the Central American countries had the highest percentage of trade with other Latin American (i.e. Central American) countries. Since the virtual collapse of the Central American Common Market, these percentages are undoubtedly lower. Paraguay, landlocked in the middle of South America, is a special case. Cuba has not published trade figures for several years; since it joined COMECON in 1972, its economy has been geared to the Soviet bloc. Its inter-American trade is minimal. Haiti, the most backward country of Latin America, does not produce reliable statistics. In all, the trade of Latin American countries with one another probably amounts to about 10 percent of their total world trade.

Foreign investors will have to work toward joint ownership, with a minority role reserved for them. Mexico and Argentina showed interest in joining the Andean group. Probably the pattern of Mexican development will be followed. After years of bitter disputes, a modus operandi has been worked out which satisfies both Mexico and the United States, although the expropriation of the telephone company in 1972 suggested that the relationship was not entirely a happy one.

Brazil is the only South American country with which the United States has excellent economic relations. Washington feels vindicated by the boom in Brazil as contrasted with the disastrous results of the anti-U.S. policies adopted by many other South American governments. Brazil is run by military-backed business-men who approve U.S. business procedures and have a business-like attitude toward investments. Brazil has shown no interest in joining the Andean group or in adopting the nationalistic and socialistic measures which the group is enforcing. Proud of its economic boom and confident of the future, it probably feels that the Andean countries should join it rather than vice versa.

However, the trend throughout Latin America is to expropriate U.S. interests, especially in critical areas such as mining. The U.S. Government says it does not oppose expropriation as long as compensation is prompt, fair, and effective (i.e. not in government bonds). Few Latin American governments respect this, and they invoke the Calvo Doctrine that force must not be used to collect debts. The United States has shown little inclination to intervene militarily in defense of its interests, and even when it reduces its aid or attempts legal redress, it is showered with insults about "economic aggression." U.S. policy seems to be to allow Latin American governments to learn from hard experience. The futurologist Herman Kahn has said that a country expropriating U.S. interests can expect a 10 percent fall in its standard of living. That may be true, but some countries are willing to cut off their nose to spite their face. Since our aim should be to improve the lot of the people, it is regrettable that the air is full of strident denunciations which cannot settle a highly complex issue.

Admittedly, large U.S. corporations have imprudently granted excessive, usually short-term credit to Latin American coun-tries; the U.S. Government and banks then lend money to these countries in order to pay off their debts to the U.S. companies. Thus the loans really are made to save the U.S. companies which have made unwise deals. The Export-Import Bank was created to make loans for the purchase of U.S. products. Latin Americans argue, therefore, that the United States is helping, not the countries which incurred the debt but, the U.S. corporations which wanted to make a sale. U.S. aid is not disinterested. It is given to help improve living conditions and increase purchasing power in Latin America, thereby preventing revolutions as well as promoting U.S. exports and business interests.

The Nixon policy of stressing businesslike loans may lead to a dead end, since now there is a wave of protests in Latin America against the outflow of funds to amortize such loans. The Latin American governments try to avoid repayment by expropriation and the presentation of deliberately concocted tax bills and other claims, or by getting the creditor nations to agree to a rescheduling of their debts. The enemies of the United States argue that loans are of no help to Latin America because the amortization and interest payments sometimes exceed the new investments and reinvestments. To this the U. S. observer replies that anyone who contracts a debt knows that he will pay back more than he received, and yet despite this he contracts the loan because it is to his advantage. No one has forced Latin American countries to accept loans. On the contrary, it is they who ask for the loans; they always ask for more loans than can be given and complain because they cannot obtain them. They justify the loans because they stimulate economic development and thus create more wealth, which makes their amortization possible. There is no way out of the dilemma, and the Soviet Union is fated to have the same problems with Cuba.

5 • The Press, Politics, and the Law

Everything in Latin America is colored by politics. In literature the bombastic poetry of Nobel Prize winner Pablo Neruda became the object of a cult because he is a Communist and, therefore, attractive to leftist intellectuals. Even in a negative way, art for art's sake, represented by Rubén Darío, alleged by some to be the greatest poet in the Spanish language, was a desperate attempt (Rubén Darío was a desperate man) to avoid and evade the pitiful spectacle of countries like Nicaragua. To attempt to understand Latin America without taking politics into account is a futile exercise.

Yet, it is extremely difficult to understand Latin American politics. It is hard to grasp the history of twenty-odd countries, and it is even more difficult to understand history in the making, i.e. politics. Although Latin Americans usually know the politics of their own country intimately, they have only vague notions of the politics of neighboring countries, despite the fact that there are some political waves, such as Peronismo and Aprismo, which sweep across national boundaries. The politics of each country are so complex that even in a neighboring country they are bewildering.

The Press

In order to follow Latin American politics, it is necessary to read the local press and journals regularly so as not to lose the thread. Yet, even this is not sufficient, since the press is often subject to government censorship and always to the censorship, however discreet, of its owners. Despite the efforts of the Inter American Press Association, freedom of the press in Latin America has been crushed in several countries. Previously, the enemies of the free press were rightwing dictatorships. The new threat comes from the Marxist or doctrinaire leftist regimes.

Mexico has several good newspapers, especially *Excelsior, Novedades,* and *El Universal,* but they are always discreet in their references to the President. In a one-party country, as Mexico really is, press freedom is always crippled. The Mexican Government exercises a veiled censorship, either by using the law against "social dissolution," which can cover almost anything, or by its control of the newsprint supply through the state monopoly known as PIPSA. The government is usually tolerant with small-circulation magazines, which are not regarded as important in the forming of public opinion.

It is probably fair to judge a country by its press, and by this criterion Castro's Cuba is an international disgrace. Whatever the shortcomings of pre-Castro Cuba, it had a varied and informative press, relatively free from censorship. When Castro seized power, he applied the Marxist-Leninist technique of reducing the press to "propaganda and agitation." *Pravda* and *Izvestia* are dull and malicious government propaganda sheets, and their Cuban counterpart *Granma* is even worse. In the Soviet Union there are numerous newspapers, even though they are monotonously alike, but in Cuba *Granma* is virtually the only one. The Communists denounce the cult of personality, but Castro's cult of his own personality is a case of egomania almost without parallel, although it has some similarity with Duvalier's self-glorification in Haiti. Every issue of *Granma* is devoted largely to the ego of Castro, with innumerable photographs and the text of his interminable speeches. The Cuban people, once among the best informed in the Americas, now live in an ignorance which facilitates Castro's trick of maintaining his authority by filling his people with anti-U.S. xenophobia.

Bogotá, the "Athens of America," has succeeded in keeping a high-level press, thanks largely to the efforts of Eduardo Santos, former President of Colombia. *El Tiempo,* which supports the Liberal Party, became under his editorship a bulwark of the enlightened and free press. Leftist university students have denounced it as the voice of the oligarchy, and the rabble-rousing dictator General Gustavo Rojas Pinilla closed it down; when he fell, it reappeared and has survived the threats from both the right and the left.

The situation of the press in Peru is confused. Traditionally, there were two noteworthy newspapers, *La Prensa* and *El Comercio.* Both were relatively conservative, but *El Comercio,* which had a bloodfeud with the socialist Apristas, began to promote relations between the Soviet Union and Peru. When the military seized power in 1968, they found an excuse to oust Pedro Beltrán as editor of *La Prensa*. Press freedom has been virtually suspended in Peru as the government, following the Communist pattern, has sought to bring all the communications media under its control.

A similar process has been going on in Chile, where there is a long tradition of freedom of the press. *El Mercurio* is the oldest newspaper in the Spanish-speaking world and, like *El Tiempo* of Bogotá, it has been admired as a responsible liberal organ by democrats and denounced as a tool of the oligarchy by the leftists. The Allende government regarded *El Mercurio* as its enemy and succeeded in ousting the publisher, Agustín Edwards. It has tried to bring all the press under its control by creating a government newsprint monopoly, but it has not dared to take formal action to restrict press freedom. However, it has forced radio and television stations to broadcast government propaganda.

Until the Perón era, Buenos Aires was the greatest city in Latin America and one of the world's cultural centers. Its two principal newspapers, *La Prensa* and *La Nación,* were known throughout the world. *La Prensa* was comparable to the *New York Times.* While *La Nación* capitulated to Perón, *La Prensa* attacked the dictator, who closed it down. After the fall of Perón, it began to reappear, but it is only a shadow of its former self. The present Argentine military-dictatorship claims that it has left press freedom intact, and in comparison with most Latin American countries this is true.

The Uruguayan press was peculiar in that every newspaper was the voice of one of the many political groups in the country. There was complete press freedom, and, for example, the magazine *Marcha* was the organ of the extreme left in South America. In 1968 Uruguay's democratic system fell apart, and the more authoritarian regime of President Jorge Pacheco Areco began to circumscribe press freedom.

Brazil has had a varied and effective press, with the Brazilian Press Association (ABI) serving as a clearing house for newspaper activities. However, the military government has muzzled the press, even *O Estado de São Paulo,* the conservative paper representing the business interests of Sã Paulo, which provided much of the support for the present regime. The junta has made any discussion of government affairs taboo, and the present censorship is worse, and indeed more stupid, than any previous one.

Political Groups and Leaders

The press tells only half the story of Latin American politics. The remainder must be painstakingly assembled from conversations. The important thing is to become familiar with the political groups and their leaders. Not too much attention should be paid to programs, since they are usually only talk. Most important are the leaders themselves, who are not very consistent in their ideas. The masses follow them even though they blithely contradict themselves. This is one of the advantages of political charisma. That the Cuban people have followed Castro with such blind devotion is either a tribute to his charisma and his control of the media or a proof of the Cubans' lack of political maturity. Although there are no Gallup polls in totalitarian states, there is some evidence that Castro's rule is no longer supported enthusiastically. The hysterical tone of the Cuban press suggests the need to whip up support.

The Peruvian Aprista leader Víctor Raúl Haya de la Torre has also used his charisma to hide a series of political non sequiturs. He started as an anti-U.S. Marxist; then he fought with the Communists and became pro-U.S. His great enemy was General Manuel Odría, during whose dictatorship he was forced to take exile in the Colombian Embassy in Lima. He spent no less than four years in the confines of the embassy building. Odría's troops kept it under siege, and, if Haya de la Torre had left it, they would have killed him. Yet when Odría was overthrown, the two men formed a political alliance. Such a pact seems to us incomprehensible.

One of the senior statesmen of Latin America, Rómulo Betancourt of Venezuela, won the support of the masses by denouncing the U.S. oil companies and their alliance with the U.S. Government and the Venezuelan dictatorship. When he became President, he came to terms with the oil companies and tried to suppress the book he had written in which he attacked them.

Political parties in Latin America are usually weak and impermanent, and power is in the hands of men who know that sooner or later they will be in the opposition and perhaps in exile; the moral is that they should take advantage of their period in office to build up a fortune which will be useful later. Dictators such as Perón and Batista, as well as the relatives of Trujillo, live in well-financed exile. The United States has shown little inclination to discourage such behavior. The one exception was Marcos Pérez Jiménez of Venezuela. He amassed a fortune and assumed he could live happily ever afterward in Florida. Wishing to make a show of supporting democratic regimes, President Kennedy acceded to the request of President Betancourt and returned him to Caracas as a common criminal, despite his claim that he was a political refugee. He was jailed in Caracas until 1968, when he was exiled to Spain. Since then, he has been trying to make a comeback into Venezuelan politics.

Unfortunately, as in the United States, these examples of corruption have been magnified to make it appear that all politicians are corrupt. For every dishonest politicial leader, there is at least one honest and outstanding democratic leader. We may name Rómulo Betancourt of Venezuela, Alberto Lleras Camargo of Colombia, José Figueres of Costa Rica, Fernando Belaúnde Terry of Peru, Eduardo Frei of Chile, and Arturo Illia of Argentina. The moral position of the United States was greatly weakened by the alliance of U.S. interests, corrupt dictators, and the local oligarchy. Some realists argue that corruption in government does not matter as long as the achievements of an administration are real. As the Brazilians said admiringly of one notorious São Paulo governor, "He steals, but he does things." It is impossible to eradicate corruption, like violence and crime, from society, but when it passes, or appears to pass, a certain level, the enemies of the regime have an excellent opportunity to smear the government and pose, rightly or wrongly, as reformers. This was one of the principal appeals of Fidel Castro. There is presumably much less corruption in Cuba now than there was under Batista, but, since the press has been reduced to a grotesque machine for the glorification of Castro and his clique, we really have no hard information.

Enemies of the United States in Latin America and elsewhere pounce upon the revelations of Jack Anderson to prove that there is large-scale corruption in the United States. President Allende of Chile used to great political and economic advantage Anderson's scoop about the intrigues of ITT (International Telephone and Telegraph), which allegedly plotted to prevent Allende's election; he seized upon this as a pretext to confiscate ITT property in Chile. If there were a Jack Anderson in the Soviet Union, Cuba, or Chile, he would certainly not come home empty-handed from his fishing expeditions. However, even in Chile, which boasts that its press is still free, a budding Jack Anderson would be jailed as an enemy of the state. In 1972 the Allende administration tried to indict former Eduardo Frei for attacking the President. In these matters what is sauce for the goose is not sauce for the gander.

Whatever the corruption of the Batista regime, even Batista, who was somewhat less than modest, did not display the egomania of Castro, which is a form of corruption. Moreover, corrupt regimes are often much more efficient than one-man shows staged by egomaniacs. For example, one of the main causes of friction between the Soviet Union and Castro was that his attempt to make the whole country revolve around him was leading to economic chaos. The Pérez Jiménez regime in Venezuela and the Kubitschek regime in Brazil were accused of corruption, but they were efficient. Jânio Quadros, who won the Brazilian presidency with the promise to clean out corruption with the broom which was his symbol, proved to be hopelessly incompetent when he came to power. The combination of dictatorship, corruption, and inefficiency, as in Haiti, is intolerable. The combination of democracy, honesty, and efficiency is, unfortunately, not too common.

The Western world has slowly and painfully moved toward orderly and democratic government, but throughout the world the belief has become widespread among the young that such government is unresponsive and unproductive and that only by violence can results be achieved. While this argument is supported by some historical evidence, its supporters fail to realize that violence breeds violence, that many innocent people suffer, and that the end result is not a just and free society. This does not perturb violent and ambitious men who know they cannot achieve their goals by legitimate means; they want to seize power by violence, which they find praiseworthy, and then to establish a system which will prevent their overthrow by violence, which they denounce as criminal. The one exception may be Allende. He won power by electoral means, and he claims he will respect the constitution. But by his attacks on Congress and the Supreme Court, he is doing his best to subvert the system, and his more radical supporters have made it clear that they will use violence rather than give up power through the democratic process.

Long before violence became modish in the United States and Europe, it was well established in Latin America; there was indeed a sharp contrast between the violent political life of Latin America and the peaceful politics of the United States. Americans were shocked at the spectacle of dictator Gualberto Villarroel's body hanging by its feet from a lamppost in the main square of La Paz, but after the assassination of President Kennedy in Dallas, no violence seems to surprise us. At the end of World War II, the body of Mussolini hung from a lamppost, and this marked a rebirth of the democracy in the name of which the war was fought.

In the Dominican Republic the assassination of Trujillo and in Brazil the ouster of Getúlio Vargas and the fall of several other dictators led, in appearance at least, to a reassertion of democracy.

In all of these cases the United States used its influence to promote the cause of representative democracy, but, as the Pentagon has become more influential in international affairs, the United States has ceased to be a vigorous supporter of democratic regimes, which we fear may open the way to a Communist takeover; our cordial relationships with the dictatorships of Brazil, Spain, and Greece are evidence that the United States has reverted to its policy of aligning itself with friendly military juntas. This brings up the important question of militarism. Realizing that old-fashioned militarism is discredited, the armies of Latin America are attempting to create a new image. The primitive army leaders who tried to run their countries like barracks are scornfully referred to as "gorillas," a reputation which the armies wish to live down. The Brazilian army, true to its Positivist tradition of science, order, and progress, through its national war college (Escola Superior de Guerra) has created an elite which now runs the country. However much we may criticize this ruthless military dictatorship, it has a record of capability and efficiency unusual in Latin America. In a more modest and more democratic way, the Colombian army, which has supported the nation's constitution, has carried out a program of "civic action," teaching the peasants to read and helping them with their sanitation and building problems. The Chilean army has tried to establish itself as the defender of the constitution, and when in 1972 Allende found himself obliged to bring several military leaders into his cabinet, it was hoped that they would insist on respect for the constitution. The Peruvian army has stolen the thunder of the leftists by using its power to bring about radical social reforms, as in Nasser's Egypt. Fidel Castro poured scorn on the old Cuban army, which he defeated and abolished; but after saying that he would turn all the barracks into schools, he created a militia which is now so strong that Cuba has become the most militarized country in Latin America.

Armies seem to be a necessary, or at least an inevitable, evil. In Bolivia the army was abolished, but it revived and again runs the country. The senseless violence which fanatics now resort to so willingly and which endangers the lives of millions of innocent people has made military repression seem less evil than in the past. The determined suppression of widespread terrorism in Brazil won the army unexpected popularity, and in Uruguay the terrorism of the Tupamaros has given the army a role in public life it never had before. Ironically, in Argentina, traditionally the center of "gorilla" militarism, the army seems incapable of doing anything right, of finding a new role for itself, or of creating a new image for itself. For this reason it is willing to return power to a civilian government.

After he was overthrown by the army, Perón fled to Madrid, where he lived while manipulating from afar the affairs of the Peronista Party of Argentina. Even though he had been totally discredited, the clumsy performance of the military governments which succeeded him allowed him to act the part of the defender of the Argentinian worker. Probably a majority of Argentinian voters supported him, but he was nonplussed by the 1972 ultimatum of the Argentinian Government to return to Buenos Aires if he wished to run for the presidency. He found it more comfortable to intervene from the outside. He reluctantly, but with much publicity, flew home in a chartered plane. The military government adroitly prevented him from using his fading charisma. Outfoxed, he flew away in a commercial plane to Paraguay, the fief of his friend, dictator Stroessner, and thence returned to the distant world where he preferred to live. The spotlight was turned off him.

A weird and macabre episode concerned his dead wife, Eva, an actress who had used her talents to appear as the embodiment of Perón's social welfare program. When she died young, Perón, in cynical disregard for her checkered personal life, tried to persuade the Vatican to proclaim her a saint. The Vatican's refusal was one of the causes of Perón's break with the Church. He then planned to have her buried in what would have been the most impressive shrine in the world, but he was overthrown before it could be built. The carefully embalmed body disappeared in the revolution, and its whereabouts was a matter of intense speculation in Argentina, a Catholic country where the traditional cult of relics is strong. Apparently, the armed forces, realizing that it might become the center of a political cult, secretly delivered the body to the Jesuits, who hid it in Italy. In 1971, following hidden negotiations between Perón and the military junta, the body was returned to him in Madrid.

Unlike the Brazilian military, the Argentinian army has shown an unfortunate lack of skill and discipline. The factional rivalries were so great that there was even a civil war between the "blue" and "red" factions of the army. There were violent outbreaks of popular unrest, especially in Rosario, Córdoba, and Mendoza.

General Pedro E. Aramburu, who had led the military uprising against Perón and had occupied the presidency, was murdered. General Juan Carlos Onganía, who then assumed the presidency, was deposed by the military. General Marcelo Levingston, who was placed in the presidency by the junta, proved incompetent and was deposed by it. General Alejandro Lanusse then became President. Whereas the Brazilian junta made it clear that it had no intention of returning the country quickly to democracy, the Argentinian junta, convinced of its inability to restore peace— there is more political consciousness in Argentina than in Brazil —prepared, as the 1973 presidential elections approached, to reestablish democratic procedures and to return power to the old political parties. The Argentinian Government no longer defied Washington; on the contrary, it sought its assistance. It had to contend with the masses who still dreamed of a Peronista dictatorship. Perón sensed their mood when, on his return to Buenos Aires, he denounced Western-style democracy as obsolete and the United States as Argentina's enemy. However, even his supporters thought he was silly when he praised the Paraguayan army as the greatest in the world. The discredited Argentinian army seemed a model of sanity in comparison. Yet his man Héctor Cámpora won the elections, which were not an exercise in rationality.

Another pillar of government throughout Latin America has been the Roman Catholic Church. Traditionally, it allied itself with the army and the oligarchy and was favorably viewed by the U.S. Government as a conservative force benevolent toward business and implacably opposed to communism. The liberals, indeed most intellectuals, disliked the Church and the clericalism it generated, but the masses, especially the women, supported it, as did the upper classes, and that was enough. The collapse of the Perón regime began when he moved against the Church. Now the laicism and anticlericalism of leftwing, especially Marxist, political parties have spread through the masses, and the Church realizes that it must acquire a new image if it is to survive as a real force in the world.

The Church claims that it represents a "third position," opposed to both capitalism and communism. This third position has a great appeal for the Third World countries, and the Arab countries, with the exception of Iraq and Syria, are trying to avoid identification with the capitalist West or the communist East. Perón claimed that his "justicialism" represented a third position, based on the Christian tradition, but this attempt to create a new and better society has not been a conspicuous success anywhere. More and more the issues appear in hard terms: state ownership or private ownership; diplomatic, commercial, and military ties with the United States, the Soviet Union and/or China. The emergence of China from its shell has modified the picture. China seems to wish to use Guyana as a basis for penetration into Latin America, as it has used Tanzania to gain a foothold in Africa. However, the Soviets have established themselves so well in most countries that the Chinese will have difficulty making headway. After flirting with the Chinese, Castro realized his total dependence on the Soviets, and in 1972 Cuba committed itself totally to the Soviet Union when it joined COMECON. Chile and Peru have established commercial and diplomatic ties with China, which wants their copper, but the Soviets strengthened their foothold in Chile with the Allende victory, and they are assisting both countries to develop their important fishing industries. Japan has become a major trading partner with Latin America, and it is sending a stream of immigrants there. Despite its trade rivalry with the United States, it represents the same capitalist outlook, but its political influence has been insignificant.

Democracy in Latin America

Western-style democracy, which swept Latin America after World War II, has disappeared from most of the continent, the victim of attacks from the left and the right. Only in Venezuela, Costa Rica, the Dominican Republic, and Mexico has democracy not lost ground. The model democracy of Latin America, Uruguay, has survived, although badly beaten by the financial chaos resulting from excessively generous social security provisions, the failure of the experiment to replace the Presidency with a Swiss-style committee, and the violence of the Tupamaro terrorists. The Uruguayan experiment was one attempt to eliminate the Latin American tradition of the man on horseback. Another way of combating the caudillo tradition was the replacing of the presidential type of government with a parliamentary system like that of England and other European countries. That too failed, and it seems to be the fate of Latin American countries to develop strongman governments. One might even say Latin governments, since de Gaulle's Fifth Republic marked the end of the parliamentary system in France. Despite Castro's Communist ideology, he is in fact a Caribbean caudillo, and he is clearly grooming his brother to succeed him. Rightist dictator Duvalier of Haiti openly proclaimed himself dictator for life and passed the title on to his son. "Continuism" is the curse of Latin America, since, as the example of Porfirio Díaz shows, years of superficial peace may end with a bang and a bloodbath.

Only Mexico has approached something like a rotating presidency by restricting the President to one six-year term. "Effective suffrage, no reelection" is the Mexican political motto. There has been talk of adopting this system in the United States, where since 1951 the presidency is limited to two four-year terms. The Mexican example should be followed in other Latin American countries. This is not to suggest that the Mexican system is really democratic. It is a one-party system with limited freedom of press and information. The spectacle of the Democratic conventions in Chicago in 1968 and Miami in 1972 makes the U.S. system seem to function badly, but at least, despite all the talk about smoke-filled rooms, it is surprisingly open. Every detail about a candidate is brought out, including health and personal problems. In Mexico the presidential candidate is called "el tapado" (the "hooded one"), since the public has no idea who it will be until the party, after long secret discussions, pulls off the hood. There is then a long and well-publicized campaign tour of the country to make it appear that the candidate is the people's choice. The PRI stresses law and order, believing that this is synonymous with order and progress. It argues, moreover, that any Mexican can join the PRI and thus take part in the election of the President. However, the ordinary PRI member has no say whatsoever in the selection.

Most Latin American countries imitated the British two-party system in the nineteenth century, and the parties were often called, as in Britain, Liberal and Conservative. The parties were very similar, except that the Conservatives tended to be clerical, the Liberals anticlerical; the Conservatives represented the land-owning interests, the Liberals the commercial interests. One party favored centralism, the other federalism, although there was no sharp distinction on this point. In most countries the parties split up, since a two-party debate does not seem to reflect Latin American mental attitudes. Only in Colombia has it survived, and even there this was possible only because the two parties agreed to form a national front to run the country for sixteen years (1956-73), with each party ruling alternately for two four-year periods. Whether the two-party system will survive the end of this pact is not sure. In the past each party could count on its unconditional supporters to the death, but now many young people regard them with indifference, accusing the two parties of being tweedledum and tweedledee, and of representing essentially the same upper- and middle-class interests. Such a situation can easily pave the way for a demagogue who claims he represents the people. Perón, Rojas Pinilla, and Castro all fit into this pattern.

This is the weakness of all one-party governments, and all kinds of excuses are found to justify what is essentially a one-party dictatorship. In Communist countries such as Cuba any criticism of the party is condemned as antiparty activity and could easily lead to political imprisonment. A one-party system often emerges as a reaction against the political fragmentation of a multiparty system, as in pre-Castro Cuba. Sometimes, as in East Germany and Mexico, small parties are allowed to exist providing that they recognize the rule of the official party. Democracy requires education, discipline, and long political experience, things widely lacking in Latin America. Moreover, only a two-party system seems to work effectively. It has been said that political parties are like fried eggs: one is not enough, and three are too many.

Much of the disillusionment with the old parties springs from the belief that they are corrupt and materialistic and that a new leader, a new system will bring in an era of honesty and justice. Perón and his wife Evita, who claimed they were bringing justice to the people, enriched themselves at public expense as no previous Argentinian President had done. Many other political saviors have behaved similarly. Such gross corruption seems to be less common under Communist Party discipline, but owing to the total lack of freedom of inquiry and of the press in Communist countries, we have little accurate information on this score. The Yugoslav writer Milovan Djilas broke with Tito and wrote *The New Class,* showing that communism breeds a new economically and socially privileged class. One of Castro's arguments with his Soviet sponsors concerned material incentives, which the Soviets believe are necessary. Castro has tried to move toward a moneyless society, and this has been one of the causes of the economic chaos in Cuba. The Soviet Union long ago gave up its scientific experiment to create a "new man," who would be entirely oriented toward social welfare rather than his own. Castro has revived the experiment of the Isle of Pines, which he renamed the Isle of Youth.

Capitalism has been criticized because it promotes selfishness and cutthroat competition. The U.S. answer is that, within the capitalist system it is possible to control these tendencies and that free enterprise is the most effective way of raising the living standard of Latin America. Capitalism in Latin America should not be overthrown but cleansed by such measures as effective income tax collection.

While this attitude is shared by the enlightened entrepreneurial class in Latin America, the masses show little interest in it. They believe that what trickles down to them is minimal, and indeed figures on income distribution in Brazil show that the present boom has not greatly improved the lot of the masses. One popular theory among U.S. academicians was that a middle class, or middle sector (as they called it in their jargon), was forming in Latin America and thus opening the way for U.S.-style democracy. This pseudoscience was wishful thinking. Pre-Castro Cuba was one of the Latin American countries where the middle class was growing fastest, and yet it was the first to to Communist.

As in the United States, an important factor is the emergence of youth onto the political scene. Because of the high birth rate, the percentage of young people in Latin America is unusually large. As a result, the hostility to traditional society is stronger than ever, while conservative forces like the family and the Church are losing their influence. However, the young rebels grow old. Castro was the idol of youth, but he is aging and, like other Communist leaders, he shows no inclination to tolerate youthful dissent. Communism is losing its attraction for youth, since the system is inevitably controlled by the older generation; Tito celebrated his 80th birthday denouncing youthful agitators.

The Law

Although lawyers are numerous and influential in Latin American society, law is everywhere subordinate to politics. Every republic has different legal codes, but almost all derive from the Napoleonic code, whereas in the United States, with the exception of Louisiana, the legal systems follow English common law. In California, property law has certain Spanish features. The conflict between Latin American civil law and U.S. common law is a constant source of legal disagreements. In general Napoleonic civil law is much more authoritarian than common law. The jury system, so characteristic of Anglo-American law, is much less important in Latin America. Generally, one judge interrogates the accused and assembles the evidence, which he passes on to another judge who gives a verdict. In the United States the jury is subject to many pressures, mostly favorable to the accused, and the delay which accompanies the selection of a jury also makes prosecution difficult. In Latin America the law is much more inexorable, and sometimes the charge of "social dissolution," similar to the Soviet charge of "antisocial behavior," is sufficient to send the accused to prison. In this way the Mexican painter David Alfaro Siqueiros spent four years in jail. Political rights are much weaker in Latin America than in England or the United States.

In times of crisis a government can proclaim a state of emergency, a state of alarm, or a state of war (i.e. internal war, sometimes called a state of siege), thus acquiring automatically the power to suspend some or all civil rights. The result is that troops are frequently sent into the streets to restore order, and the military are thus led to believe that they control the country. This is one of the sources of militarism. The officers in charge of barracks are usually colonels, and they have a power base from which to stage a coup. For this reason "revolutions of colonels" have been frequent. The new government forces into retirement army generals who are a nuisance, and the colonels promote themselves to the rank of generals. Obviously, the usual motive is personal ambition, and any pretext is used to justify a coup, even though political liberties usually suffer. The result has been antimilitarism, and because of their unpopularity and their inability to run a modern government, many officers do not wish to become involved in military coups. However, in general Latin American armies are still happy to seize power when the opportunity presents itself.

In the United States the tripartite division of government according to the formula of Montesquieu—executive, legislative, judicial—gives rise to an uneasy balance of power. In Latin America there is no doubt that the executive is in command; if necessary it dismisses Congress and represses the Supreme Court. If there is a coup, the Supreme Court, which is supposed to defend the constitution, simply declares that a new legal state exists. The judiciary seldom dares to look into political deaths, such as those of Castillo Armas in Guatemala or Getúlio Vargas in Brazil.

Since political rights are so weak, special value is attached to the right of asylum. A politician fleeing from the police or the army takes refuge in a Latin American or Spanish embassy. He cannot take refuge in an American Embassy, since the U.S. Government has never recognized the right of asylum, although very exceptionally American embassies have granted asylum to individuals like Cardinal Mindszenty in Budapest. Political asylum is not recognized for common criminals, so a government trying to lay its hands on an opponent who has taken refuge in an embassy usually tries to prove that he is guilty of some common crime. A Latin American government can exile its enemies, something the U.S. Government cannot do. There are thousands of Latin Americans living in exile, and Americans find it hard to understand what this means. On the one hand, the exile suffers great privations, but on the other, he acquires prestige. It would be logical to suppose that an exiled person would soon be forgotten, but often he becomes more famous in exile than he would have been at home. This was true of Rómulo Betancourt of Venezuela. Perón of Argentina hesitated to leave his exile in Madrid, since he had there a mystic position he lost when he went to Buenos Aires. This phenomenon is dangerous, since a leader such as Juan Bosch, who was exiled by Trujillo, may easily lose contact with the reality of his own country. After twenty years in exile, Bosch returned to the Dominican Republic as President, but he failed miserably because he was a stranger in his own country.

In the past, mystic and poetical figures often rose to the presidency, only to be cut down and thus achieve martyrdom. The Cuban José Martí was not President because the island had not yet achieved its independence, but he was recognized as its revolutionary leader. He was killed in Dos Ríos, in eastern Cuba, when he rode into the Spanish lines on a white horse, clearly seeking martyrdom. He is now referred to as "the Apostle." Francisco Madero, the first President of Mexico after the Revolution of 1910, was assassinated and became a martyr. Had he lived, his administrative incapacity might have left him a more inglorious name.

It is surprising that in all this lawlessness so much attention is paid to law and constitutions. Great Britain has no constitution; the United States has had one; but some unstable Latin American republics have had a whole series of them. Lawyers delight in drafting constitutions and in juggling with their clauses. In the Mexican constitution of 1917 some articles are well known by number: article 3 on education, article 33 on the expulsion of undesirable foreigners, and article 123 on labor unions. Article 135 of the civil code on "social dissolution" has been the subject of sharp polemics since it gave the government carte blanche in dealing with its opponents. This constitutional game has little appeal for the younger generation. In any case, a constitution is easily swept aside by an authoritarian government. Fidel Castro's government is not constitutional; he defends it as "direct democracy," but these words are meaningless. Castro fought his campaign proclaiming that he was going to restore the constitution of 1940. He abandoned this pretext as soon as he had power, since he did not wish to be subject to the constitution and to have to accept a legal opposition. "Direct democracy" is simply a phrase to camouflage an illegal regime.

6 • Religion and Philosophy

The Roman Catholic Church

Because of its Spanish and Portuguese heritage, Latin America is nominally the continent with the greatest number of Roman Catholics, and Brazil is the Catholic nation with the greatest population. The viewpoint of Latin American traditionalists is that Catholicism is an essential part of the national culture, and not to be a Catholic is a form of treason. Protestants are subversive heretics, the agents of U.S. imperialism. This argument was used in countries like Colombia and Peru to force the government to limit the activities of Protestant missionaries. A similar situation prevails in Franco Spain. With few exceptions the upper hierarchy of the Catholic Church defends this position, although in the past few years it has not spoken bluntly on the issue.

In the past the Catholic Church was a disciplined force, with a remarkable information network. In every village in Latin America there were churches where, through confession, the priests had a real control over the women; hence, much of the anticlericalism of the men. The Church could make or break a government, and most governments, even those which were declaredly anticlerical, found it wise to make their peace with the Church. All this has changed. The Catholicism of Latin America has proved to be more apparent than real, and the Church no longer presents a united front. Some clerics are old-line conservatives, but a majority are going willy-nilly with socialist trends. Pope John XXIII had sought to modernize the Church and make it responsive to the needs of the common people, although neither he nor the Church faced up to the problem of the population explosion, which is one of the main causes of the misery in Latin America. While the Church sought to dissociate itself at least in appearance from the oligarchy, it proposed a moderate solution, represented by Eduardo Frei and the Christian Democrats in Chile or Rafael Caldera and the Christian Democrats in Venezuela. However, many clerics went far to the left and, like Camilo Torres in Colombia, even took up arms with guerrillas, reviving with a vengeance the concept of the Church militant. The result has been deep dissension within the Church, and the disappearance of its old comfortable relationship with the army, the oligarchy, and the United States.

By the same token, old-fashioned anticlericalism has disappeared. It had little to do with communism, since it reached its peak in the nineteenth century. In 1835 in Madrid there was a ruthless massacre of friars, and during the Mexican Reform (or Reformation), Juárez's troops burned churches and convents. Such anticlerical violence would be almost inconceivable in Latin America today, although Perón's *descamisados* set fire to churches when he broke with the clergy.

Freemasonry was the organization which led the anticlerical fight. The Masons claim that their history goes back to ancient Egypt; it certainly goes back to the Middle Ages. The stonemasons whose labor and genius built the great cathedrals resented the tyranny of the clergy, who forced them to work in inhuman conditions. It was not until the eighteenth century that the Freemasons became, in Europe and North America, an important political force, whose task it was to promote the cause of freedom by breaking the tyranny of the Catholic Church. Freemasonry reached Latin America at the end of the eighteenth century, and the Lautaro lodge was especially important in the South American independence movement. During the early years of Mexican independence, Mexican politics was largely a struggle between the pro-British Scottish Rite and the pro-U.S. Yorkist Rite. As a result of its role in the wars of independence, Freemasonry was built into the political structure of most Latin American countries. Politics makes strange bedfellows, and many governments were allied with both the Church and the Freemasons. In Brazil a serious crisis occurred when the Vatican told the government of Pedro II that this *ménage à trois* was uncanonical and that a good Catholic could not be a Mason. In Venezuela, where the Church was weak, the government of Antonio Guzmán Blanco and the army allied themselves openly with Freemasonry, which became the official state religion. Usually, the Liberal Party, which in countries like Colombia was anticlerical, made its peace with the Church once it came to power.

The case of Castro's Cuba is noteworthy. The Church was

The frontispiece of the first scientific book printed in America. Produced in Mexico in 1557, the book is a treatise on physics, written in Latin by Fray Alonso de la Vera Cruz, an Augustinian friar and a teacher at the Mexican Academy in New Spain. The saint, identified in the band behind his head, is seen surrounded by members of his order, holding in his right hand a house symbolizing "The City of God" (the title of St. Augustine's famous work). The book in the other hand proclaims, "Ante Omnia Diligatur . . . . " (The most important thing is to love God).

The Roman Catholic Church in colonial Spanish America, built great churches and fostered traditional learning; Diego Rivera saw it otherwise. (Diego Rivera's "View of the Spiritual Conquest of America" from Stuart Chase, *Mexico*.)

never very strong in the island; there was an active anticlerical movement, and Freemasonry played an important role in the independence movement. The Masonic triangle on the Cuban flag recalls the role of Freemasonry in the struggle. In Havana there was even a Masonic university. Castro, who studied in a Jesuit school, became violently anticlerical, like so many Spanish American alumni of the Jesuits. When he seized power, his attitude was sharply anticlerical, especially toward the numerous Jesuits and other priests of Spanish origin. He was guilty of gross ingratitude toward the Archbishop of Santiago de Cuba, a Spaniard who had defended him after his capture following the attack on Moncada barracks.

Nevertheless, he changed his attitude and now, although a Communist, has a working relationship with the Church. He maintains diplomatic relations with the Vatican and allows himself to be photographed with priests. This does not mean that Castro has been struck by religious zeal, but rather that he has acted in terms of two pragmatic considerations. The first is that the Spanish Republic of 1931 made a serious mistake in following an anticlerical policy, since the result was that the Church became the principal ally of General Franco, which in large measure ensured his victory and the defeat of the Republic. The Church, likewise, played an important role in the overthrow of Perón and Rojas Pinilla. Castro's ideological mentors realize that it is still dangerous to engage the Church in battle in Spanish-speaking countries. The prudent course is to leave the Church in peace and let it wither on the vine, according to the inexorable laws of history.

The second consideration influencing Castro is that the Church and communism are trying to find what they have in common. It is assumed in the United States that Christianity is the ally of capitalism and the enemy of communism. This dovetails with the Calvinist tradition in the United States, but not with the biblical Christianity, which was an antimaterialist communism. While the role of private property has long been the subject of canonical debates, the Catholic Church, like the Protestant, became the ally of property and wealth. It will not be easy for the Church and communism to reach a modus operandi, as the case of Poland shows. Atheism is built into the Marxist-Leninist system, and, while militant anticlericalism is no longer a feature of Communist society, Marxist theoreticians say that any attempt to reconcile Marxism and Christianity is vain. Within the Church, there are sharp differences on this point. The Franciscans and the

Maryknoll Fathers, among others, accuse the Church, and especially the Jesuits, of having forgotten the basis of Christianity and of having sold out to capitalism. On this issue there is a cleavage within the Jesuit and the Dominican orders, whose traditional discipline has been severely strained. The Vatican has said many times that it opposes capitalism (for material reasons) and communism (for spiritual reasons). It occupies a third position. In fact, in countries like Italy, Germany, France, Spain, Chile, and Venezuela, the Catholic parties are bourgeois and anti-Communist. However, just as the right wing of the Church blends into capitalism, so the left wing approaches communism, and since 1971 the Communist labor unions have been seeking the cooperation of the Catholic labor unions, much to the annoyance of the unions affiliated with the AFL-CIO. This issue is of great importance in understanding Latin American politics. The recent rapprochement between Communist and Catholic labor unions may explain why the Christian Democratic government of Venezuela has turned against the U.S. oil companies. The youth of the Christian Democratic Party have long been critical of large corporations and foreign investors. Of all the Communist countries, Cuba is the one which has the best relations with the Church. In Peru and Chile the Church used to be very conservative, but in both countries it has come out in favor of the anticapitalist measures of the leftist governments. This is in some measure just protective coloration, but many clerics now proclaim themselves "Marxist Christians."

To defend the Catholic tradition of Latin America, the Church created the Latin American Episcopal Council (CELAM) in 1955, with its headquarters in Bogotá, reputed to be the most Catholic capital in Latin America. At first CELAM was militantly Catholic and conservative. During the papacy of John XXIII (1958-63), CELAM became less intransigent, and it began to speak openly of the misery of the Latin American people, of the abuses of the capitalist system, and of the need for social reforms. Nevertheless. its basic purpose remained the same: to defend the Catholic tradition of Latin America. The visit of Pope Paul VI to Bogotá in 1968 to participate in a CELAM conference reinforced the conservative attitude of the organization.

However, Latin American Catholicism is largely a façade like the baroque architecture typical of Latin American churches. The President of the Spanish Republic, Manuel Azaña, once said, "Spain has ceased to be Catholic." This remark enraged the Catholics and turned many of them against the Republic, but it contained a bitter truth. We may likewise ask: Has Latin America ceased to be Catholic? Has the United States ceased to be Protestant? Has the Western world ceased to be Christian? The honest answer to all these questions must be a modified "yes." The Latin American case must be viewed in the context of the crisis of Christianity in the modern world.

Despite appearances, Latin American Catholicism is hollow. One proof is the shortage of priestly vocations and, therefore, of priests. This is surprising, because in poor Catholic countries (and most Latin American countries are poor), the clerical life opened the door to material security. Poor, ambitious boys entered the Church or the army, which were practically the only areas of society in which there was a certain vertical mobility. Now, Latin American youths do not wish to become priests, and as a result there are many churches without clergy. In the past, and even today, the remedy was to import priests from Spain, but there has been a reaction against this custom, which suggests that the Spanish American republics are still ecclesiastical colonies. Moreover, it was suspected that Spanish priests were reactionaries and even partisans of Franco. From time to time, Spanish priests have been expelled from Latin American countries, but they always return.

In the last decade or two, there has been a flood of U.S. missionaries to Latin America. Some orders, such as Maryknoll, have as a special mission the evangelization of areas like Latin America. U.S. Catholics have enough money to maintain missionaries and, moreover, there is more religious fervor among U.S. Catholics, who are a minority, than among Latin American Catholics, who are a majority. In the past there was an abundance of clerical vocations among U.S. Catholics, although in recent years there has been a decline.

At first U.S. Catholic missionaries were well received, but now they arouse opposition. The Maryknoll Fathers wished to strengthen Catholic orthodoxy in countries like Guatemala, where the Catholic faith was corrupted by paganism. This task did not make them popular among the folk Catholics of Guatemala. Then, after the wave of support for the United States during World War II, came the anti-U.S. reaction, and Catholic as well as Protestant missionaries were accused of being agents of U.S. imperialism. Soon after the opposite accusation was made; U.S. missionaries began to show their indignation at the social injustice prevalent in Latin America, and then they were accused of being subversive. In 1968 the expulsion from Guatemala of a group of Maryknoll Fathers accused of having joined a guerrilla band received international publicity. It is evident that Latin America cannot be dependent on foreign missionaries for the staffing of its churches. Latin American anticlericalism is prevalent among men, who go to church simply to be baptized, married, and buried; many of them refuse to set foot in a church on any other occasion, although others accompany their wives to Sunday mass for appearance's sake. The Church has its principal strength among women, but it refuses to ordain them. The result is often a frustrating formalism or phariseeism.

As elsewhere, the Catholic Church (like the Communist Party) has attempted to secure the allegiance of youths through education: primary, secondary, and university. This is sometimes doubly counterproductive: the youths rebel against the Church, and the anticlericals attack it for using this maneuver to take over a task which they believe should be the responsibility of the state and of the family, and for its retrograde attitude. Church schools praise the Spanish tradition and describe Darwinism as a heresy. There is also a class issue, since the upper classes, which can afford the tuition charged by Church schools, think, often rightly, that their children can get a more exacting education in private than in public schools. The snob appeal of a private education has diminished somewhat in the last few years as private schools have suffered from turmoil similar to that which has shaken public schools, but it is still true that in general Church schools do a better job of educating children than public schools. The Jesuits were the most famous educators, which was one reason why they were attacked with special vehemence, since they were charged with teaching ultramontane ideas incompatible with state sovereignty. The expulsion of the Jesuits from Spain and its empire in 1767 set a pattern which has been followed repeatedly when a liberal government comes to power. The Jesuits have been expelled many times from different Spanish American countries.

The case of Mexico is interesting. The aim of the Reform (or Reformation) proclaimed by Benito Juárez in 1859 was to put an end to the power of the Church. The 1910 Revolution continued Juárez's fight against the Church, which had allied itself with Porfirio Díaz. The 1917 constitution is clearly anticlerical, reducing the Church to the level of a civic organization, or less, since Church buildings are technically the property of the government, which allows the clergy to use them, although it may allow a Protestant sect or any other civic organization to do so. The Church is forbidden to engage in educational activities, and Jesuits are not allowed to enter the country. Priests are not permitted to wear cassocks in public, and religious processions may not leave the precincts of a church.

The Catholic reaction against these anticlerical provisos was violent. In the northwestern part of the country, around León and Guanajuato, the Cristero movement developed; its cry, from which its name derived, was "Christ the King!" The Cristeros took up arms, and a Cristero killed President Obregón in 1928. The government took terrible revenge; a famous photograph shows a line of telegraph poles along a railroad, with the body of a Cristero hanging from every post. Thousands of refugees, mostly Catholic conservatives, fled to the United States, somewhat like the Cubans who have fled from Castro. In the United States there was a revulsion against the Mexican Revolution similar to that against Castro's atrocities.

Since World War II, the war between Church and State has abated. When Mexico entered World War II against the Axis, the government did not wish to have the Catholic Church as a Trojan horse. When Manuel Avila Camacho, who was President from 1940 to 1946, made his famous statement "I am a believer," he was discreetly ending the Church-State war. Since then, the anticlerical provisions of the constitution have become a dead letter. After a sharp debate, the proviso of article 3 of the constitution that education must be "socialist" (i.e. anticlerical) was rescinded. The Church owns property through straw men. In many parts of the country, the priests wear clerical garb in public, and religious processions parade through the streets. The Church is active in education; not only have the Jesuits returned, but they even have a large university, the Universidad Iberoamericana. This has all been possible because the government has been in the hands of pragmatic businessmen who want to cooperate with the Church and the United States. However, were a doctrinaire leftist government to come to power, it could revive the dead letter of the constitution and impose its observation.

Mexico, like other Latin American countries, has found that the Catholic cult can promote nationalism, and the Church has found that nationalism can promote religion. In a symbiosis which recalls the use in France of Joan of Arc to make Catholicism and nationalism seem synonymous, and in disregard of the basically international character of Christianity, there is scarcely a country in Latin America which does not have its special, national Virgin Mary. Famous in Argentina is the Virgin of Luján. The best known, however, is that of Guadalupe in Mexico. The shrine of the Virgin of Guadalupe, near Mexico City, is really a symbol of colonialism. The name derives from the Spanish shrine of Guadalupe, even though some fanatical Mexican nationalists claim that it really has nothing to do with the Spanish sanctuary but is a deformation of an Aztec name. The legend of the Indian Juan Diego, to whom the Virgin appeared with the message that a shrine to her should be built where there was then a pagan shrine, is the symbol of the conversion of the Indians to the religion of the conquerors. Another important shrine near Mexico City was that of Our Lady of the Remedies, a little image which Hernán Cortés brought from Spain. When the Mexican priest Miguel Hidalgo led the revolt against Spanish domination, he took as his symbol the Virgin of Guadalupe, since the "brown Virgin" was the protector of the Indians and the poor, whereas the Virgin of the Remedies was the symbol of the white aristocracy. Since then, the Virgin of Guadalupe has been the symbol of "Mexicanity," while the Virgin of the Remedies has been forgotten.

Despite the official anticlericalism of the government, no one dares to criticize the Virgin of Guadalupe. A Catholic historian, Joaquín García Icazbalceta, at the end of the last century studied the legend of the Virgin of Guadalupe and came to the conclusion that it was false, since it appeared many years after the date of the supposed miracle. Mexicans should reject this myth as one of many pious legends, but even the anticlericals prefer not to discuss the matter; they simply say that the Virgin of Guadalupe is part of the history of Mexico. The Virgin of Guadalupe is used to promote an uncritical nationalism. Her motto is the verse from the Psalms "Non fecit taliter omni nationi," i.e. God has singled out Mexico for a special favor. The cult of the Virgin of Guadalupe is an example of what Protestants denounce as the idolatry of Latin American Catholicism. In Latin America the Church promotes the cult of the Virgin, or rather of statues of the Virgin. Christ is practically forgotten. This is the "Mariolatry" which Catholics themselves denounce.

The Protestants

There are many forces working against the Church, which is trying to impose itself in an atmosphere of indifference. Historically, the most important has been rational skepticism and the anticlericalism which found its clearest expression in Freemasonry. Other enemies of the Church were the Protestant or, as they are called in Latin America, Evangelical sects. At the end of the last century and the beginning of this, the major Protestant sects—the Baptists, Methodists, and Presbyterians—were welcomed in several countries, especially Brazil, which is the most tolerant of the Latin American countries. These sects were respected as the embodiment of Protestant ethics, which seemed so desirable in the amoral atmosphere of Latin America. They founded schools and colleges, such as Mackenzie University in São Paulo. The Protestant was regarded as a serious individual, and his dedication to work usually ensured his material success. However, as they became more conspicuous, Protestant missionaries were denounced as agents of U.S. imperialism by nationalists and Catholics.

In the last few decades, some of the less orthodox varieties of Protestantism have had considerable success; we may mention the Seventh Day Adventists, the Mormons, and the Pentacostal groups. The Seventh Day Adventists travel through the hinterland, distributing medicine and helping the peasants. The Mormons, with their racial beliefs, would not seem to be destined to enjoy much success in a continent of such varied racial background, but they have won some success because they pay attention to poor people, whom the Catholic Church has neglected.

There is disagreement as to the success of Protestant missions in Latin America. The missionaries themselves naturally tend to assess it highly, since they must maintain the support of the churches which sent them. Catholics place the degree of success much lower. It is safe to say that the growth of Protestantism has not been sufficient to offset the spread of secularism. In recent years relations between Protestants and Catholics have improved markedly. To offset the charge of being foreign agents, the Protestants have been training local pastors to replace the American missionaries. The ecumenical movement has mitigated the frictions between Catholics and Protestants. Both realize that they face common enemies: atheism and indifference. In the past there were frequent clashes between Catholic and Protestant missionaries in the interior. Now, they help each other. The Catholics now have a problem with the "protestants" within their own ranks. These protesters seldom become Protestants, because they regard Protestantism and Catholicism as equally corrupt. Sometimes they leave the Church; at other times they assert that, despite their protests, they remain good Catholics. In 1968, just before the visit of Pope Paul VI to Bogotá, a group of young Catholics, among them priests and nuns, occupied the cathedral of Santiago de Chile in protest against the unprogressive attitude of the Church. The Archbishop of Santiago forced them to make an act of contrition.

The tension in the Catholic Church has reached a point unknown since the period of Martin Luther. Certainly, the Church does not arouse the popular enthusiasm which is inspired by movements which hope to bring about social justice even at the cost of violence.

Positivism

In Latin America there have been religious and philosophical movements, outside of orthodox Christianity, which have had a great influence on the life of the continent. These movements have usually represented a reaction against the Catholic tradition. In the second half of the last century and in the first years of this one, Positivism played an important role, especially in Mexico and Brazil. Positivism derives from the system developed by the French philosopher Auguste Comte, who, following the arguments which Immanuel Kant had developed in his *Critique of Pure Reason,* argued that theology and metaphysics are a waste of time because they present problems which human reason is incapable of solving. Humanity must, therefore, devote its efforts to the study of the positive sciences (mathematics, physics, chemistry, etc.), which alone can bring progress and well-being to humanity.

Comte's Positivism, known as the Religion of Humanity, enjoyed an extraordinary success in Latin America. It seemed to offer a solution to the problems of a backward and poor society, where intellectual energy was dissipated on Catholic theology and metaphysics, to the great detriment of the sciences, which are the key to progress. In Mexico, Positivism mixed with Darwinism provided an ideological basis for the "scientists" who served the dictatorship of Porfirio Díaz.

The Brazilian republic of 1889 came in under the auspices of Positivism. According to Positivism, there can be no progress without order, and the Brazilian Government took as the national motto Comte's phrase "Order and Progress," omitting the final words "and above all, love." In Brazil, as in Mexico, Positivism developed into an authoritarian ideology and even became virtually the state religion. In his last years Comte became a mystic. He built a church on the dogma of Positivism. In Positivist temples the service seems to be almost a parody of the Christian rite. In Rio de Janeiro a Positivist temple was built, and services are still held there each Sunday. Until their death, it was attended by many of the founders of the republic. It is the only Positivist temple in the world where services are still held, but few young people become Positivists, and probably the Positivist temple in Brazil will cease to function. It is strange that Positivism has had more success in Brazil than in France, where it was born. Comte's home in Paris is maintained as a museum by Brazilian Positivists.

A parallel phenomenon is Krausism, which likewise derived from Kant through Karl Christian Friedrich Krause, a pupil of Hegel who is completely forgotten in Germany. By a historical accident Krause's philosophy had an enormous repercussion in Spain, where it had a great influence on public life. After demonstrating in the *Critique of Pure Reason* the contradictions inherent in theology and in the attempts to explain the evidence of God, Kant insisted in the *Critique of Practical Reason* that humanity cannot live without morality. The conclusion: less theology and more morality. Kant was abstruse and even physically remote (he lived in East Prussia), but Krause knew Spanish intellectuals and spoke a language they understood, less metaphysical and more practical. His ideology had a great appeal for Spanish liberals, who lived in a country where there was an abundance of theology and a scarcity of morality. In Spain, Krausism filled the vacuum which Positivism filled in many Latin American countries. Krausism had some success in Uruguay and Argentina, but very little in the other republics. Unfortunately, Krausism, like Positivism, demanded reason and discipline. It made few concessions to fantasy, traditional superstition, and laziness, and it was, therefore, unable to survive. Today it is even deader than Positivism.

Spiritualism

Latin American intellectuals, dissatisfied with the austerity of Positivism and Krausism, and not wishing to return to the Catholic religion, looked for something to fill their spiritual vacuum. They found it in idealism and spiritualism. Seeing that the Positivism of the scientists had led to an arid and inhuman society, a group of young Mexicans founded the Atheneum of Youth, taking as their doctrine the idealism of the French philosopher Henri Bergson. The Atheneum supported the presidential candidacy of Francisco Madero, the leader of the movement against the dictatorship of Porfirio Díaz. Partisans of Díaz murdered Madero shortly after he reached the presidency. It is difficult to imagine what his administration would have been like, since he believed in spiritualism and consulted the Ouija board before making decisions.

The country in which spiritualism is most widespread today is Brazil. Alain Kardec, the Frenchman who systematized spiritualism, is as forgotten in his country as Krause is in Germany, but in Brazil every educated person knows of him. In Rio de Janeiro there is a street named after him, and the Brazilian postal service has issued a stamp in his honor. Visitors to Brazil are surprised at the development of spiritualism there, and a visit to a spiritualist session is a noteworthy experience. In Rio de Janeiro and São Paulo there are several sessions a week in different places, and sometimes over a thousand people attend. Most of them are middle-class whites, and the seances are conducted in a serious spirit revealing a great intellectual concern about the mysteries of life and immortality. Spiritualism enjoyed a great vogue in Europe in the last century, attracting leading intellectuals such as Victor Hugo, who is greatly admired in Brazil. It is probable that spiritualism will fade away as Positivism has done.

Existentialism

The younger generation leans toward existentialism, which, in the form given it by Jean Paul Sartre, is atheistic and hedonistic. The Catholic existentialism represented by Gabriel Marcel, which seems to be an attempt to prove that Catholicism reflects the latest philosophical movements, has had little success outside of Catholic circles. Sartre's existentialism is a serious philosophical movement, but the majority of Latin American "existentialists" have not read Sartre, for the simple reason that they read nothing. They follow Sartre like a hippie following a guru. Like youth everywhere, Latin American youth has little interest in religious and philosophical structures. They seek material or emotional satisfaction, and when they fail to achieve it, they sometimes become anarchists. In the Spanish-speaking world there is a long tradition of anarchism and anarchosyndicalism; it derives intellectually from another forgotten figure, the Frenchman Georges Sorel. In Buenos Aires, especially, there are many youths who say they are "Trotskyists," but this is merely a façade to hide the chaos in their ideas.

Paganism

A curious movement in Latin America is the return to paganism; despite centuries of missionary effort, paganism has not died. It mingled with Christianity in the process known as syncretism. To

A Mayan stela. (From John L. Stephens, *Central America*.)

use the title of a book by Anita Brenner, there are idols behind the altars. In the picturesque Guatemalan town of Chichicastenango, the Indians go up into the hills to burn copal incense in front of their stone idols before going to mass in the church. The behavior of the Indians in church clearly has elements of pagan origin. The pagan and Christian elements blend perfectly, since the pagan tradition also is full of poetry. It is touching to see an Indian with his family kneeling on the floor of the church of Chichicastenango, speaking with God as though he were the local lord and making designs on the floor with flower petals. The Church has tended to tolerate this syncretism, although in Mexico the Archbishop of Oaxaca forbade the famous plume dance in the courtyard of the church on the grounds that it was pagan. Among the Indians of the highlands of Peru syncretism has taken a curious form. They believe that they have lived through the periods of God the Father and God the Son and are now living in the period of God the Holy Ghost. This period will end when the Inca returns and sweeps aside the Christian religion.

The problem of paganism is especially serious in Brazil. Among the blacks, mulattoes, and poor whites there is a rebirth of Afro-American cults. This coincided with the "black power" movement in the United States, with its return to African ways of which hitherto the blacks had been ashamed. As in the United States, the movement has been pushed by leftwing intellectuals. The popular novelist Jorge Amado promotes macumba uncritically; in a nonsensical way he declares that it is the true religion of Brazil. Macumba, again, is a syncretic religion. In appearance it is Christian, since in its temples there is an altar, with statues of Christian saints. The cult of the goddess of the sea is African, although the Catholic Church also blesses the sea. The custom of putting on the sea little boats with candles is picturesque, but pathetic; the blacks who throw cheap jewels into the sea as an offering to the goddess do not have enough money for their own basic needs. In Brazil there are some blacks who descend from African Muslims, but as yet there is no evident Black Muslim movement, as in the United States.

What has happened to the Brazil which prided itself upon being the greatest Catholic nation in the world and the intellectual heir of France? The Catholic Church is fighting this neo-paganism, and, in order to reach the people, it is promoting Christian Democracy within the framework of the "modernization" of the Catholic Church. In two countries, Chile and Venezuela, this movement won the Presidency, although, as in Europe, this may be a transitory political phase. Elsewhere, its political success has been extremely limited, although some Christian Democratic intellectuals, like the Brazilian writer Alceu Amoroso Lima, have won widespread esteem. The rebels in the ranks of the Brazilian clergy, such as Archbishop Helder Câmara of Recife, are in exile, in jail, or muzzled. The Brazilian army, supported by most of the Church hierarchy, has made it painfully clear that a cassock does not protect "subversives." In Peru the new-style army has been more understanding, although it too wishes there to be no misunderstanding that in this world at least the army controls the Church.

7 • Inter-American Relations

Relations between the United States and Latin America are complex, as are those between this country and Europe, Africa, or Asia. The United States has to develop a general policy between the "two Americas" and a specific policy for each of the Latin American republics, as well as Puerto Rico, the Commonwealth countries, and the French and Dutch territories. There is a constant flux in this matter. Following President Allende's expropriation of U.S. properties in Chile, President Nixon announced that instead of a blanket policy for Latin America, the United States would operate primarily on a country basis, the implication being that Washington would adopt a benevolent attitude toward those governments which showed benevolence to the United States. As always, a basic problem is that the same issue appears quite differently from different capitals. For the United States, the Monroe Doctrine was a generous attempt to defend Latin America against aggression; for most Latin American countries, it was a humiliation, since in effect it declares them to be U.S. protectorates. The expropriation of U.S. interests in Cuba, Peru, and Chile is judged in New York to be theft, whereas in those countries it appears to be a legitimate assertion of sovereign rights.

Historically, the basic phenomenon in inter-American relations was the growth of U.S. power and the relative decline of Latin American power. The independence of the United States was well received in almost all of Latin America. For the conservatives loyal to Spain (which took part in the war not for love of freedom but because it was allied with England's enemy, France), U.S. independence was a victory for Mother Spain and a defeat for England, the leader of the Protestant, liberal world. For those who aspired to liberate Latin America, the U.S. example was a model to follow. The thirteen colonies were not exactly a world

Дополнительный 10-процентный налог на импортные товары, введенный США, тяжело отражается на торговле латиноамериканцев с их северным соседом. **(Из газет).**

— Заходи, сосед, поторгуем...   Рис. Д. Агаева.

INTER-AMERICAN RELATIONS AS SEEN FROM MOSCOW

Source: Pravda.

The Soviets lose no opportunity to arouse Latin American resentment against the United States. The imposition by the Nixon administration of a 10 percent additional tax on imports gave them a fine opportunity to depict Uncle Sam sitting behind a 10 percent barrier which the Latin Americans cannot possibly surmount. They do not respond happily to Uncle Sam's invitation: "Come on, neighbor, let's bargain!"

power. The admirers of the new republic thought of it as Latin American liberals thought of Uruguay when that country seemed to be a model democracy, or as leftists viewed the Castro revolution in Cuba. Latin Americans did not suspect that the United States would become "the Colossus of the North." When Bolívar said that "America speaks Spanish and is Catholic," he revealed that for him the United States and Brazil were almost accidents, two clusters of cities along the coasts of North and South America respectively, clinging to the great mass of Spanish America. When the Spanish Americans obtained their independence, they did not imagine that one day the United States would control the Caribbean; they wondered simply if Mexico or Colombia would exercise hegemony in the area. The Monroe Doctrine was at first received with indifference, because the United States did not have sufficient power to impose it. Indeed, the independence of Latin America was guaranteed primarily by the British fleet.

Little by little, Latin Americans came to realize that the United States was not simply a liberal and democratic Arcadia. They found themselves confronted with the ruthless expansionism which the doctrine of "manifest destiny" justified. First came the acquisition of Louisiana and Florida; the Stars and Stripes were hoisted on the shores of the Caribbean. Bolívar, who assumed that "Greater Colombia" would dominate in the Caribbean, in his later years spoke of the United States in brutal terms which are seldom quoted.

Mexico

Mexico is a special case because it is the only Latin American republic with which the United States has a common border. It has been a constant source of friction. Mexico, which claimed that it had inherited from New Spain the whole continent from Alaska to Panama, lost not only Central America, which declared its independence, but also Texas, New Mexico, Arizona, and California, and, naturally, everything which lay to the north of these states. The indignation with which Mexicans accuse the United States of imperialism is hypocritical, since, by declaring its sovereignty over the aforementioned territories, Spain and later Mexico were committing an act of imperialism, and, in fact, they had never occupied most of them effectively, which is an established criterion for claims to sovereignty. Moreover, the population of the territories was very mixed ethnically, and there was much resentment against Mexico among the inhabitants, who often received the U.S. armies as liberators.

It is a common mistake to believe that California had a well-established Spanish American society, with a significant culture. In reality the population was made up largely of primitive Indians and a few Europeans of mixed origin and a rather disreputable way of life, who lived in simple communities. Only the missions and to some extent the military posts *(presidios)* were outposts of Spanish civilization. To get some idea of the way California really was, we should read *Two Years before the Mast* by Richard Henry Dana. In the Southwest, the Spanish domination had been brutal, as demonstrated by the suppression of the Great Rebellion of 1680 in which the Indians who rose against their Spanish oppressors were massacred. They had no reason to lament the end of Spanish-Mexican domination. There was a small "Spanish" population which engaged in sheep raising and had tense relations with the Indians, who resented the invasion of the sheep. This population, still known in New Mexico as the "Hispanos," remained faithful to Spain and had little affection for the Mexican republic. This is the historical reality, but the Mexicans do not see it thus. They know merely that they lost half of their territory, or rather of the territory they claimed, and they blame the United States for having reduced Mexico to the rank of a second-class power.

Mexico has accepted the present boundary between the two countries, and, since President Kennedy solved the issue of the Chamizal (a small slip of territory between the Rio Grande and the city of El Paso, which an international court had awarded to Mexico, but which the United States refused to give up), there have been no border disputes between the two countries. Nevertheless, Mexican resentment over the loss of its territory is not dead. In the last few years, the cadets who defended Chapultepec castle in Mexico City against the U.S. invaders, and who are known as the "boy heroes," have become national figures, and there is an impressive monument to them. There is doubt about the historic truth of the story as the Mexicans tell it, but, like the Virgin of Guadalupe, it now forms part of the patriotic mythology of Mexico. It is something like the Betsy Ross legend in the United States, but it has more tragic overtones. It stimulates Mexican xenophobia, as the Joan of Arc legend does in France.

There was serious tension along the border until World War II. The Americans scorned the Mexicans, and the Mexicans hated and feared the Americans. During the Mexican Revolution, the bloody fighting surged up to the border. Sometimes Americans would go to watch the frays on the other side of the line, and on one occasion the fighting even crossed the border. When Pancho Villa attacked the border town of Columbus, New Mexico, the U.S. Government sent an army under General Pershing to capture him. Pershing, who later led the U.S. troops to victory in World War I, scoured northern Mexico but could not catch Pancho Villa; this was a foretaste of the current paradox that it is easier to fight a large army than a small guerrilla band. The hostile atmosphere lingered long after the end of the Mexican Revolution. Now it has practically dissipated, although the Chicano movement has to some degree revived it. The border states have cooperative programs under which California helps Baja California Norte, Arizona helps Sonora, etc. There are banquets and friendly speeches, and the Lions and the Rotarians swear eternal friendship across the border.

Although Mexico has more or less cordial relations with California, New Mexico, and Arizona, the case of Texas is different. The defeat in the 1846-48 war was humiliating for Mexico, but the loss of Texas was a crushing blow. For Texans "Remember the Alamo!" is a patriotic cry, but Mexicans regard the Alamo as treachery committed by foreigners whom Mexico had admitted into its territory. The battle of San Jacinto is for the Texans a glorious victory, but for the Mexicans it is a defeat for which they blame the incompetent government of a scurrilous President, Antonio López de Santa Anna. For Mexicans, Texas symbolizes their national humiliation. Despite all the border ceremonies, the Mexican has little love for the Texan, whom he considers big, overbearing, and somewhat coarse. President Kennedy, from distant Massachusetts, was a thousand times more popular in Mexico than President Johnson of Texas. Johnson spoke affectionately of Mexicans; he had taught in a school with Mexican pupils, and he knew Spanish; but he had the disadvantage of being Texan. John Connally, successively Governor of Texas, Secretary of the Treasury, and adviser to President Nixon on international affairs, is for the Mexicans the embodiment of the Texan. Unlike Johnson, he deals with Latin Americans in a matter-of-fact way and does not attempt to convince them that he holds them in special esteem.

The picture is not entirely black, especially after the settling of the Chamizal case. The Texans of Mexican origin, known as the Texmex, are no longer scorned by other Texans, and one even became mayor of El Paso and later a U.S. ambassador.

Monterrey, a very Americanized city, has close relations with the United States. The Technological Institute of Monterrey, which wants to become the MIT of Mexico, has working agreements with U.S. universities; and the opening of a branch of the National Autonomous University of Mexico in San Antonio will greatly enhance the cultural prestige of Mexico in the area. The National Border Program of the Mexican Government has as its aim to improve the border cities so as to brighten the U.S. image of Mexico. The plan includes making the Chamizal the site of a permanent exhibit and conference center to the greater glory of Mexico, and to promote relations of equality with the United States. The plan was extremely ambitious; to date it has had a limited success.

With the other states, Mexico has had fewer problems. There is still some resentment over the 1853 Gadsden Purchase by the United States of a strip of territory now belonging to Arizona. Americans regard the acquisition with satisfaction, and a few years ago the U.S. Post Office issued a stamp commemorating it. Mexicans are ashamed that a Mexican Government should have stooped to selling a piece of the national territory.

To avoid new losses and danger to its sovereignty in the border zone, Mexican law forbids foreign ownership of any land within 100 kilometers of the border or 50 kilometers of the coast. The law is directed primarily against U.S. purchasers, but those who want to buy a house or land on the Mexican coast do so through a legal device by which title is nominally owned by a Mexican company or individual. Many U.S. citizens do in fact own houses in Baja California, attracted by the climate and the low cost of living.

While the historic resentments have ebbed, the status of the population of Mexican origin in the United States has, with the development of Chicano "brown power," complicated Mexican-U.S. relations. The Mexican Government has started a campaign to encourage Americans of Mexican origin to remember and reinforce their Mexican identity. At first this campaign was given a cultural façade, but as various ethnic groups began to assert their identity and demand special political rights, the essentially political character of the scheme became evident. In the past Mexicans regarded Americans of Mexican origin as "pachucos" or "pochos," degenerate traitors to the Mexican tradition. Now the Chicanos (the term currently used) are regarded as political allies of the Mexican Government. When President Luis Echeverría visited the United States in 1972 on a supposedly friendly visit, he intervened in the internal affairs of this country when he urged Mexicans resident here not to take out U.S. citizenship. The aim evidently is to build up a foreign body politic in the United States. The issue has been aggravated by prevailing Mexican hostility to population control programs; this has encouraged the growth of an excess population in Mexico for which the only solution is migration to the United States. Unlike the blacks, the Chicanos have the advantage of a common U.S.-Mexican border and the presence across the border of a government which clearly supports them. Incidentally, Soviet propagandists are stirring up unrest among both the blacks and the Chicanos. However, the Mexican Government wishes to avoid a direct confrontation with Washington; it refused to assist the New Mexican leader Reyes López Tijerina in his militant campaign for Chicano power.

It is impossible to say how this situation will evolve. Historically, the "Hispanos" and the Indians were enemies, but now they have united, at least to some degree, in the campaign to restore "Aztlán," a mythical Eden that once was supposed to exist in the area now occupied by Mexicans. The problem is complicated by the fact that some old "Hispano" families in the Southwest still imagine they are displaced Spaniards and look down on the Chicanos, who stress their Indian heritage. The attempts to bring together all the Spanish-speaking people of the United States (Puerto Ricans, Cubans, Central Americans, Mexicans, and others) have been fairly successful. In some places such as New York, relations between the black and the Spanish-speaking (or as they now say "Hispanic") groups have been tense, but at the Democratic convention in 1972 it appeared that all the minority groups were forming a coalition. This was one of the reasons the labor leaders were not enthusiastic in their support for McGovern, since labor has traditionally been hostile to minorities and to Mexican workers in the United States.

Union attempts to expel Mexican workers clash directly with the Echeverría scheme to have them retain their Mexican citizenship. A further complication is the presence of many "wetbacks" in this country, Mexicans who have entered illegally and who are deported if the Immigration Service can catch them. Since many of these illegal immigrants are good workers and accept low wages, employers, especially farmers, welcome them, but the labor unions use every possible pressure to have them deported. The unions succeeded in halting the bracero program initiated during World War II, under which contract laborers were imported from Mexico during the harvest season because of the shortage of U.S. farm workers. Mexicans are willing to do stoop labor which the ordinary American refuses to accept. Because of the increasing difficulty of obtaining cheap Mexican labor, and because of César Chávez's unionizing activities, an effort is being made to mechanize U.S. agriculture in order to reduce to the minimum the need for manpower. As the United States ceases to be a safety valve for the excess Mexican rural population, the Mexican Government is reluctantly beginning to consider population control measures.

Legally, Latin American immigration to the United States is limited to 120,000 a year; in addition many Mexicans have a "green card," which allows them to cross the border daily to work in the United States. A vast desert separates the border zone from central Mexico. The Mexican Government has allowed the border zone to trade fairly freely with the United States, and many Mexicans from the border towns still shop in the United States. Now the border zone has good communications with the rest of Mexico, and the Mexican Government has slowly been abolishing the special privileges of the border zone. Mexican border cities must sell Mexican-manufactured goods, even if the same articles could be purchased more cheaply across the border. The border zone itself is becoming industrialized, and, since wages there are much lower than on the American side, a number of American corporations are shipping semimanufactured goods across the border for those parts of the production process which are labor intensive. U.S. labor unions object to this practice, since it favors Mexican factories at the expense of U.S. workers.

An acute problem in the border area concerns water, especially the water of the Colorado River, which, after forming the boundary between California and Arizona, flows across Mexico to the Gulf of California. There is a treaty arrangement dividing the water among California, Arizona, and Mexico, but the Mexicans accuse Arizona farmers of using the water to irrigate their lands and of returning salty water to the Colorado River. The Mexican farmers of Baja California Norte say that the salt water is killing their crops, and this bitter complaint figured conspicuously in the 1972 discussions between Presidents Nixon and Echeverría. The United States has suggested all kinds of remedies, including the building of a large desalinization plant on the coast near Tijuana, but still the problem remains. In reality Mexican agriculture benefits greatly from the United States, which offers a vast market for the agricultural products, particularly of the Pacific coast area.

Americans who cross the border to towns like Tijuana have the impression that the chief industry is vice, and in recent years the problem of drug smuggling across the border has become serious. The Mexican Government has cooperated with the U.S. authorities in locating and destroying poppy and marijuana plantations, but, especially in the state of Sinaloa, it is difficult to police a border where cars are crossing day and night, giving U.S. customs officials only twenty seconds to inspect each car. The situation is similar to that which prevailed during Prohibition, when some Mexicans made fortunes running liquor across the border. Many of the drugs smuggled across the Mexican border come from distant points such as Turkey, Bolivia, or Chile. It is curious that, despite the drug traffic, Mexico has less of a drug problem than the United States.

An examination of the peculiar problems of the U.S.-Mexican border leads naturally to the general problem of U.S.-Mexican relations. Basically, the problem may be defined as the issue of U.S. hegemony in North America, indeed in the Americas. The Monroe Doctrine was defied when, during the Civil War, Emperor Napoleon III of France set up in Mexico an empire under French influence, with the Austrian Maximilian as ruler. During the Civil War there was little Washington could do, but after the defeat of the South, Napoleon was warned to take his troops out of Mexico. Washington also helped Juárez, who had withdrawn to the border town of El Paso, opposite the Texas city of the same name; it is now called Ciudad Juárez. With U.S. help, Juárez defeated Maximilian and shot him. After this victory, he crushed the power of the Catholic Church and of the old oligarchy. For Mexican liberals he is the great national hero, but for Catholic conservatives he is a traitor who sold out to the United States. The official party of Mexico, the Partido Revolucionario Institucional, has gone to great pains to prove that Juárez was not a tool of the United States, indeed that he resented and ridiculed Lincoln. but the historic truth is that U.S. aid made the victory of Juárez possible.

After being accused of intervening on behalf of liberal forces, the United States, during the dictatorship of Porfirio Díaz, was faced with the opposite charge, which has plagued it ever since, that of supporting the oligarchy and a reactionary dictatorship. With a total disregard for the rights of Mexicans, U.S. businessmen and the U.S. Government used servile flattery to obtain economic concessions from Porfirio Díaz. When the 1910 Revolution broke out, the U.S. Government clumsily attempted to help the partisans of the dictator and to clip the wings of the new democracy. Worst of all, after a minor incident, President Wilson ordered U.S. Marines to occupy Veracruz, a fresh humiliation for the long-suffering Mexicans. The German Government tried to promote anti-U.S. feeling among Mexicans by offering, in the eventuality of a German victory in World War I, to return to Mexico the territories ceded to the United States in 1848. This was one reason why the United States entered the war.

President Lázaro Cárdenas (1934-40) followed leftist policies which deeply offended the United States. The expropriation of U.S. oil companies and of U.S.-owned lands, such as those of William Randolph Hearst, triggered a new press campaign against Mexico. The help that Cárdenas gave the Spanish Republic during the 1936-39 Civil War, and his good relations with the Soviet Union, seemed to substantiate the charge that he was a Communist.

Only during World War II, after the Cárdenas presidency, did U.S.-Mexican relations improve. Hitler's racism deeply offended all of Latin America (even the whites of the "Southern Cone" are not Nordics), and it shocked Mexicans, among whom the Revolution had developed the cult of the Indian. It was, therefore, fairly easy for President Roosevelt to win over the Mexicans to his fight against the Axis, but this did not mean that Mexico had sold out to the United States. Any Mexican politician who appears to be too much under U.S. influence immediately loses his popularity. Mexico wishes to follow an independent foreign policy. It formulated the Estrada Doctrine, in favor of nonintervention and against the use of nonrecognition as a diplomatic weapon. Mexico has not been consistent in that it refuses to recognize the Franco government in Spain, but it invoked the Estrada Doctrine when it refused to break with Castro's Cuba, being the only Latin American government which did not join the anti-Castro front. However, its relations with Castro have in general been formal and cold, since Castro agents are accused of provoking serious disturbances in Mexico.

Cuba

Mexico and Cuba are the two horns of the Latin American bull. Unlike Mexico, Cuba does not have a common land boundary with the United States, but there is a gap of only ninety miles between Cuba and Florida. Before Castro, Havana had close ties with the United States. However, this very proximity created problems, and Havana became a glorified Tijuana. Despite the appearances of easy conviviality, Cuba felt, like Mexico, an uneasy resentment toward the United States. Americans assume that Cuban hostility toward the United States is a Castro product. but in fact it is much older. It is evident in the writings of the Cuban national hero José Martí. He knew the United States well, since he was here as a refugee from the Spanish Government of the island. He had little affection for the United States and feared U.S. expansionism. He saw the famous Oklahoma land rush and realized what a danger this behavior pattern might become for Cuba.

There has been a curious reversal in the Latin American attitude toward Castro. The governments, the affluent, and the middle classes felt, like the United States, a mixture of hostility and fear. The masses saw in Castro a defender of their cause, while many, perhaps a majority, of intellectuals and nationalists sympathized with him because he was a David successfully confronting the "Colossus of the North." For most European intellectuals, he was a mixture of Byron and Bolívar. The pro-Castro movement peaked when "Che" Guevara became a martyr in Bolivia and the young French intellectual Régis Debray, author of *Revolution in the Revolution*, was jailed as an accomplice. The "Che" myth still survives, albeit weakened, and in a way it casts a shadow over Castro. European and other admirers turned critical as Castro ceased to symbolize democratic freedom and became a hypertrophied example of egotism. When a French admirer, René Dumont, dared to question Castro's policies in *Cuba, est-il socialiste?*, Castro bridled. It further angered him that a group of leading European intellectuals criticized him when he jailed the poet Hcriberto Padilla for speaking too freely and made him recant publicly.

The Latin American masses lost their initial enthusiasm for Castro more slowly. He outstayed his welcome in Chile (where there were demonstrations against him), apparently in the vain hope that the Broad Front would be victorious in the Uruguayan elections and allow him to land there in glory. The Broad Front was defeated, and all that Castro netted was a reprimand for interfering in Uruguayan internal affairs. On the other hand, the ice of the official blockade of the island was cracking, largely as a result of President Nixon's journeys to Peking and Moscow. Would not a reconciliation with Castro be a logical consequence? The Allende regime in Chile had been quick to recognize Castro. The Peruvian junta, wishing to improve its image as a government of and for the people, raised the issue in the Organization of American States. When the vote was negative (not resoundingly so), Peru decided to go ahead itself and recognize Castro. Jamaica, Barbados, Trinidad and Tobago, and Guyana announced their intention to do so. At the Democratic convention in 1972, a proposal to recognize Castro became part of the McGovern platform. President Nixon showed no inclination to make up with Castro, but some of his advisers, such as Ambassador Keating, said the matter should be considered. These breaks in the hostile inter-American front gave Castro an opportunity again to denounce the whole inter-American system with typical truculence. A conciliatory spirit is not one of Castro's characteristics.

Panama

A second and related sore point in inter-American relations is Panama. Americans regard Teddy Roosevelt as one of their great presidents, but in Panama he is remembered less admiringly for his remark "I took Panama." The very fact that Cuba and Panama owe their independence to the United States makes them resentful rather than grateful. The Colombians, who should be bitter because of the amputation of their territory, have almost forgotten the episode. The Panama case involves painful lesions which are not present in Cuba. Panama is cut in two by a zone over which the United States claimed to exercise sovereign rights. The United States pays Panama a rental for the Zone, but the Panamanians believe that the United States receives the lion's share of the profits from the Canal. There is the brutal contrast between the slums of Panama City on one side of the boundary and the attractive U.S. residential area on the other side. The United States is useful to Castro since he can arouse nationalistic support by denouncing the imperialist giant across a channel. Panamanian politicians are even better off, since they can rant across a fence, backyard style.

When Nasser seized the Suez Canal, Secretary of State Dulles used incredible language in his protests against British, French, and Israeli intervention. Yet, when the Panamanians, who followed the Suez episode carefully, made similar demands about their Canal, the U.S. attitude was entirely different. To the Panamanians and to the Europeans the United States is displaying gross hypocrisy. The 1967 war resulted in the blocking of the Suez Canal, with a total loss of revenues for Nasser, so the idea of nationalizing their Canal has become less attractive to Panamanians. On the other hand, they have made it clear that they do not want the Canal internationalized. The question really breaks down into two parts: the Canal Zone and the Canal itself. The United States agreed to an apparent condominium over the Zone, with the Panamanian flag flying at the same height as the U.S. flag. As in Puerto Rico, the altitude of the flags gives only an illusion of authority to Panama. Real power still resides with the United States. When there was an alleged insult to the Panamanian flag in the Zone in 1964, Panamanian students invaded the Zone but were repelled, with the loss of nineteen lives; these students have become martyrs, and their graves are national shrines.

Negotiations concerning the Zone and the Canal have been going on for years in great secrecy. Occasionally, strongman Omar Torrijos harangues a mob about U.S. refusals to meet his demands. Presumably, his real desire is total sovereignty over the Zone and ownership of the Canal, with the United States (or some other country) providing technical assistance. The United States is clearly unwilling to meet either of these demands, and it has the power to say "No." The Panamanian Government realizes that the Canal is obsolete and should be replaced with a sea-level canal wide enough to allow the largest tankers to pass through. If Panama pushes too hard, the United States might decide to build a new canal through Nicaragua (which is much more friendly to the United States) or even Colombia. The political tug-of-war is complicated by technical reports which recommend only Panamanian sites for a new canal. These confidential reports have received less publicity than the protests from ecological groups which claim that a sea-level canal would permit a dangerous cohabitation of marine species of the Caribbean and the Pacific. They dramatically call attention to a viciously poisonous yellow sea snake which is abundant in the Pacific and which would endanger the whole marine life of the Caribbean were it able to swim through the canal. The surge of anti-U.S. nationalism manifest in Cuba, Chile, and Peru, with the expropriation of important U.S. properties, has aggravated the situation and made Panama more intractable. In general it may be assumed that a Democratic administration in the United States would be more receptive to Panamanian demands than a Republican administration. The Nixon administration was embarrassed when in 1973 the U.N. Security Council agreed to hold a session in Panama to allow the Torrijos government to vent its resentment.

The Dominican Republic

An episode which loomed large for a while in inter-American relations, but now is largely forgotten, was the U.S. occupation of the Dominican Republic in 1965. It has been compared with the Soviet occupation of Czechoslovakia in 1968, but, whereas the Czech Government is still criticized internationally for its persecution of dissidents, the Balaguer regime in the Dominican Republic has shown a remarkable degree of tolerance. However, the defeated President Juan Bosch and the pro-Communist students at the University of Santo Domingo try to keep the episode alive in their denunciations of Balaguer.

Venezuela

Venezuela, which is even more Americanized than pre-Castro Cuba, reminds the visitor of Texas. Both have boomed in this century, thanks to petroleum. It is essentially a new society, and the typical Venezuelan has much in common with the typical Texan, in regard to both the modern urban type and the cowboy of the cattle country. Since World War II, Caracas has boomed like Dallas, Fort Worth, and Houston, with similar architectural expressions. The bolívar is almost as strong as the dollar, and Venezuela is the only Latin country where gasoline is measured in gallons.

It would be logical to assume that such a country would be unquestionably pro-United States, but, whereas in Cuba the pro-American façade was blown away violently, in Venezuela it is merely crumbling. While there are special circumstances in each case, an important factor in both countries was the eagerness of the U.S. Government and U.S. corporations to make deals with dictators who became for the people the epitome of tyranny. A logical consequence of overthrowing a dictator and forcing him to flee was to overthrow and expel his U.S. allies. In a curious reversal of roles, Rómulo Betancourt's Acción Democrática, which came to power as a crusading force against the oil companies, reached a modus vivendi with them, while the Christian Democrats of Rafael Caldera, regarded as more friendly to foreign capital, began to fight them after they came to power. The explanation is partly that Betancourt, once a Communist, turned against the Party, and Castro incited and armed guerrilla forces to overthrow him, while the Christian Democrats, traditionally bitter enemies of the Communists, suddenly found themselves throughout the world the object of the friendly advances of the Marxists in 1971. For years many young Christian Democrats had favored a coalition with the Communists.

About the same time, even the capitalist oil-producing countries of the world began a program of slow takeovers of foreign oil companies, triggered by the seizure of these companies in Algeria, Libya, and Iraq. The Venezuelan army, long the main support of the oligarchy and the oil interests, was infected with the "national socialism" of the Peruvian army, with which it has had close relations. It has shown a readiness to invade Guyana and seize territories Venezuela claims. It has been restrained by Brazil, which once lost a boundary dispute with Guyana and would now like to bring the whole country into its orbit. Brazil has built a road connecting the Guyanese capital, Georgetown, with Manaus. While neither the United States nor Brazil would permit a Castro-type takeover in Venezuela, the Somoza-style relationship the United States once had with Venezuela is gone forever.

The Andean Republics

Relations with Colombia have in general been excellent, largely because of the moderate and responsible leadership of both major parties by such men as Alberto Lleras Camargo. The sixteen-year national front agreement between Conservatives and Liberals ends in 1973. If the country returns to the political chaos which almost led to a civil war and triggered the burning of Bogotá in 1948, the future of U.S.-Colombian relations will become complicated and dangerous.

Ecuador lives in a constant state of hypertension and views the loss to Peru of the eastern territories it claimed somewhat the way the Irish Republican Army views Northern Ireland's association with Britain. Ecuadorian politicians have an excellent opportunity to present themselves as the defenders of their small nation against three bullying giants: Peru, which "took"the territories; Brazil, which played host to the 1942 conference at which the present boundary line was established; and the United States, which prompted the conference since it did not wish inter-American relations to be complicated by a Peruvian-Ecuadorian boundary dispute which could weaken the common front in the struggle against the Axis. In its desire to make its existence felt on the international scene, Ecuador has acted with a tragicomic petulance. In 1967, after the President of Ecuador attacked the Alliance for Progress, the U.S. Ambassador felt obliged to defend it in moderate terms. The President declared that he had been insulted and demanded that Washington withdraw the Ambassador. No Latin American country has shown the aggressiveness of Ecuador in asserting its claim to a 200-mile-wide strip of territorial waters, although many Latin American countries make the same claim. It has used warships given by the United States to seize U.S. fishing ships in these waters, to arrest their captains and crews, and to impose heavy fines.

The Eleventh Conference of American States was to have been held in Quito. The United States generously provided funds for a splendid new building, which was later to be used to house the Ecuadorian Congress. The Ecuadorian Government made it clear that for it the conference was to be primarily a sounding board for its complaints against Peru, so the conference was canceled. That was the end of these meetings, which had been held at five-year intervals in different capitals since 1889.

The politician who made a public career out of such international blackmail was the demagogue José María Velasco Ibarra, who once boasted, "Give me a balcony and I will rule the country!" Five times he won the presidency, but only once did he finish his term. He was elected President in 1968 and overthrown by the army in 1971; he seems to have gone for the last time, but, like Santa Anna of Mexico, he keeps popping up. The Ecuadorean army feared that free elections would have led to the victory of a leftwing demagogue; its nationalism has imitated to some extent the "national socialism" of the Peruvian army. It will be for the United States an obstinate negotiator, but at least the world can hope for some respite from the rantings with which Velasco Ibarra has been filling the air for so long. Ecuador has suddenly become a major oil producer, second in Latin America to Venezuela; the U.S. companies operating there feel like geese that have laid golden eggs in an area of quicksands.

Peru once had a rather special relationship with the United States, like that now enjoyed by Brazil. It was the typical pattern of a dictatorship allying itself with Washington and U.S. business interests. W. R. Grace and Company owes its existence to this relationship, and until recently it occupied in Peru a position similar to that of the United Fruit Company in Central America. The 1968 military coup which led to the expropriation of the large estates has changed all that, and the Grace Company no longer has any major operations in Peru. The military government has established relations with most of the Communist countries and is developing an especially active relationship with the Soviet Union. All this has led to serious tensions with the United States; but Washington is showing moderation and restraint, since it hopes the situation will not deteriorate as badly as that in Chile.

Castro's prophecy that the Andes would be the Sierra Maestra of South America, and "Che" Guevara's attempt to make this prophecy come true, seemed, despite Guevara's death, to be close to realization in Bolivia under the leftist administration of Juan José Torres. However, after a short but bloody civil war, conservative General Hugo Banzer seized power in 1971, and a large number of Soviet agents were expelled. The new government clearly has the support of the Brazilian Government, which regards Chile as a focus of Communist infection even more dangerous than Cuba, since a large number of Brazilian radicals have taken refuge there and are conducting a campaign against the Brazilian junta. Bolivia claims the northern strip of Chile, which was once its coast, with the vehemence displayed by Ecuador in its claims to its lost eastern territories. The "Day of the Sea" is a national holiday devoted to be theme "Antofagasta will be ours!" Bolivian feelings on this issue run so strong that, if there were chaos in Chile, the Bolivian army might seize the opportunity to attempt to recover the lost coastal area.

The key problem in the Southern Cone is the uneasy relationship between Argentina and Chile. The Argentinian army detests Allende as much as the Brazilian army does, and it is concerned about the Chilean minority in southern Argentina. Lanusse took a conciliatory attitude, but in the summer of 1972 a group of young Argentinian extremists highjacked an Argentinian plane and forced it to fly to Chile. Allende rejected Lanusse's request that the highjackers be returned to Buenos Aires and allowed them instead to go to Havana. There is little likelihood that Chile's traditionally cold relations with Argentina will greatly improve.

Historically, the relations between the United States and Chile have not been cordial. In the last century Chile had excellent relations with Britain, and the United States was doing everything possible to eliminate British competition from South America. In the War of the Pacific (1879-83) the United States supported Peru and even threatened to intervene on its behalf. Chile won the war, but there was a legacy of resentment against the United States. In 1891 came the notorious episode of the U.S. warship "Baltimore," which landed sailors in Valparaíso. Since World War II leftist parties have grown considerably in Chile. The Christian Democrats came to power when Eduardo Frei won the presidency in 1964, and it seemed that cordial U.S.-Chilean relations could be established on a modified basis. However, this hope proved vain when a coalition of Socialists and Communists under Socialist Salvador Allende defeated the badly divided opposition in the presidential elections of 1970.

The result was not a complete break, like Castro's revolution in Cuba. The Chilean Socialists are to the left of the Communists, and Allende recognized Castro's government and gave him a triumphant welcome when he made his first trip to a Latin American country since his government was expelled from the Organization of American States. However, Allende, who had come to power legally, said he would act constitutionally, probably fearing that if he did otherwise the army would stage a coup against him. Extreme leftist groups which had supported him were impatient with his constitutional methods and resorted to violence, including the illegal seizure of lands in disregard of the government-sponsored legally constituted land reform program. The Soviets were elated by the Allende victory, but they did not wish to provoke a complete break with the United States, which might burden the Soviet Union with the responsibility of keeping Chile going; Cuba was enough.

The Christian Democrats, allied with the National (i.e. Conservative) Party, still controlled both houses of Congress, and the prestige of Eduardo Frei grew, despite Allende's personal attacks on him. Accusing the Christian Democrats of blocking his reforms, Allende made a futile attempt to replace Congress with a "People's Parliament" and the judicial system, from the Supreme Court down, with a system of people's courts. The U.S. administration of President Nixon met Allende's unceasing insults with a stony silence, to his disappointment. When Allende seized the large U.S.-owned copper mines and juggled figures to avoid paying complete, prompt, and effective compensation, the U.S. Government took steps to hold up loans and credit for Chile, to which Allende responded by accusing Washington of economic aggression. There was a short-lived trading boom when Allende came to power, because he raised wages and because those who had money were trying to convert it into goods, but then the day of reckoning came. Allende, who had urged the workers to make claims against the owners of factories, mines, and other enterprises, now told them that they must work hard and uncomplainingly, since to do otherwise would be almost treasonable. Chilean democracy survived, but Chileans had lost their reputation as mature and restrained citizens. Like Uruguay, Chile had ceased to be regarded as a model democracy. However, a battered democracy has fared better there than in many other Latin American countries. The 1973 congressional elections were conducted fairly, and, since the result was a stalemate, it would prove almost impossible for Allende to push through the radical constitutional reforms he had announced.

The River Plate Republics

Traditionally, Argentina had regarded itself as the great rival of the United States for hegemony in Latin America. Wealthy and developed, proud of its white, highly educated and Europeanized population, it thought it had a manifest destiny to be the natural leader of South, and even of Latin, America. The last manifestation of this continental ambition was the attempt of Perón to exercise control of the working classes of Latin America through labor attachés in Argentine embassies. At one period Argentina, with Brazil and Chile, promoted an anti- U.S. bloc. It attempted to persuade these neighbors that the "ABC countries in the south were a natural counterbalance to the United States, but this alliance never became effective because of Brazilian and Chilian resentment of Argentina. Indeed, Argentina's haughty attitude won it few friends in the rest of Latin America. However, the ideas expressed in books such as Manuel Ugarte's *The Destiny of a Continent* (1923) fit into the intellectual and political history of the pan-Latin American movement, which has grown visibly, or at least verbally, in the last decade.

Argentina was less than helpful to the United States in World War I, and in World War II it was openly hostile. Buenos Aires became the center of Nazi activities in Latin America. The U.S. Government attempted to cut off Latin American trade with the Axis by publishing a blacklist of such traders, and it prepared and distributed a "Blue Book" revealing Argentine connivance with the Axis. However, publication of the "Blue Book," with its account of the career of Perón in the service of fascism, gave the Argentinian dictator an opportunity to pose as the victim of U.S. calumnies. Suddenly, Washington and Perón decided that it was to their mutual advantage to come to terms. As a result, both lost moral standing, and Perón was overthrown. When Perón returned to Buenos Aires on the eve of the 1973 presidential elections, he proclaimed his old charge that the United States was the great enemy of Argentina. The rather surprising clear victory of his man Héctor Cámpora did not bode well for inter-American relations.

The United States had long assumed that it would count on Uruguay as a safe democracy and on Paraguay as a safe dictatorship. Now, it was no longer sure of either. The guerrilla activities of the Tupamaros, especially the cold-blooded murder of a U.S. police officer on loan to the Uruguayan Government of Jorge Pacheco Areco, incensed the American public. The leftists formed a "Broad Front" in the presidential elections of 1972 but were defeated, and President Juan María Bordaberry governed with a severity previously unknown in modern Uruguay. Most Western countries, especially the United States, Brazil, and Argentina, were relieved that Uruguay had not become another Cuba. When in 1973 the armed forces staged a coup to force Bordaberry to govern with more severity, it seemed that, thanks to the Tupamaros, the much-vaunted Uruguayan democracy was following in the footsteps of Argentina.

In Paraguay the dictatorship of General Alfredo Stroessner presented the old pattern of a stable government by a strongman allied with U.S. promoters and working easily with the American Embassy. The Church at first supported the dictatorship, but in 1971 it became openly hostile. There were signs that the old order was changing, giving place to new. However, Stroessner easily won the presidential elections of 1973.

Brazil

Brazilians believe that their country is now much more important than any Spanish-speaking republic, and they are convinced that in the future it will be a great power. Even Brazilian atheists believe that "God is Brazilian," and there is a marked obsession with national greatness in contemporary Brazil. Sometimes Brazilians, in their euphoria, forget the obstacles which their country faces. They point out that Brazil has three million square miles of territory, so it is about three times as large as the second-biggest Latin American republic, Argentina. The population of Brazil is nearly 100 million, half of the population of South America and a third of the population of all of Latin America.

Like U.S. history, a dominant feature of Brazilian history has been the "March to the West." Brazil began as a chain of coastal cities, and the westward movement has been a continual policy of the government. The moving of the capital to Brasília and the building of the east-west highway through Amazonia were important steps in this process. In some places such as Paraguay the Brazilians are even spilling across the border, whereas there is little migration from Spanish America to Brazil.

Brazil is the Latin American country with which the United States traditionally has had the most cordial relations. There is a psychological barrier between Brazil and Spanish America, and the anti-U.S. psychosis which at different periods has affected Mexico, Cuba, Panama, Argentina, Chile, Peru, and Ecuador has had little repercussion in Brazil. Argentina was a rival of both Brazil and the United States, and this tended to draw the two countries together. During the empire, Brazil, in politics and trade, was oriented primarily toward England. Under the republic, its orientation in these fields has been toward the United States, even though culturally it was attuned to France until recently.

There has been some anti-U.S. feeling in Brazil, as was expressed in the notorious book *The American Illusion* (1893) of Eduardo Prado. This book by a disgruntled supporter of the old empire so enraged the U.S. and Brazilian governments that it was suppressed. Anti-U.S. feeling came from pro-fascist groups during World War II, and more recently from leftists. The United States was blamed first for supporting Vargas, then for overthrowing him, and finally for causing his suicide. The leftist government of João Goulart was hostile to the United States, which welcomed and even abetted the military coup which overthrew him. Relations between the military government and the Nixon administration have been very good. Brazil does not regard itself as just another Latin American country, and the United States seems inclined to recognize it as, at the same time, a major power and a leader of the Third World. Brazil was the only Latin American country to participate actively in World War II, and this was quite different from the verbal participation of the other countries. Brazil has formal diplomatic relations with the Soviet Union, but it is resolutely anti-Communist, and there is a willingness in Washington to treat it virtually as a member of NATO.

Brazil occupies a special place in U.S.-Latin American relations. President Nixon is alleged to have said "As Brazil goes, so goes Latin America," a remark which pained the Spanish Americans but in the minds of many U.S. leaders reflects the truth. The disillusionment of Washington with Spanish America was expressed in Treasury Secretary Connally's remark that "We haven't got many friends there anyway."

"Progress" and Indifference

In response to the Castro revolution and the wave of sympathy for his ideas in Latin America, President Kennedy tried to revive the spirit of Roosevelt's Good Neighbor Policy, and in 1961 he launched the Alliance for Progress. The Kennedy charisma, his Catholicism, and his death created the "Kennedy myth." He won a popularity somewhat similar to that of Perón in Argentina. In both cases popular enthusiasm obfuscated a cold analysis of achievements.

The Alliance for Progress did not prevent a Communist-Socialist victory in Chile or the adoption of anti-U.S. policies in other Spanish American countries, so the Nixon administration is, as it is politely expressed, maintaining a low profile in Latin America. Nixon must feel a certain hostility for the Latin Americans after the treatment he received when as Vice President he made a tour of the area in 1958. There were student riots, he was spat upon, and President Eisenhower sent the Marines to Puerto Rico, ready to invade Venezuela, if necessary, to protect Nixon. President Nixon's feelings have sometimes surfaced, as when in 1969, referring to U.S. student riots, he said that U.S. universities were imitating Latin American universities, "which are the worst in the world." Nixon's evaluation of Latin America was not improved when he sent Nelson Rockefeller to the various countries of Latin America, hoping that the Rockefeller name would work magic. The treatment he received was similar to that accorded Nixon earlier; in Bolivia his visit had to be canceled, and his group never left the airport. Rockefeller's report, based on a series of hasty visits, was a pathetic finale to a disastrous adventure. Secretary of the Treasury Connally visited several Latin American capitals in the course of a worldwide tour in 1972. He is disliked in Latin America as a tough Texan who made it clear he would tolerate no nonsense, but his trip did not trigger the protests which accompanied the visits of Nixon and Rockefeller, who had shown an eagerness to dialogue with anti-U.S. elements.

Traditionally, the United States believed its manifest destiny lay in Latin America and that it had no reason to concern itself especially with the Old World. Latin America was described, in a peculiarly unflattering phrase, as "our own backyard." Now the United States is concerned primarily with Europe, the Soviet Union, and China. Latin America and Africa have been down graded in U.S. priorities, and the attitude of most Americans is that they do not particularly care what happens in Latin America.

Even Castro has ceased to bother them. The Organization of American States (OAS) is a regional organization under the United Nations, but it has less general support than the parent body, which is widely viewed as a rather tawdry organization of colorful politicians. In the Department of State the officers in charge of relations with the major world areas have the title of Assistant Secretary. Several times the proposal has been made that the United States should show its special appreciation of Latin America by giving the officer in charge of relations with it the rank of Under Secretary, but this proposal wisely has been shelved, since other areas of the world would then demand equal status.

One reason why U.S. relations with Latin America have cooled is that the structure of inter-American organizations has changed. In the old days the Pan American Union was clearly controlled by the United States, and the director was an American. Since the 1948 reorganization, when the name Organization of American States was adopted, this is no longer true. Both the secretary general and the assistant secretary are Latin Americans. Since the United States provides two-thirds of the budget of the OAS, it could be assumed that two-thirds of the officials would be Americans, but this is far from being the case. All the inter-American organizations are now staffed largely by Latin Americans, who receive tax-free salaries which are high by Latin American and even U.S. standards. Congress is critical of the overstaffing of U.S. Government departments, and it is doubly critical of the staffing of inter-American agencies. Another criticism of the OAS is that the United States has one vote, like any Central American republic, and, were it not for the pressure it can bring to bear on other delegates, it would frequently be outvoted. The OAS should have a security council, as has the United Nations, so that great and small, responsible and irresponsible nations would not be placed on the same illusory level. The present tendency of the U.S. Government is to deal with other American governments directly on important political issues and to use the OAS as a vehicle for less important and more technical matters. Even here, there is an unwillingness to put too much faith in the OAS. The most pressing problem facing Latin America is, in a variety of forms, the population explosion, but, being under constant pressure from Latin Americans, the OAS has shown an almost complete unwillingness to tackle the subject.

Latin American indifference or hostility to the OAS is also marked. A tendency in the last few years has been to promote a pan-Latin Americanism which would confront the United States with a bloc of comparable size. The United States has traditionally opposed such a bloc, realizing that it would weaken U.S. control of the hemisphere. Indeed, the Soviet Union is actively supporting the movement because it would assist the Soviet plan of isolating and weakening the United States. The Latin American Parliament, a rather sporadic organization which meets from time to time in different capitals, has become a sounding board for anti-U.S. propaganda. During the administration of President Lyndon Johnson, there was a sharp change in U.S. policy; Washington began to promote the idea of Latin American unity. There was a false analogy with the European Economic Community (EEC); the EEC had brought prosperity to Europe, so would not LAFTA (Latin American Free Trade Association) do the same for Latin America? There was the belief that a Latin American common market would permit U.S. subsidiaries in Latin America to enjoy the advantages of economies of scale. Unfortunately, LAFTA has had only a modest success, and even the Central American Common Market, which was looked upon as a model, virtually collapsed as a result of the "football war" between El Salvador and Honduras and subsequently of Costa Rica's virtual withdrawal. Efforts to revive it have had only modest success. Now, no one talks much about LAFTA or the Central American Common Market. There is also an Andean subregional grouping, comprised of Chile, Bolivia, Peru, Ecuador, and Colombia, with Venezuela finally in. The aim of this organization was to allow the Andean countries to compete with Argentina and Brazil. Some publicity has appeared about the integration of the economies of Chile and Argentina—an old proposal which has been revived. We are never told the plain truth about these bureaucratic shufflings. Integration, both inter-American and Latin American, is made difficult by the proliferation of organizations which duplicate each other's functions. Most of these organizations respond largely to the desire of Latin Americans to have a steady government job.

In summation, it may be said that at present the United States necessarily has bilateral relations with all Latin American countries (except Cuba) but that inter-American relations, in the broad sense, continue only at a modest level.

8 • World Relations

The United Nations

The inter-American system creates a special relationship among the countries of the Western Hemisphere; this chapter is devoted to the world, or extra-hemisphere relations of Latin America. The inter-American system gives the Latin American countries a means to exercise pressure on the United States, but at the same time they realize that the U.S. hegemony of the system makes it impossible for any one country to defy the United States without suffering the consequences. In the United Nations they feel freer, since they can count on broader support. Isolated in the inter-American system, Castro finds solid support among the Communist-bloc countries in the United Nations. For both the United States and Latin America, the United Nations is the major, the Organization of American States the minor, league.

It should not be supposed, however, that the United Nations is a free and open forum. There, also, the Latin American governments vote with the United States, not only by conviction but also because they expect material rewards to be the recompense for their support. This is not only the U.S. modus operandi. Other countries, such as the Soviet Union and Israel, keep careful count of voting in the United Nations and allocate their aid funds to influence this voting. When the United Nations was founded, the twenty Latin American votes had considerable weight, and the Soviet Union accused the United States of having these votes in its pocket. The United States denied this vehemently, and it is true that this country does not control Latin American votes as the Soviet Government controls those of the Ukraine or Byelorussia, or even the Soviet-bloc countries. Yet, it knows that in an emergency it can count on most of the votes of Latin America.

The equality of votes in the General Assembly of the United Nations would be an absurdity without the Security Council, where real power and responsibility rest. The Latin Americans complain that the Security Council is antidemocratic because there the Latin American bloc has only two votes. This is really a more reasonable representation, especially as the United States, which makes a far greater contribution in every way, has only one vote, admittedly with veto power. The countries in the General Assembly have no real international responsibilities. The Latin American nations are unhappy since the admission of a large number of African countries, which now form the largest voting bloc in the General Assembly, replacing Latin America in this artificially favored position. No one Latin American country has a permanent seat on the Security Council, although Brazil, which withdrew from the League of Nations because it was not given one, still aspires to this rank in the United Nations.

The abject role of Cuba in the United Nations shows how relatively benevolent the United States is. The Cuban representative rants constantly about imperialism, but when the Security Council in 1968 sought to condemn the Soviet Union for its invasion of Czechoslovakia, Castro issued a statement supporting the Soviet action. If anyone should have condemned this occupation of a small neighbor by a super power, it was Cuba, which had so loudly denounced the Bay of Pigs invasion in which the United States had participated only in a secondary way. Castro was paying his debts, past and future, to the Soviet Union.

Latin American Isolationism

The general attitude of Latin America is isolationist; the rest of the world seems a long way away, and national problems are immediate and pressing. The United States should understand this mentality. Only Brazil, with its aspiration to be a great power, has shown any real willingness to take part in international military operations, and even Brazil's role in World War II was of secondary importance in the total picture of the war. The Latin American countries are willing to take part in peacekeeping missions, such as the U.N. force which once held the Gaza strip. Latin American countries like also to be entrusted with international missions giving them prestige. Such missions are usually not entrusted to major powers, and Latin American countries have the triple advantage of occupying an intermediate position between the major powers and the Third World, of not being directly involved in most conflicts, and of having a strong legal tradition. The present secretary general of the OAS, Galo Plaza, played an important role as mediator in Cyprus. Latin Americans like to be appointed to leading posts in international organizations: the Mexican writer Jaime Torres Bodet was director of UNESCO, the Brazilian physician Marcel Candau was director of the World Health Organization, and the Brazilian ecologist Josué de Castro was director of the Food and Agriculture Organization.

The Latin American isolationist attitude in world politics does not necessarily imply intellectual or cultural isolation. It should be remembered that "South" America is really "South East" America, being located between Europe, North America, and Africa. It has close relations with all of these areas, Europe predominating in culture, the United States in trade. Historically, relations with Europe have been most important. After World War II it seemed that the United States would be preponderant in every field, and there is no other country whose influence can compare with that of the United States. However, the boom of the European Economic Community has coincided with sharp attacks on U.S. economic interests in Cuba, Chile, Peru, Ecuador, and Venezuela. The United States is unwilling to meet Latin America's demands for arms, so the Latin American countries have turned to France, England, and, in the case of Cuba, the Soviet Union. Even in technology, the United States is no longer supreme; the Concorde has made demonstration flghts to South America, while the United States has abandoned its plans for a supersonic transport. Leftist groups promote anti-U.S. feeling among Latin American youths, who show little inclination to criticize European countries. These generalizations apply in different ways to each country. Since there are some twenty Latin American countries and a like number of European countries, the network of relationships is extremely complex.

Spain

Spain has a special historical place in Spanish America. For traditionalists, Spain is the Mother Country, but this attitude is becoming less and less common. Few are the Latin Americans who believe that Franco's repressive militarism offers a model for Latin America. Even the Spanish American military, following the Peruvian pattern, now believe that their role is to lead the people forward rather than to hold them down. The old-fashioned con-

servatives have almost disappeared, and the Christian Democrats, who have taken their place, see models in Italy or Germany
but not in Spain. For the leftists who have achieved considerable
power from Cuba to Chile, Franco is the epitome of what they
detest, even though they proclaim their affection for the Spanish
people. Spain and Greece, controlled by military juntas allied
with the United States, are viewed alike. The Brazilian junta is
somewhat like that of Spain, but Brazil is attuned to Portugal,
not to Spain. The Argentine militarists have good relations with
Franco's army, but the colonial heritage of Spain there is slight
in comparison with the overwhelming Italian immigration of
modern times and the rise to the top of Italian families, who
were long under the shadow of the old Spanish, especially Basque,
oligarchy. Since there is no great Indian tradition in Argentina
and since the Indians were virtually annihilated, not by the
Spaniards but by the Argentines in the nineteenth century, there
is, at the same time, no great hostility toward Spain.

Hatred of the Spanish colonial regime has long been a part of
the official liberal doctrine of Mexico. The Catholic conservatives, who were ousted from power by the 1910 Revolution,
admire Hernán Cortés as the bearer of Spanish culture, language, and religion, but for the Indianists he is the devil incarnate
who destroyed Aztec culture and reduced the Indians to virtual
slavery. His Indian mistress, Malinche, whose assistance as inter-
preter made the Conquest possible, has become a symbol of
national betrayal. The term *"malinchismo"* is still used in the
meaning of "to sell out to a foreign power" (now especially, the
United States). Emperor Maximilian represented the same Catholic
conservative Europe as Spain, and Benito Juárez led the Indian
crusade to recover the rights lost by the Conquest. The frescoes
of Diego Rivera, with their idealized depiction of Aztec society
and their monster-like caricatures of Cortés and his fellow Spaniards, brought the liberal interpretation of Mexican history to
the people and, more recently, to tourists. President Cárdenas'
support of the Spanish Republic in the Civil War and Mexico's
refusal still today to recognize the Franco regime reflect in large
measure this historical attitude toward Spain. There is some
mellowing, as is evident on the plaque in the Square of the Three
Cultures in Mexico City, where the remains of a pyramid, a
colonial church, and the modern skyscraper housing the Foreign
Ministry stand dramatically side by side. The plaque says that the
Conquest did not represent the victory of one side over the other
but rather the painful birth of a new nation.

An anti-Spanish attitude provides an appropriate background for the heroic lives of liberators such as Venezuelan Simón Bolívar and Colombian Francisco de Paula Santander, and there are still some people who speak as though Spanish atrocities had been committed yesterday. Santander has become the hero of the Colombian Liberals and Bolívar of the Colombian Conservatives; the anti-Spanish attitude is more marked among the Liberals. The militarists, who regard Bolívar primarily as a general and dictator, view Franco Spain favorably, and many of them took refuge there when they were overthrown. That these enriched dictators in exile (Perón, Batista, Pérez Jiménez) as well as their heirs (such as those of Trujillo) live so happily in Franco Spain, where they have been welcomed, has not enhanced Spain's image. Under its old military dictators, Peru was the focal point for the cult of the Spanish tradition, but the 1968 coup, which has aims similar to those of the Mexican Revolution, has changed this glorification of the colonial order, which had survived in Peru better than anywhere else. The Pizarro Room in the National Palace has been renamed the Tupac Amaru Room.

Castro's Cuba is a special case. In its attempt to shake off the legacy of U.S. imperialism, it cultivated to some degree the Spanish heritage which was detested by the old liberals represented by José Martí and the Freemasons. If any country should hate Franco Spain, it is Castro's Cuba, but after an initial exchange of insults, Castro decided to keep on good terms with Spain, partly because the Havana-Madrid air connection provides a bridge to Europe. Canning's famous phrase might be parodied by saying that Castro has called upon the Old World to redress the balance of the New. Franco propaganda says that the Civil War of 1936-39 was fought to free Spain (and the West) from communism, but Spain maintains good relations with Castro. One psychological reason is that Spain has still not forgotten the humiliating defeat of 1898 in which the United States brutally wrenched Cuba from the Mother Country. In any case, politics makes strange bedfellows.

Traditionally, anti-Spanish propaganda included charges that the Spanish people were lazy, incompetent, corrupt, and cruel, and Spanish culture the quintessence of obscurantism and fanaticism. These charges are seldom heard now, since Spanish culture is viewed as part of the national heritage. Taking advantage of this, the Franco regime created in Madrid the Institute of Hispanic Culture, the aim of which is to win the sympathies of Latin Americans by cultural propaganda, which forms an attractive screen for ideological and political activities.

Portugal

In Latin America there is a general indifference toward Portugal, except in Brazil. Brazilians do not regard Portuguese as foreigners, and indeed they now have virtual common citizenship. Since the Portuguese did not destroy any high Indian culture, as did the Spaniards, there is nothing comparable to the propaganda against the Spanish Conquest in Mexico. Portugal and Brazil separated without bloodshed, so there is no need to paint in lurid colors the misdeeds of the Mother Country in order to enhance the prowess of a liberator. Culturally, Brazil has been oriented toward France, and interest in Portuguese culture is limited largely to Camoens' epic *The Lusiads* and Portuguese colonial architecture. Yet the Brazilians feel a kinship with Portugal which they do not feel with Spanish America. Politically, the dictatorships of Portugal and Brazil are attuned to each other, and official speeches refer to a "community" embracing Portugal, Brazil, and the Portuguese territories in Africa.

France

In the nineteenth century Latin America was almost a cultural colony of France. Ashamed of the much-maligned cultures of Spain and Portugal, which were expressions of the colonial past they were rejecting, the young Latin American republics turned to France, whose culture radiated from Paris throughout the Western world. Especially in Brazil, a knowledge of French and a visit to France were part of the cultural baggage of all men aspiring to elitist standing. This attitude explains why movements such as Positivism had such an impact in Latin America. The attachment to France was such that in Brazil people wept in the streets when they heard the news of the fall of France in World War II.

Throughout the world the prestige of the French language and of French culture declined in the post-war period, and, despite the efforts of General de Gaulle, who visited Latin America and tried to revive the idea of a Latin World with Paris as its focus, the Latin American fixation on French culture has gone forever. However, France is still respected, and movements such as existentialism have a vogue in Latin America. Before World War II, many Latin American countries had a French military mission, and the French army provided a model to be copied. During and immediately after World War II, U.S. military missions achieved almost a monopoly in Latin America, but beginning about 1960

Latin America began to turn again to France for military equipment because of the prestige of Mirage fighters and the unwillingness of the U.S. Congress to provide large quantities of advanced equipment to Latin America. Significantly, as Venezuelan relations with the United States soured in 1972, the Venezuelan armed forces turned to France for their equipment.

Italy

Italy has cordial relations with Latin America, especially where there are large Italian colonies, such as Argentina and the state of São Paulo, Brazil. Mass Italian immigration to Latin America has stopped, and personal ties are dwindling, but Italian commerce remains very active. Italian fascism had many admirers in Latin America, but with its collapse the Italian image suffered. Rome and the Papacy give Italy a certain prestige, but Latin America is fundamentally not very Catholic, and the liberals, even liberal Catholics, view them as part of the impedimenta of Latin America. Publicity about the Mafia has harmed the good name of Italy in the United States, but this phenomenon is almost entirely absent in Latin America. However, Paraguay, Argentina, and Chile have recently been singled out as among the main sources of the drugs which are smuggled into the United States by the Mafia.

Britain

Of the non-Latin countries of Europe, England is the one which has had the most influence in Latin America. During the colonial period, with the contraband trade, came books bringing English ideas of freedom. The Spanish Government condemned these books as subversive, but they found eager readers among Spanish American intellectuals. For the British, the Spanish empire was a dangerous monster and Sir Francis Drake a hero. For the Spaniards, he was an impious pirate, attacking Spain's God-given heritage. The Spanish empire collapsed anyhow. Nelson, who was in a way the heir of Drake, is something of a hero to Latin Americans, since his victory over the French and Spanish as Trafalgar was an important contribution to the independence of Latin America. Bolívar and the other liberators had a great admiration for British political institutions, and, while France provided the cultural model for Latin America, England was the political model, although only Brazil became a constitutional monarchy.

Britain played a major role in the economic life of Latin America, especially Argentina. At first Latin American governments requested, even pleaded for, loans and investments, but after these had been granted the inevitable happened. Latin Americans began to denounce the "economic imperialism" of Great Britain, as they now do that of the United States. Nationalists and leftists promote this propaganda assiduously, and Latin Americans frequently forget that, without these loans and investments, the development of their countries would have been much slower. The economic position of Great Britain in Latin America is now weaker than before World War II because Britain had to sell many of its investments to pay the cost of the war. Britain's fight against Hitler won general admiration, and, with the end of Britain's dominant position in the economies of Latin America, the resentment virtually disappeared.

Until World War II there was a symbiotic relationship between England, which supplied manufactured goods, and Argentina, which provided Britain with beef, having imported prize breeding cattle from England. Under this arrangement, Argentina prospered, but the Argentine nationalists accused Britain of impeding the industrial development of Argentina. The British had built a good railway system, but after making it virtually impossible for the British to operate it, the Argentine Government under Perón nationalized it and destroyed whatever efficiency was left. The farmers, whose principal market was Britain, were ruined when Perón taxed them to industrialize the country. In retrospect the period of the trade alliance between Argentina and Britain may be seen as Argentina's golden age. One irritant in British-Argentine relations has been the British-owned Falkland Islands. The British Government has declared it would turn the islands over to Argentina if the inhabitants so desired, but they have emphatically rejected the suggestion. Possession of the islands would not help Argentina in the slightest and would even deprive the country of an international complaint, which is useful in arousing nationalist feelings which the government can exploit. A similar situation exists regarding British Honduras (Belice), whose black English-speaking Protestants have little desire to be absorbed by the Indian Spanish- or Mayan-speaking Catholics of Guatemala.

The British form of government no longer seems a dazzling model to Latin Americans, and indeed many young Latin Americans reject representative democracy as slow, ineffective, and incapable of solving critical social problems. Nevertheless, a majority of Latin Americans still prefer English-style democracy to left- or right-wing dictatorships, even though the failure of democracy has produced dictatorships of both types through much of the area. British relations with Latin America remain cordial, but they will never regain their earlier importance.

Germany

The United States, Spain, Portugal, France, and England have all had serious conflicts with Latin America. Germany has the advantage of never having had direct clashes with Latin America, despite the unpopularity of Nazism during World War II. Germany, indeed, has been able to pose as the defender of Latin America against U.S. and British imperialism. In the sixteenth century the German bankers of Charles V, the Welsers and the Fuggers, played an important role, especially in Venezuela, but nothing remains of this except romantic memories. In the nineteenth century several German scientific expeditions went to Latin America, and Germany gained a reputation as the scientific center of the world. The name of Alexander von Humboldt is respected throughout Latin America. This extraordinary man explored Venezuela, Colombia, Ecuador, Peru, Mexico, and Cuba, and left us valuable descriptions of these countries on the eve of independence. Besides making scientific observations of every kind, von Humboldt described the cultured society of the Spanish colonies; in fact, since as a member of the aristocracy he was idolized by Creole society, it is suspected that his picture of Spanish America is somewhat idealized. Bolívar met him in Paris, and the possibly legendary story is told that he advised Bolívar to lead the Spanish American colonies to independence. He is, therefore, respected not only as a scientist but almost as a prophet of the independence movement.

Under Bismarck, Germany was transformed from a federation of small states with an intensive cultural life into an empire with an army which soundly defeated the French army of Napoleon III in 1870. This defeat marks the end of the Napoleonic legend in Latin America and the beginning of a German cult among the militarists. Germany sent military missions to several Latin American countries, especially Argentina. Ironically, in Allende's Chile the army still uses the goose step it learned from its German missions, which reorganized the Chilean army in 1891. The defeat of Germany in the two world wars punctured the German military balloon, and now its military presence in Latin America is minimal.

Alexander von Humboldt (1769-1859) traveled with Aimé Bonpland through much of Spanish America during the period 1799-1804, gathering scientific data. (From Ronald Hilton, *The Scientific Institutions of Latin America.*)

There is still some sympathy for Nazism among nationalist groups, especially in Argentina, where some leading Nazis took refuge after World War II; the kidnapping of Adolf Eichmann by Israeli agents and his trial and execution became headline news. However, the defenders of Nazism are only a small minority, and the democratic government of the new Germany has generally excellent relations with Latin America. The Christian Democrats had especially close ties with the Adenauer and Kiesinger governments in Germany, while the leftists are sympathetic to Willy Brandt's Socialists. East Germany has made a determined attempt to gain a foothold in Latin America, especially among the German colonies of southern Brazil, but it has won little support. It has established active relations with Castro's Cuba and with the Allende government in Chile. The West German Government has protested against the eviction, legal and illegal, of farmers of German descent in southern Chile, many of whom have left the country, but East Germany has accepted this as part of the revolutionary process.

Austria

There are many traces of Austria in Latin America's past. The Conquest was carried out under the auspices of the Hapsburgs. Pedro II of Brazil was the son of an Austrian princess, and documents discovered in the archives of Vienna show that for Austria Brazil occupied a key position in the Empire's American policy, which was to support a conservative monarchy in Brazil as a bulwark against New World republicanism. Whatever the hidden diplomatic motives, Brazilians recall Pedro II and old Austria with affection.

Austrian relations with Mexico were less fortunate. The empire of Maximilian was imposed by Napoleon III, whose troops invaded and occupied Mexico. The Mexicans are proud of the victory of Puebla (May 5, 1862), and General Zaragoza, who defeated the French army there, is a national hero. The Maximilian interlude complicates France's relations with Mexico, but it scarcely affects Austria. Mexicans regard Maximilian as a man of good faith who had been misled by Mexican conservatives guilty of *malinchismo*. Mexicans are also secretly ashamed that Juárez shot Maximilian despite appeals from all over the world. All this is past. The new truncated Austria plays a very minor role in Latin America.

Holland

Holland is another small country which in the past played a significant role in Latin America. Like Austria, Holland once had a great empire. It needed tropical products, and, like England, it was a Protestant country in a life and death struggle with Catholic Spain, which wished to reduce it to submission. Holland not only preserved its independence, it carried the struggle to the New World. It took advantage of the annexation of Portugal by Spain (1580) to attack the Northeast of Brazil, which had become part of the domains of the King of Spain. The Dutch West India Company, established in 1621, occupied Bahia in 1624, but it was forced to withdraw in 1625. The Dutch established a more permanent colony in Recife (Pernambuco), which they seized in 1630. Maurice of Nassau arrived in 1637, and his government, which lasted until 1644, was the golden age of Dutch rule in the Brazilian Northeast. The Brazilians reconquered Recife in 1654. They talk rather proudly of the Dutch legacy in the Northeast, even though it has been shown that this legacy is a myth, except perhaps for the stimulus given to improved sugar cultivation. When the Dutch were expelled from Indonesia after World War II, many settled in Brazil, where their experience as tropical farmers was a valuable asset. The old Colonial Institute in Amsterdam, which concerned itself with Indonesia, is now the Institute for the Tropics, and it maintains an active interest in Brazil. However, this is only a modest contribution to the giant Brazil. Apart from its ties with the Netherlands Antilles and Surinam, Holland plays only a minor role in Latin America today.

Switzerland

Switzerland has played a curious if minor role in Latin America. In the past it was regarded as a model democracy, and José Batlle y Ordóñez initiated the unsuccessful experiment to introduce Swiss-style democracy into Uruguay. The Swiss were regarded as good farmers and engineers, and they were welcomed as immigrants, especially in Brazil. In recent years the Swiss image has been tarnished. Switzerland is no longer a people's democracy which welcomes refugees but rather a resort for the oligarchy. Latin American politicians who have enriched themselves illegally smuggle their money out of the country and invest it in a Swiss secret account so that they may later live a life of ease in some pleasant spot in Europe. Swiss secret bank accounts have become a cause of friction between Switzerland and the United States, as well as Latin America. This subject has received so much publicity that the world tends to forget the solid virtues which the Swiss possess.

The Soviet Bloc

The Soviet-bloc countries have been playing a growing role in Latin America. The Soviets' policy is to weaken the U.S. position there and at the same time to improve their own chances by encouraging anti-U.S. propaganda and activities. The two cartoons from *Pravda* (see pp. 94, 150), with the commentaries from the *World Affairs Report* of the California Institute of International Studies, are typical of the unceasing campaign in the Soviet press to blame all of Latin America's woes on the United States. The Soviets have no scruples about distorting the facts. Their greatest success has been in Cuba, but it has been so costly that they do not want to promote more revolutions as expensive as Cuba's. Until World War II the Soviet Union actively sought to promote revolution in Latin America, except in Mexico, where it maintained excellent relations with the government. Mexicans insist that their Revolution, which began in 1910, could not have been inspired by the Russian Revolution of 1917, but there were deep ties. President Cárdenas was a friend of the Soviet Union, and Diego Rivera's paintings reflect the Marxist, pro-Soviet viewpoint. After Cárdenas, the "new class" set Mexico upon a capitalist course, and the present Mexican Government is sharply anti-Communist. Leftist student groups have been violently repressed, and in 1971 a number of Soviet Embassy officials were expelled. A similar pattern of events occurred in Bolivia, where in 1972 almost all the Soviet Embassy staff was expelled. Soviet tactics around the world are to win the sympathy of students who may later seize power. This, rather than direct promotion of unrest, would seem to have triggered the trouble in both Mexico and Bolivia.

Another Soviet tactic is to try to gain power through a popular-front-type government, which the Communists take over when the occasion presents itself; this was how the Communists came to power in Czechoslovakia, and it is the pattern they would like to follow in Chile. However, the operation must be carried out in such a way that the new government does not become an excessive financial burden for the Soviet Union. In December 1972, after making in the United Nations an anti-U.S. speech which the pro-Soviet delegates loudly applauded, President Allende, the Socialist head of a popular-front coalition, visited Moscow. On his return to Santiago his opponents formally accused him of making secret deals with the Soviet Union.

However, these charges merely offset the charges against ITT and Kennecott made by anti-American elements, with the result that the 1973 congressional elections, which gave neither side the victory it hoped for, did little to change the picture of Chile's international relationships.

Only in Paraguay and some Central American countries does the old pattern exist of a Communist underground fighting an uncompromising dictatorship. The Stroessner regime in Paraguay is the target of steady Soviet attacks, as is the Somoza regime in Nicaragua. The Soviet Union is trying to infiltrate Central America through its new embassy in Costa Rica. It has good relations with the leftist military dictatorships of Peru and Ecuador. In principle it should detest the Brazilian military dictatorship, but it seeks normal relations and an active trade exchange. Criticism of the Brazilian regime is conspicuously absent in the Soviet press. The Soviets should likewise hate the Argentine military, but the Argentine situation is so confused that the Soviets are clearly bewildered. The Soviet Embassy in Montevideo used to be a focal point for Soviet activities in South America, but this has changed since the Uruguayan Government became more authoritarian. The defeat of the Broad Front in the elections of 1972 seems to have convinced Moscow that it will have to live with the status quo in eastern South America for some time. As part of its plan to establish working relations with the Latin American governments of all shades, the Soviet Union has initiated regular steamship service to South America. It also sent YAK-40 passenger planes on a demonstration tour of Latin American countries, in the hope of interesting their governments in purchasing some.

Soviet propaganda has not been very effective, partly because of psychological differences. It was for this reason that the Soviet bloc assigned a special role to Prague in Communist propaganda relations with the Third World. Czechoslovak agents were active in Castro's move toward Communism. The calculation apparently was that a small, Western, largely Catholic country like Czechoslovakia was the best agent to promote Communist ends. However, the Soviet intervention which crushed Czechoslovakia's democratization in 1968 ruined this calculation, even though Castro tried to curry favor with the Soviets by declaring his approval. East Germany, which participated in the intervention, is viewed as being on about the same level as the harsh Czechoslovak regime. The Poles are especially strong in the Brazilian state of Paraná, but, since the Polish state has a running feud with the Catholic Church, it does not benefit much from this. The Polish Jews who fled to Latin America during the Nazi period have no special affection either for the Polish state. As part of its plan to achieve some degree of diplomatic independence by developing relations with countries all around the globe, Romania, which views itself as an outpost of Latinity in a Slavic sea, has paid special attention to Latin America, with modest success.

Yugoslavia provided many immigrants to Chile, and Yugoslav names are fairly common there. However, many of them came from Split (Spalato) and Dubrovnik (Ragusa), which were Catholic, Italian cities. Some leftists regard Yugoslavia as a political model, combining communism with some degree of freedom. However, the Croatian-Serbian feud which exploded in 1971 and Tito's reconciliation with the Soviet Union in 1972 impaired the attractiveness of this model.

Israel, the Arab World, and Africa

Israel has generally failed to win the solid support of Latin America, as it has failed in black Africa. At first it too seemed to offer a model, and Israel gained considerable sympathy by inviting Latin American intellectuals to Israel and by offering technical assistance to Latin American countries. The Arabs were far less skillful in their propaganda. However, Israel now appears as a militaristic state supported by Washington, which needs the votes of American Jews, a state which refuses to abide by U.N. decisions on the Near East. Anti-Semitism is still fairly common in Argentina. When Fidel Castro visited North Africa in 1972 on his way to Moscow, he proclaimed Cuban support of the Arab cause against Israel, and even non-Marxists feel that the status of Latin America is similar to that of the Arab countries. This was apparent at the meeting of Third World countries in Lima and the UNCTAD (United Nations Conference on Trade and Development) conference at Santiago, Chile, in 1972. As a member of the Organization of Petroleum Exporting Countries, Venezuela has a close relationship with the Arab states. Very seldom now does a Latin American public figure raise his voice on behalf of Israel.

The only Latin American country which has significant relations with Africa south of the Sahara is Brazil. Ever since the colonial period, Brazil has had relations with the Portuguese colonies there, and the present Brazilian Government is cooperating with Portugal in the development of Angola and Mozambique. It has been said that the South Atlantic will become a Luso-Brazilian lake. There is direct air service from Rio de Janeiro to Capetown, and Brazil has cordial relations with the South African Government, which is closely allied with Portugal.

Japan and China

Japan and, more recently, China have developed active relations with Latin America. Both are interested in the copper of Chile and Peru. Japan is concerned primarily with business, China largely with political ideology, so the rivals of the Chinese in

Latin America are not the Japanese but the Soviets, and this ideological war has been getting worse. Japan is happy to have, especially in Brazil, an outlet for its excess population, but China, so many of whose people migrated to Latin America in the last century, does not seem interested in exporting people; this may come later, but the Chinese know that this is a sensitive issue.

Japan and China are both, in different ways, special cases. In general Latin American relations with Asia and Africa are minimal The solidarity of the Third World is not very real, and it is often offset by trade and political rivalries. Latin America is still proud of being a cultural and even a religious extension of Europe, and it does not regard itself as being on the same level with most of the countries of Africa and Asia. It may be classed with the Third World economically, but not in terms of its general orientation, which is toward Europe and the United States. However, the Japanese impact on Latin America is extraordinary, and it may prove to be one of the salient features of Latin American development in the twentieth century.

9 • The Languages

In Latin America there are three major languages: Spanish, Portuguese (in Brazil), and English (in the former British colonies and on the east coast of Central America). French is the official language of the French territories and Haiti, but the Haitian people speak Creole; it is a formality to maintain French as one of the official languages of the Organization of American States and of its secretariat, the Pan American Union in Washington.

Spanish

Fortunately, Spanish has maintained its unity in America, thus assuring it the international status which has led to its being one of the five official languages of the United Nations (the others are English, French, Russian, and Chinese). In the nineteenth century it was not certain that Spanish would survive as a single language. In the Spanish American republics there was such a hatred of the Spanish tradition that the ancient name "Castilian" was used instead of the word "Spanish," as though the name had somehow a less colonial connotation. (Today the common usage is to say "Castilian" in South America and "Spanish" in Spain, Mexico, and Central America.) To call American Spanish "Castilian" is erroneous in view of the fact that, despite the theories of some philologists, it has a clearly Andalusian character, since Seville and later Cadiz had a monopoly on communications between Spain and America. The Spanish spoken in Venezuela shows the influence of immigrants from the Canary Islands. The Canary Islanders were so different from the Spaniards of the Peninsula that, in his proclamations, Bolívar denounced "the Spaniards and Canary Islanders!"

Not only did the new independent republics hate the Spanish tradition, the "patriots" (i.e. the founders of the new republics) thought that every republic ought to have its national language as an expression of its cultural personality. Thus, Spanish Americans would no longer speak Spanish or Castilian, but Mexican, Colombian, Peruvian, and so on. It recalls the nationalities theory of the contemporary Soviet world. To designate the cultural personality of the republics, new words were invented like "Mexicanity," "Peruvianity," and "Argentinity." The most extreme case was Agentina, where rabid nationalists proclaimed that they did not speak Spanish or Castilian but "the national language of the Argentinians" and that this language would have as its basis *lunfardo,* the language of the Buenos Aires dock area. This would be somewhat comparable to Brooklynese becoming the official language of the United States. The nationalist idea that every republic should have its own language was based on an analogy with the fate of Latin in Europe. Latin was the official language of the Roman Empire. When the Empire broke up, Latin split up into Romance languages (Italian, French, Spanish, Portuguese, and Romanian), which became the official languages of the new nations into which the Roman Empire divided. Likewise, with the dissolution of the Spanish Empire and the creation of the new Spanish American republics, Spanish would break up as Latin had done.

This analogy proved false. The creation of the new republics was the work of the cultured oligarchy and not the masses of Indians or of barbaric, illiterate invaders. The times had changed. The Spanish American oligarchs wished to show the world that they were not crude, illiterate Americans. While some nationalists urged the need to create national languages, the oligarchy and the cosmopolitan intellectuals strove to speak polished Castilian. A rivalry began among the various republics as to which spoke the purest Castilian. For a Spaniard of a certain social level, to speak and to write well is a proof of culture, and it is partly for this reason that Spanish is one of the most beautiful languages in the world. In some Spanish American countries, the elite spoke more correctly than the elite in Spain, where no one felt the need to prove that he was not an illiterate Indian or a black. The Spanish American uses less profanity than the Spaniard. In Spain some uneducated individuals are incapable of opening their mouths without using a crude word; this type is uncommon in Spanish America. In some republics there is an artificial academism. For example, the Chilean Government for a long time required that Chilean schools teach the difference in pronunciation between "b" and "v," a distinction which is not made in Spain or indeed in the rest of Spanish America. The Spanish Academy, the official arbiter on language matters, had issued a decree, and it was followed in Chile, although in Spain itself it passed unnoticed.

This preoccupation with good speech led to the development of linguistic studies in Spanish America. It is curious that one of the founders of Spanish linguistic studies, Andrés Bello, came from a country, Venezuela, where Spanish was badly spoken. In Colombia, and more precisely in Bogotá, a much more cultured Spanish is spoken because during the colonial period Bogotá was the seat of a viceroyalty and an important cultural center. After Bello, the most important linguist was the Colombian Rufino José Cuervo. The Spanish grammar written by Bello and revised by Cuervo is a standard manual in all of Spanish America and even in Spain. Cuervo's dictionary of the Spanish language was a landmark in Spanish lexicography, although Cuervo never completed it. Another great Colombian linguist was Miguel Antonio Caro. Bogotá claims to be the "Athens of America," although the violence which characterized Colombia during the decades following World War II has distracted national attention from matters of linguistic purity.

In the Spanish world, as in France, there is an authoritarian tradition in language usage which does not exist in the English-speaking world. The instrument of this authority is the network of academies of the Spanish language, which have as their prototype the French Academy. The Royal Spanish Academy of the Language was founded early in the eighteenth century, but the authoritarian tradition in language is much older. It goes back to the Middle Ages. During the Reconquest of the Peninsula from the Moors, the Castilians, as they moved south, conquered lands which did not speak Castilian (originally the language of the Burgos area), but other Romance dialects and Arabic. The Reconquest, which was completed in 1492 with the capture of Granada, was followed in the same year by the discovery and subsequent Conquest of the New World, with its millions of Indians. The Spaniards realized that, for Castilian to become not only the official language but also the lingua franca of that vast area which was the Spanish Empire, it had to have a well-organized grammar, a reasonable spelling, and a vocabulary which did not create confusion. The first grammar of a Romance language was that of Antonio de Nebrija, who stated clearly in his *Castilian Grammar* (1492) that he wrote it because language is an instrument of empire.

The unity of the Spanish Empire was broken by the wars of independence in the nineteenth century, and, together with linguistic nationalism and Hispanic academism, an attitude developed which finally has prevailed, namely that Spanish America is more important than Spain and that consequently the Spanish language is no longer the property of the Mother Country but of the American republics. Spanish America now has an authority in linguistic matters independent of that of Spain. It was in this spirit that Bello proposed a spelling reform to make Spanish spelling absolutely phonetic. The Bello spelling had some success at first, but it was later adandoned. Of course, Spanish spelling is still far from being as absurd as English.

Despite these assertions of linguistic independence, the belief prevailed that there must be a norm for every language. In Spanish it was Castilian, as in English it was the King's English, which was really the educated speech of southern England. In French it was the language of Tours, in Germany the language of Hannover (which was the German dialect most similar to the artificial Bühnensprache, or theater language). In Italy it was a curious combination, "Tuscan language in a Roman mouth." In Spain, as in France, the choice of one dialect as a norm had the official sanction represented by the Academy. It was said that the purest Spanish was that of Toledo.

Spanish Americans speak of "American Spanish," which in fact does not exist. There are, in reality, many varieties (the word "dialect" would suggest unacceptable provincialisms). The two most important are Mexican and Argentinian, but there are more differences between them than between Castilian and Mexican or Castilian and Argentinian. When it is said that the best Spanish in America is spoken in Bogotá, it means (although it is not quite true) that Bogotá Spanish is the closest to Castilian.

This hard fact upsets the linguistic Americanists, who, in an attempt to prove that there are two varieties of Spanish, namely Castilian and American Spanish, have stressed the lisp, which is a peculiarity of the Spanish pronunciation of "c" before "e" and "i." To make Castilian appear reactionary, antidemocratic, and ridiculous, they spread a story about the origin of this lisp. The legend states that, primarily because of the jutting jaw which was characteristic of many Spanish kings, they were unable to pronounce the "s" and lisped. The courtiers were so servile and submissive that they imitated this lisp, which thus became general in Castilian. This explanation is absurd for a number of reasons. First, historical linguistics prove that the lisp did not develop in this way. Moreover, if the kings lisped, they would have done so always and not just when a "c" preceded an "e" or an "i." In any case, it is incorrect that the lisp is general in Spain; those who speak that way are probably a minority. In the south (Andalusia) it is almost entirely absent. When American Spanish is described as "Andalusian," it generally refers to the absence of the lisp. It is incorrect to say that the lisp does not exist in Spanish America. It may be heard not only in formal speeches, such as sermons, but also in isolated places where speech is archaic. Those who say that the lisp is not heard in Spanish America simply have not traveled throughout the area. The claim that the pronunciation of the "ll" as "y" is another distinguishing American trait is also a gross oversimplification.

Despite all this talk about two speech traits among hundreds, there is no uniform pronunciation in Spanish America. One can tell immediately if a speaker is from Mexico, the River Plate area, or the Caribbean. One general difference is that the pronunciation in the hot lowlands is more slovenly than in the highlands, where the pronunciation is more precise. For this reason the way of speaking in Madrid is similar to that in Mexico or Bogotá, whereas in Andalusia it is like that of Havana or Caracas. According to this theory, it is incorrect to speak of American Spanish generally as Andalusian. Some have even argued that, since the best Spanish is spoken in the highlands, the purest variety is that spoken in La Paz, Bolivia, the highest capital of the Americas (3,632 meters).

There are variations in the syntax of American Spanish, especially in the forms of address. The vocabulary varies from country to country. These differences are most marked in the nouns referring to trees, foodstuffs, and animals. Often the local words are Indian words which have been given a Spanish form. Some Spanish words vary in meaning from one country to another; a word which is polite in one country many be obscene in another. These differences sometimes create confusion among Spanish Americans, but they should not be exaggerated; there are some vocabulary differences among the variants of the English language.

Castilian Spanish had a historical prestige and was generally accepted as the norm until World War II. The Royal Spanish Academy of the Language promoted the creation of "Corresponding Academies," which were, so to speak, branches of the Academy in Madrid. Their main task was to impose the norms emanating from the Spanish capital. This pattern was reflected in the teaching of Spanish in the universities and schools of France, England, Germany, and even the United States. Spanish was taught according to Madrid norms; Spanish literature was studied, while Spanish American literature was almost unknown. Even in California there were many professors of Spanish, some very famous, who visited Spain frequently but never went to Spanish America; they never even crossed the Mexican border.

World War II brought about a fundamental change. Franco Spain aligned itself ideologically with the Axis, and this antagonized both the U.S. Government and almost all Spanish American intellectuals. In Washington, the Office of the Coordinator of Inter-American Affairs was created; an important part of its activities was cultural propaganda. The study of Latin American culture, and especially of Latin American literature, was encouraged in U.S. universities and colleges. The Spanish American way of speaking and writing thus won acceptance and even prestige. A rather synthetic cult was promoted of the Nicaraguan poet Rubén Darío, who was eulogized as the greatest poet in the Spanish language. It was, therefore, no longer possible to regard Spanish Americans as linguistic barbarians. In general Spanish American intellectuals responded enthusiastically to these overtures from Washington; their disdain for Spain was similar to that which prevailed during the wars of independence. At present the United States is not excessively popular in Latin America, and it is hard for us to imagine the admiration of the people of Latin America for the U.S. struggle against fascism. In the United States, universities and colleges began to teach "American Spanish" and "Brazilian" instead of Portuguese. No one could say exactly what "American Spanish" was.

With the defeat of fascism and the victory of cultural Americanism, the Spanish Government realized that it could no longer exercise even a tacit linguistic hegemony over the Spanish American republics. The Spanish American academies ceased to be corresponding academies of the Spanish Academy and became independent. Together with the Spanish Academy, they formed an association of academies and began to hold congresses in different capitals. Meetings have been held in Mexico (1951), Madrid (1956), Bogotá (1960), Buenos Aires (1964), and Quito (1968). The dictionary of the Spanish Academy has ceased to regard Americanisms as barbarisms and has admitted them with full rights of citizenship. Outside of Madrid, Mexico City, Buenos Aires, and Bogotá the academies have only limited prestige.

What is the future of the Spanish language? The major languages of the world are becoming standardized, not only by the actions of governments and academies but above all by the spectacular improvement in communications. Henry Mencken spoke of "the American language," but the fact is that, because of air communications, radio, and television, the speech of the north and south of the United States, of Canada, England, Ireland, or Australia is slowly becoming more uniform. A "general English" is developing. Likewise, albeit slowly, a "general Spanish" is forming.

The fact that Spanish America speaks a relatively uniform Spanish has an enormous importance in international life. Although the Organization of American States has four official languages (English, Spanish, Portuguese, and French) Spanish is becoming the working language of the organization. It is the native language of most of the workers there. Almost all the officials of the Inter-American Development Bank are likewise Spanish Americans. If most of the officials of the inter-American organizations speak Spanish, it is natural that Spanish should have a preferred status among the four official languages. There are eighteen Spanish-speaking republics. Until recently the only English-speaking country was the United States, and one reason why some republics opposed the admission to the OAS of former British colonies such as Jamaica, Trinidad, and Barbados was that they did not want the preponderance of Spanish-speaking delegates to be diluted. In the OAS, Portuguese is the language of Brazil alone. Unlike the elites of Asia and Africa, only a minority of Spanish-speaking leaders speak English.

When a Spanish American complained to Secretary of State Rusk that some U.S. ambassadors in Latin America did not know Spanish, Rusk replied, with justified annoyance, that the number of Latin American ambassadors in Washington who did not speak English was higher, and he gave the precise figure. Since in inter-American meetings many of the Spanish American delegates do not speak English, it is common for the U.S. delegates to speak Spanish. Brazilian delegates often do the same, although there is a Brazilian Government regulation which states that in inter-American meetings the Brazilian delegates must speak Portuguese. In the past, Latin Americans used to say scornfully that the Pan American Union was the colonial ministry of the United States. Now perhaps we should say that inter-American organizations have become the colonial offices of Spanish America.

Portuguese

The fact that Spanish is one of the five official languages of the United Nations is due in large measure to the division of Spanish America into eighteen republics, which has given rise to the expression "the Disunited States of Latin America." If Spanish America had maintained its unity, as Brazil did, it would not have eighteen delegates in the United Nations and probably would not have been able to muster enough votes to have Spanish declared an official language. We are told that nothing succeeds like success, but in this case it is not the success represented by Brazilian unity which has been rewarded but the failure represented by Spanish American disunity. Partly as a result of this international situation, Spanish is much better known than Portuguese throughout the world.

Linguistic studies developed in Europe in the nineteenth century, when it was natural that from the English viewpoint foreign languages should have this hierarchy: French, German, Italian, and Spanish. Portuguese was the language of a country on the distant edge of the continent, a country which had long since lost its importance. Few foresaw the status which Brazil would achieve in the twentieth century. Not even the Portuguese understood this; the theme of the national epic of Portugal, *The Lusiads* by Camoens, is the Portuguese discovery and conquest of Africa and India. Camoens names Brazil only incidentally, as if it had no great importance.

It is difficult to foresee population developments in Latin America, but it is possible that in the next century half of the population will be Brazilian and will speak Portuguese. Brazilians are annoyed by the ignorance of the Portuguese language abroad. They become irate when a foreigner assumes that in Brazil Spanish is spoken. Even educated foreigners make this mistake. In the universities and colleges of Europe and the United States, for every student of Portuguese there are at least twenty studying Spanish (instead of the mathematically correct proportion of one to three). In many schools Portuguese simply is not taught. In the United States this is due not only to the European tradition in language studies but also to the fact that the United States has as its southern neighbors Spanish-speaking countries such as Mexico and that for this reason there is a considerable Spanish-speaking minority in the United States. Brazil is a long way away. Rio de Janeiro is farther from many places in the United States than is Moscow.

It must also be recognized that Portuguese is a more difficult language than Spanish. We have spoken of the variety and complexity of the Spanish vocabulary, but Spanish pronunciation and grammar are clear and simple in comparison with almost all the other languages of the world. This is one reason why the Spanish language spread so easily. The Portuguese phonetic system is far more complicated than that of Spanish, which does not have the Portuguese diphthongs, triphthongs, and nasal sounds. Because of these sounds, a foreigner finds it much harder to understand Portuguese than Spanish. A Spanish-speaking person has great difficulty understanding Portuguese, whereas a Portuguese-speaking person has little difficulty understanding Spanish. Admittedly, the Portuguese of Brazil is clearer and easier to understand than the Portuguese of Portugal.

Castilian and Portuguese are more similar in the written than in the spoken form, and it is easier for a person knowing Spanish to read Portuguese than to understand the spoken language. However, Portuguese words which look almost the same as their Spanish cognates frequently have a slightly different meaning. For students of Portuguese it is difficult to grasp these differences of meaning between words which seem identical.

Brazilian Portuguese is more or less uniform. In the Portuguese of Brazil there are not the marked regional differences which occur in American Spanish. The Brazilian Government (then located in the former capital, Rio de Janeiro) once declared that Rio Portuguese was normative for the whole country, a decision which annoyed the jealous Paulistas. Since the capital has moved to Brasília, which is a kind of neutral territory, it is probable that "general Brazilian" Portuguese will in fact become normative. It is easy to tell if a Brazilian comes from the north or the south by his pronunciation of certain letters (final "s," initial or double "r") and by his vocabulary. However, this is not a serious problem, and when they defend their language Brazilians stress their country's linguistic unity, which is almost unique in countries of its size.

In most other countries there are minorities which speak their own languages. In the United States, for example, the Spanish-speaking minority is becoming ever more assertive in the use of its language. Such minorities do not exist in Brazil. Until World War II, German was the language of the German colonies in the south of the country, but President Getúlio Vargas closed the German schools and forbade the public use of that language. In cities like Blumenau, in the state of Santa Catarina, German is still heard quite frequently, and even children speak it, but it is certain that within one or two generations it will have virtually disappeared. The same is true of the Italian language in São Paulo; formerly it was heard frequently in the Braz district of that city, but no longer.

In the interior there are still Indian tribes who speak a variety of native languages, but in Brazil there were never important centers of native culture. The Tupí Guaraní languages were spoken in much of what is now Brazil, and in colonial Brazil a curious lingua franca called *lingua geral* (general language) developed. Indian languages are now spoken only in a few remote areas, and Brazil has an almost total linguistic unity.

The linguistic frontiers of Brazil coincide with the political frontiers. Since Spanish and Portuguese are so similar, it is curious that there is a fairly sharp linguistic boundary, which does not exist in North America between English and Spanish or English and French (in Canada). This reflects the historic development of Brazil, the pride and nationalism of Brazilians, and their distaste for the whole Spanish tradition. It is noteworthy that Portuguese has persisted and spread, even though it is a difficult language facing the expansive power of Spanish, which is relatively simple.

While the Portuguese of Brazil has unity, the relationship with the Portuguese of the Mother Country is different. Brazilian nationalism has led some Brazilians to speak of "the Brazilian language," just as Mencken spoke of "the American language." However, the common name is "Portuguese of Brazil." The attitude of the Brazilian toward Portugal and Portuguese speech is ambivalent. The traditionalists and the Brazilians of Portuguese origin speak with affection of the Portuguese tradition. After the 1964 military coup, the Brazilian Government stressed the glorious Portuguese tradition, which is used to embellish both the Portuguese and the Brazilian dictatorships. However, since most of the Portuguese who come to Brazil are illiterate peasants, the Brazilian regards them with rather disdainful affection, like work donkeys. Portuguese speech impresses him as being rough and less refined than Brazilian speech. When Napoleon invaded the Iberian Peninsula, the Portuguese court took refuge in Rio de Janeiro. Brazilians believe, possibly correctly, that the aristocracy which accompanied the court brought with it elegant speech habits, whereas the uncouth peasants remained in Portugal. It is also true that the imperial court, which was succeeded in 1889 by a cultured elite, tried to develop in Brazil a focus of good speech. The Portuguese resent the Brazilian attitude and correctly say that the Portuguese speak a grammatically more correct Portuguese than the Brazilians, among whom tropical sloppiness has led to all kinds of vulgarisms.

Both the Portuguese and the Brazilians agree that their language should have greater recognition in international affairs (only in inter-American organizations does it have a rather hypothetical official status), and they would like to cooperate to achieve such recognition. One way would be to settle linguistic differences, and the two governments have entrusted their respective academies with the task of settling the discrepancies. The academies have held many meetings, but, because of national pride, the agreements reached have not been effective. The Brazilians believe that, since their country is so much more important than Portugal, they should have priority in linguistic matters. The Portuguese reject this claim. They are proud of their tradition, and they believe that, with their African possessions of Angola and Mozambique, they still have an important role to play in the modern world.

The debates between the two academies have often involved spelling. Portugal uses a traditional etymological spelling, whereas Brazil has introduced a simplified phonetic spelling. However, the differences are not great and may be compared to those between the English and American varieties of English. It is probable that the remarkable unity of the Portuguese language will be strengthened and that throughout the Portuguese- speaking world a conservative Brazilian speech will become the norm. Many of the world's languages will, and indeed should, disappear because they complicate world communications unnecessarily. Portuguese will certainly survive. Its importance is comparable to that of Arabic (which is now one of the official languages of UNESCO), and it is possible that in time its status may be similar to that of Spanish.

English

English is spoken in the former British colonies of the Caribbean. Even though Spanish has borrowed many words from English, the two languages do not really mix. In Venezuela, for example, the English word "ticket" ("tiquete") is used rather than the Spanish word, but the number of those who know English is small. Linguistic distances cannot be measured in miles. Cuba can be seen from the north coast of Jamaica, but the two islands are worlds apart. In Havana there are still psychological ties with the capitals of the Spanish-speaking world, whereas Jamaica is linked with Britain and the English-speaking countries. This is slowly changing as, with a stimulus from the United States and Britain, the teaching of English is developing in Latin America. Within a generation or two many young Latin Americans probably will know English. There is no comparable movement between Brazil and Spanish America, since the Brazilians do not feel the need to study Castilian, and vice versa.

French

Except for Spanish, Portuguese, and English, other European languages are disappearing in Latin America. As we have seen, this is true of German and Italian. In the nineteenth century and until World War II every cultured Latin American claimed to know French. The ignominious defeat of France by Hitler was fatal to the position of French as a second language in Latin America. Most young people do not wish to study French, which they do not regard as a truly international language. This is even truer in the United States. In Haiti the cultured class, which spoke French rather than Creole, has gone into exile or has lost its social position.

Dutch

In the Netherlands Antilles and Surinam, the official language is Dutch, which is the language used in schools. However, this relic of Dutch colonialism annoys the young, who are obliged to learn a language almost unknown even in Europe and which does not open for them the door of the important Spanish- and English-speaking worlds. Both the Netherlands Antilles and Surinam are slowly moving toward independence, and it is probable that within a few years the predominant language there will be English. Because of the growth of tourism, this is in large measure true already in the Netherlands Antilles.

There are two pidgin languages in the Dutch territories, papiamento in the Netherlands Antilles and talki-talki in Surinam. They are a mixture of Dutch, English, French, Spanish, and Portuguese, with some Amerindian and African words. A papiamento newspaper is published in Curaçao, and there is some demand that papiamento and talki-talki be made the official languages of the two territories. Given the nationalist frenzy which reaches insanity in the modern world, such an eventuality is possible, even though some black African countries now realize, as the Spaniards did early in the last century, that it is self-defeating to cut one's country off from one of the great linguistic areas. A nation shut up in papiamento or talki-talki would be a prisoner in a cage much smaller than the cage of the Dutch language.

Indian Languages

The problem of the native American languages is complicated by a series of political, religious, and academic factors. When the Spaniards arrived in the New World, a great variety of languages were spoken in what is now Latin America, somewhat like black Africa when it was opened up by the whites. Each of the great pre-Columbian cultures had its own language: the Aztecs of Mexico spoke Nahuátl, the Mayans of Yucatán and Central America spoke Mayan, the Incas of Peru spoke Quechua. In these areas the subordinate tribe often spoke other languages, such as Aymara in the Andes of Peru and Bolivia. In Brazil and Paraguay, various forms of Tupí-Guaraní were widely spoken. In addition there were many minor languages whose relationship, where it exists, has slowly been worked out. The unity of Latin America is largely the result of the creation of a linguistic community by Spain and Portugal. As Nebrija said, language is an instrument of empire. Without the linguistic imposition by Spain and Portugal, there would be no "Latin America" today.

It is evident that native American languages are disappearing. Even in the Indian areas, the spread of Spanish in the last few decades has been remarkable. Thanks to radio, the movies, and increased mobility, the Indians, who do not wish to stay in their villages, are learning Spanish. They want to learn it, and their governments want them to learn it. In an attempt to bring knowledge to the Indians in their own language, a new "university" of Haumanga has been established in Ayacucho, Peru (it claims to be a revival of the colonial university there). This is an isolated case, and it is probable that within a generation or two there will be no monolingual Indians, i.e. Indians who speak only their native language. Some specialists claim that because of the population explosion among the Indians the number of those speaking native languages is growing. This is not impossible; but not only are there fewer monolingual Indians each year, the bilingual Indians prefer more and more to speak Spanish. In many places bilingual Indians use their native language only in their homes. In Argentina, Uruguay, Chile, Cuba, the Dominican Republic and Costa Rica native languages have disappeared almost completely. They are spoken by marginal groups in El Salvador, Honduras, Nicaragua, Panama, Venezuela, Colombia, and Brazil. Only in southern Mexico, Guatemala, Ecuador, Peru, Bolivia, and Paraguay do they show some vitality.

Paraguay is a special case. Because of the Jesuits, who in the colonial period administered this remote area and tried to convert it into a theocracy controlled by them and peopled by Indians whom the use of Guaraní would keep isolated, Paraguay is today a bilingual country. It is the only country of Latin America where the whites have learned the language of the natives. Today there are practically no pure whites or Indians in Paraguay, but mestizos. Nevertheless, the oligarchy is still almost white and speaks Guaraní. It is strange to see groups of more or less white Paraguayans at international conferences speaking Guaraní among themselves. Modern Paraguayan culture is almost entirely Spanish in origin, but Paraguayans believe that they have a great Indian tradition reflected in the Guaraní language, whose beauty and delicacy they frequently praise. It is common for a Paraguayan speaker addressing a country audience to say at least a few words in Guaraní as a tribute to the native language. Paraguay was practically destroyed in the War of the Triple Alliance (1865-70), an alliance formed by Argentina, Brazil, and Uruguay, and as a result nationalist feeling was aroused to the limit. This feeling finds its expression in Guaraní. There are societies for the defense of Guaraní, and poetry is often written in Guaraní.

Nevertheless, despite the pride with which the Paraguayan preserves the Guaraní language, it is slowly disappearing. It is heard less and less on the streets of Asunción. There are no Guaraní newspapers, and on the radio Spanish is almost always used. There are no Paraguayans who speak only Guaraní, so the final triumph of Spanish will be easier than in Peru, Bolivia, Ecuador, and even Mexico, where there is still a considerable native population which does not know Spanish. It is probable that within fifty years native languages will have disappeared from all of Latin America. Many linguists may dispute this affirmation, but the problem of native languages is viewed through a series of prisms which deform reality.

Historically, missionaries, first Catholic and then Protestant, studied native languages in order to convert the Indians to their particular brand of Christianity. As a result of this missionary activity, which began with the Conquest and continues today, there is an abundant scientific literature on native languages, written to facilitate proselytism. In the colonial period the Jesuits were outstanding in this regard. They wanted to impose their authority on the Indians by learning their languages. This gave them a great advantage over the civil and military authorities who always used Spanish. In the very complex relations between the Spanish crown and the Roman Catholic Church, the Company of Jesus represented the tradition of the superiority of the Pope over civil governments, even in nonecclesiastical matters. What the Jesuits really wanted was worldwide theocracy, and it was this which provoked the crisis between the Company of Jesus and the monarchies of Portugal and Spain, which expelled them from the two empires in 1759 and 1767, respectively. Many Jesuits took refuge in Italy, but the Pope abolished the order. It was reestablished in the nineteenth century.

Following the wars of independence and the opening up of the former colonies, waves of Protestant missionaries came to Latin America from England and the United States. They began working among the Indian tribes, which the Catholic missionaries regarded as their preserve. The latter protested bitterly, and in Colombia they even persuaded the government to declare all the southeast sector of the country territory reserved for the Catholic missionaries, and Protestant missionaries were forbidden to enter there. In recent years, inspired by the ecumenical spirit, the two groups of missionaries have made a truce, and they even cooperate. Now the study of Indian languages is carried on, primarily by certain groups of American missionaries. First come members of the Summer Institute of Linguistics, who study the native languages and give them a written form. Then come the Wycliffe Bible Translators, who translate the gospels, at least in part, into the native languages. Thanks to this proselytizing effort, we now have excellent studies of most of the native languages of Latin America.

The ordinary American has no idea of the scope of this enterprise. There are thousands of young American missionaries working in Latin America. They even have small planes to reach isolated areas. This is all subsidized by the Protestant communities in the United States. When the missionaries are asked why they concentrate on native regions where neither Spanish nor Portuguese is spoken, they reply that they want to reach the Indians with the Christian message before they are corrupted by so-called civilization. One result of these activities has been that an inordinate amount of attention has been paid to the native languages, out of proportion with their importance in the total Latin American picture.

Anthropologists have also been active in the study of native languages and cultures. They concern themselves primarily with primitive tribes, and they have given the world a one-sided account of Latin America. Now, political scientists, economists, and sociologists are actively interested in Latin America, so we have a more balanced picture of the continent. The heavy interest in anthropological and archaeological studies coincided with the nationalist passion in Latin America to seek the origin of the Latin American nations in their native tradition. There are more or less white Mexican and Peruvian scholars who consider the last Indian chiefs, Cuauhtémoc of Mexico and Atahualpa of Peru, as national heroes, while they depict the Spanish Conquistadores Hernán Cortés and Francisco Pizarro as barbaric invaders who wrecked the civilizations of Mexico and Peru.

Recently, international politics has introduced an element of passion and intrigue into the study of native languages, above all of Quechua. After coming down from the Sierra Maestra mountains to conquer the flat areas of Cuba in 1959, and establishing a Communist regime in the island, Castro declared that "the Andes will be the Sierra Maestra of South America." The famous expedition of "Che" Guevara to Bolivia was an attempt to implement this declaration. Radio Havana and Radio Moscow began to broadcast Quechua language programs to the Andes, so the United States did the same. The study of Quechua was developed in universities like Cornell and the University of California at Berkeley. These Quechua language campaigns may well be misdirected, since many of the political agitators in the Andes do not know Quechua, and it is doubtful if there is a single one who does not know Spanish. Those who run the programs try to justify them on the grounds that Spanish was the language of the Conquistadores, while Quechua is the language of the Indians, who are still seeking vengeance through revolution. All this seems rather romantic; the total failure of Guevara indicates that Castro had miscalculated. However, since the Soviets and now China are doing all they can to arouse anti-U.S. feeling among the native populations, perhaps the United States should leave no stone unturned.

In conclusion we may state that Latin America will be a region with two main languages, Spanish and Portuguese, with some English-speaking areas in the Antilles. French will have virtually no importance, and Dutch and the native languages will disappear. As a result, Latin America will have few serious language problems. Only a few other areas, such as North America and Australasia, will be equally fortunate. Many aspects of Latin America arouse concern, but as far as language goes we should be happy that it does not suffer from the chaos which marks India, or even Europe.

Literacy

More important than linguistic unity is literacy, and in this, unfortunately, Latin America presents a sorry picture. There are millions of Latin Americans who speak Spanish or Portuguese but who can neither read nor write. The percentage of illiterates varies greatly. It is difficult to give exact figures because statistics are unreliable and there is no uniform definition of illiteracy. It is very low in Argentina, Uruguay, Chile, and Costa Rica, i.e. in the white countries, but it is high in countries like Ecuador, Peru, Bolivia, and Haiti. Britain, France, and the Netherlands did an excellent job of bringing literacy to their colonies. Fidel Castro has carried out a large literacy campaign in Cuba, but we should view with skepticism the claim that illiteracy has been wiped out in the island. Some countries have tried the Laubach system— "each one teach one"—but such a voluntary system cannot replace regular schooling. Even in countries like Mexico which have built large numbers of schools, the population is increasing so fast that many children find no places in the classrooms. It has been calculated, perhaps correctly, that although the percentage of illiterates is declining their numbers are increasing because of the population explosion.

In many Latin American countries it is hard to maintain schools because of lack of funds, but in military-controlled governments the allocations for the armed forces are constantly increasing. It is true that often illiterate peasants are taught to read and write while they are doing their military service, but this does not justify the heavy expenses on modern military equipment which the countries do not need. Latin Americans reply that no Latin American country spends as high a percentage of its national budget on arms as does the United States, that Mexico, for one, spends more on schools than on its armed forces, and that Costa Rica is proud of being a nation of teachers but has no army.

The linguistic unity of Latin America will mean little unless illiteracy is reduced as soon as possible. Otherwise, Latin American hopes for a better future will be vain. However, the linguistic unity, or rather unities, of Latin America has received a great impulse from the communications revolution of the last fifty years. The linguistic walls between the language groups of the various countries, indeed of the whole continent, are falling down. This should open up new perspectives and new horizons.

10 • Literature, the Arts, and Science

Spanish American Literature

The complex problem of the relationship between literature and the social reality of Latin America is the subject of vigorous arguments among specialists. At one extreme are the aesthetes who, taking the theory of art for art's sake to its logical conclusion, affirm that there is no direct relationship between art and reality, that art is an experience apart. Indeed, the poetry of Rubén Darío and other modernist poets has little relationship with the life of Nicaragua (where Darío was born) or of the other countries where they lived. This poetry is a flight from reality, something like that of the Golden Age Spanish poet Luis de Góngora, whom the partisans of art for art's sake greatly admire.

Admittedly, if Rubén Darío had reflected Nicaraguan life he would never have won the general admiration of the Spanish-speaking world. Indeed, Darío devoted himself to poetry and to alcohol because the reality of Spanish America nauseated him, even though in his famous ode to President Theodore Roosevelt he said there were still countries which (unlike the United States!) spoke Spanish and believed in God—a boast which hid his despair. Admittedly also, there are works which give a well-documented account of a country or a region but which, from the literary viewpoint, have very little value.

Yet aesthetic reputations are most unreliable, and they are often inflated by nationalism or ideological sectarianism. In any case, style is usually lost in translation. Most works are difficult to read in the original, if only because American Spanish has a great variety of regionalisms, which appear abundantly in novels. We shall not attempt here to give aesthetic evaluations but rather to call attention to those works which are valuable for the understanding of Latin America.

The chronicles of the Conquest bring us dramatic accounts of this remarkable phenomenon. Hernán Cortés wrote five letters to Charles V between 1519 and 1526, describing the conquest of Mexico in such a way as to impress the Emperor with his exploits. Another work exalting the achievements of Cortés was the *Chronicle of New Spain* (1552)), written by Francisco López de Gómara, who was Cortés' chaplain after the Conquistador returned to Spain. Gómara never crossed the Atlantic and relied entirely on what Cortés told him. Unfortunately, the Emperor did not respond to Cortés' boasts, and Cortés died a disappointed man in a village near Seville. Resentful that Cortés claimed all the glory for himself, one of his captains, Bernal Díaz del Castillo, who spent his last years in Guatemala, wrote a *True History of the Conquest of New Spain*, stressing the role of the ordinary Spanish soldier. The manuscript was sent to Spain in 1575, but it did not appear in print until 1632. Perhaps the most picturesque and even the most extraordinary Conquistador was Alvar Núñez Cabeza de Vaca, who told the story of his wanderings through North and South America in *Shipwrecks and Commentaries* (1555). Orellana's voyage of discovery from Quito down the Amazon to the Atlantic was narrated in *Relation* by Gaspar de Carvajal. The conquest of the Inca empire by Francisco Pizarro is the subject of the *Chronicle of Peru* (1553) by Pedro Cieza de León. A companion of Pedro de Valdivia, Alonzo de Góngora Marmolejo, narrated the conquest of Chile in the *History of Chile* (1575).

While the conquerors were boasting of their exploits, some friars were denouncing their inhumanity. The most famous of these was the Dominican Bartolomé de las Casas, who accused the Spaniards of genocide in his *Brief Relation of the Destruction of the Indies* (1552). The priests were competing with the soldiers for primary authority in the New World, and they tried to contrast the brutality of military rule with the reign of justice they wished to establish.

The Conquest inspired many literary works, the most famous of which was the heroic poem *La Araucana* (1569-89) of Alonso de Ercilla y Zúñiga, describing the resistance of the Araucanian Indians of Chile to the Spanish Conquest. Like the work of Las Casas, it belongs to what might be called the counterculture of the period, since the author does not exalt Spanish achievements. Ercilla's attitude may be explained by the fact that he quarreled with his commanding officer and was condemned to death. Even though the punishment was reduced to dismissal and exile, his bitterness is reflected in the way he describes his old companions as the enemies of the real heroes, the Chilean freedom fighters. The poem seems artificial to us, since the Indians make speeches in octosyllabic strophes reminiscent of the Italian poets Ariosto and Tasso. The Chileans later adopted the poem as the epic of their national struggle, and the Indian Caupolicán has become a symbol of national resistance comparable to Cuauhtémoc in Mexico.

Other chronicles give us a general account of America at the time of the Conquest and of the history of the period before the Conquest. The *Natural and Moral History of the Indies* (1590) by José de Acosta provides general information, while *The General and Natural History of the Indies* (1535-37) of Gonzalo Fernández de Oviedo is especially valuable for information about flora and fauna. The *Royal Commentaries* (1609-17) of Garcilaso de la Vega ("el Inca") give us an excessively generous history of the Incas. Garcilaso was a halfbreed who settled in Córdoba, Spain, and he felt the need to describe and praise the Inca society from which his mother came. His book is our principal source of information about the Incas, but it was responsible for speading the belief that the Incas were living proof that man is naturally good.

Much of the literature of the colonial period was an imitation of the baroque literature of Spain. The best-known writer of colonial Mexico is Sor Juana Inés de la Cruz. Even though she is known in Mexico as "the Tenth Muse," her literary productions seem artificial to us, but the biographical information she provides is fascinating. She was born near Amecameca, at the foot of the volcanoes Popocatepetl and Ixtaccíhuatl. By her precocity she attracted the attention of Viceroy Mancera, who brought her to the viceregal court. At the age of sixteen, following apparently an unfortunate love affair, she became a Carmelite and spent the rest of her life in the convent of Saint Jerome in Mexico. At the age of forty-four, Sor Juana was a victim of an epidemic of the plague.

Colonial literature must be read with great care because it is full of exaggerations and legends. Among these are: the Fountain of Youth, which Ponce de León sought in Florida; el Dorado, who was not a golden man but a Chibcha Indian who covered himself with gold dust and dived into a lake near Bogotá; the Amazons, female warriors who gave their name to the great river of Brazil;

and the Seven Cities of Cíbola, supposedly wealthy cities which in reality were wretched pueblos of New Mexico.

Because of this literature, Europeans had a false idea of America. Instead of gilded cities peopled by virtuous Indians, the reality was the tyranny of Spain, which built cathedrals and palaces while the people lived in misery, which fostered an artificial literature but stifled free thought and political development. From colonial literature, it would have been impossible to foresee the convulsions which would lead to the dissolution of the empires of Spain and Portugal. Because of the Inquisition and censorship, there could not be in Latin America writers like Locke, Montesquieu, Voltaire, and Rousseau, but these authors are much more important than the authors of the colonial period to explain contemporary Latin America. It was, above all, travelers who brought to the Spanish world the ideas of liberal thinkers, men like Pablo de Olavide, a friend of Voltaire who took part in the French revolutionary convention.

The American Revolution and even more the French Revolution shook the intellectual life of Latin America; since then there have always been writers prepared to risk exile or death on behalf of their liberal ideas. In 1794 the Colombian Antonio Nariño translated *The Rights of Man*. The influence of French and English liberal thinkers is evident in the writings of Simón Bolívar. The Mexican José Joaquín Fernández de Lizardi wrote a picaresque novel, *The Itching Parrot* (1816), to spread his radical ideas about society.

The most noteworthy intellectual of the independence period was the Venezuelan Andrés Bello. A man of vision and learning, Bello spent the years 1810 to 1829 in England, where he mingled with intellectual groups and developed his culture and scholarship. In 1829 he settled in Chile, where he exercised a great influence and where he died. He founded the University of Chile and wrote important works on language and law.

Of comparable importance is the Argentinian Domingo Faustino Sarmiento, a liberal enemy of the Dictator Rosas. He fled to Chile, where he had a famous polemic with Bello, whom he accused of being too conservative and too purist. More important was his battle against the tyranny of Rosas and the barbarity of the Argentina of that time; we have already mentioned his famous work *Facundo, or Civilization and Barbarism*. A comparable work is the novel *The Slaughterhouse* (1871) by Esteban Echeverría, which could not be published in the author's lifetime. The title refers to a slaughterhouse where Rosas' secret police met; the novel is full of brutal scenes, such as the death of a young Unitarian (the Unitarians were the enemies of Rosas). The vast novel *Amalia* (1851-55) by José Mármol gives an equally unpleasant picture of the Rosas dictatorship. Amalia hides her fiancé, a young Unitarian, but the secret police find and kill him. The novel makes it clear that the Unitarians, who represented liberalism and progress, belonged to the white upper and middle classes, while Rosas had the support of the masses, the blacks and the Indians. Even today support for Western-style democracy comes primarily from an intellectual and social elite. This explains in part the popularity of dictators like Perón or Castro and the difficulty of establishing parliamentary democracy in Latin America; liberalism has never been a people's movement there.

The struggle against Rosas had parallels in other countries. In Ecuador the liberals had to fight the clerical conservative dictatorship of García Moreno. His great opponent was the polemicist Juan Montalvo, whose most famous essays appeared under the title *Seven Treatises* (1882). When García Moreno was assassinated, Montalvo declared that he had killed him with his pen.

Naturally, these politically inspired works are only a part of the literature of the past century. More popular were the romantic works such as *María* (1867) by the Colombian Jorge Isaacs. The novel gives us an idyllic picture of life in the Cauca valley, but the sad love story seems too romantic. This was also the reaction of young Latin American intellectuals. Romanticism gave way to realism, with its brutal descriptions of Latin American life.

However, the flight from reality continued in different forms. The Peruvian scholar Ricardo Palma lived during a tragic period. Peru was defeated in the War of the Pacific (1879-83), and Chilean troops occupied Lima and sacked the National Library. As its director, Palma had the task of rebuilding the library and its collections. He took refuge in the past, and the ten volumes of *Peruvian Traditions* (1872-1906) make virtually no mention of the tragic years in which they were written. With skill and irony, Palma tells curious, amusing, but usually rather insignificant episodes of Peruvian history. Most of the stories are about the colonial period, which gives them a special local color. Palma avoids tragic themes, the blood and horror of the wars of independence.

Another flight from reality was poetry. The melody of his verses has won for Rubén Darío the reputation of being the greatest poet of the Spanish-speaking world. His volume *Azure* (1888) made

him famous and transformed him from a young unknown Nicaraguan into a poet of international stature. Nevertheless, his personal life was a disaster, and his melodious lines were a flight
from the sad reality of it and of Latin America. His inspiration
came from France, above all from the Parnassians and the Sym-
bolists; he was writing at a time when Latin Americans thought
it was elegant to imitate the latest Parisian fashion. The symbol
of Parnassianism was a white swan on a blue lake—not a
typically Latin American scene. Dictators appreciate harmless
writers like Rubén Darío, who have no libertarian urges to free
the world from tyranny. The Nicaraguan dictatorships have promoted the cult of Darío; his tomb is in the cathedral in León, and
there is an impressive statue of him, complete with swans, in
Managua.

This flight to the imaginary gardens of Versailles was even
more irrelevant to Latin America than the romantic novel about
Latin America, and the Mexican poet Enrique González Martínez
said the swan should be seized by the neck and strangled. For
him, the symbolic bird should be the owl, which, in disregard of
ornithology, humanity has made the symbol of wisdom. However,
the owl was about as poetic as Darwinism and Positivism, and he
never really got off his branch. More successful was the high-
flying condor, the symbol of the Andes, which became the symbol of sonorous, totally Spanish American verses. The most famous poet of the condor school was the Peruvian José Santos
Chocano, whose bombast seems archaic today. Both he and the
Uruguayan prose writer José Enrique Rodó, author of *Ariel*
(1900), are commonly called "modernists," which shows how
meaningless the term has become in Latin American literature.
Their main concern was not style but the destiny of Latin America. Rodó reads better than Santos Chocano because he under-
stands the complexity of reality, whereas Santos Chocano relies
on passion and eloquence. The approach of Santos Chocano and
similar prophets of a new Latin America seems to us a little
naïve, but they are attuned to the current Latin American vogue
for "consciousness-building," i.e. making Latin Americans aware
of their problems as a means of stimulating them to action.

In addition to the Guatemalan Miguel Angel Asturias, mentioned earlier, two Chilean writers, Gabriela Mistral and Pablo
Neruda, have won the Nobel Prize for Literature. Gabriela Mistral was a sweet poetess, but not a major figure. As so often happens, the award of Nobel Prize for Literature is determined by a
number of accidents, including transitory fame. Gabriela Mistral

was selected when it was the turn for a Latin American, but most leading writers, including Pablo Neruda, were too controversial; for many years Neruda, a Communist, was on his government's blacklist. Neruda is the Spanish American poet most admired by youth, who are attracted to his Marxist politics. His most famous work is *Residence on Earth* (1925-31). He was profoundly influenced by the Spanish Civil War, and since then he has been uncritically anticapitalist. He refused to condemn Stalin and still today will not speak out against intellectual oppression in the Soviet Union. His hatred of the United States is apparent in his 1968 play *Joaquïn Murieta,* in which the California bandit becomes a Chilean who came to the United States at the time of the Gold Rush and was a victim of American oppression. Politically, Neruda, who served as Allende's Ambassador to France, is biased and doctrinaire. His writings are generally bombastic, and when history sorts out values, he will probably be placed with Santos Chocano. There is at present a cult of another poet, the Peruvian César Vallejo, who died as the result of his activities in the Spanish Civil War. The current attempt to promote him to the top rank of poetry is unconvincing. The black Cuban poet Nicolás Guillén expressed in *Spain* (1937) the agony he felt because of Spain's agony. He is now one of the leading official writers of the Castro regime.

Sarmiento's *Facundo* opened in Argentina the mainstream of literary concern about the reality of the Argentine hinterland. There was the peculiar combination of a civilized capital, Buenos Aires, looking at the interior with distaste, grudging admiration, horror, pity, or amusement. Distaste mingled with admiration characterizes the work of Hilario Ascásubi, a monstrous poem (13,000 lines long) entiled *Santos Vega* (1851) about a bad man (a typical figure in both gaucho and cowboy literature) who repents on his deathbed and dies a good Catholic. Amusement was the attitude of Estanislao del Campo, whose poem *Fausto* (1870) is about a simple gaucho who came to Buenos Aires; in the famous Colón theater, he saw Gounod's *Faust,* and later he tells a friend the story of the opera as though it were a drama of the pampas.

Pity for the gaucho is the keynote of the famous poem *Martín Fierro* (1872) by José Hernández, who brings out the qualities of the long-suffering gauchos and the abuses of which they are the victims at the hands of "civilized" men. Persecuted by the Establishment and above all by the army, Martín Fierro in his despair and resentment becomes a bad man and joins the Indians. Rebellious American youth will doubtless find him an attractive figure. At the time of writers like Maurice Barrès and D. H. Lawrence, there was a reaction against civilized values and a cult of primitive passions. One manifestation of this was the novel *Don Segundo Sombra* (1926) by Ricardo Güiraldes. It is an admiring account of an idealized gaucho by an orphan boy who is so impressed by the gaucho's free-riding career around the pampas that he regrets the time he wasted in school when he could have been riding with his hero. Some writers such as Byron and Espronceda have idealized the pirate, but this praise of an illiterate gaucho is uncomfortably like the attitude of those Argentines for whom Rosas is the national hero. Buenos Aires, the most civilized city in Latin America, has a contradictory strain of rural anti-intellectualism. During World War II, the Nazis published there a newspaper called *El Pampero*—the wind from the pampas.

While the works about the pampas mixed realism with romanticism, novels about Buenos Aires and the other large cities were, in general, painfully realistic or naturalistic. The most famous novelist writing in this vein was Manuel Gálvez, whose *Normal School Teacher* (1914) depicts the misery of a woman teacher. *The Shadow of the Convent* (1917) takes us to Córdoba, traditionally the center of Argentine clericalism (but now a major industrial city) for an account of the struggle between clericals and anticlericals. *Nacha Regules* (1919) describes the horrors of prostitution in Buenos Aires, in the manner of French naturalists. It is possible to interpret the work of Gálvez as a protest against conditions in Buenos Aires. This may be why he was one of the few Argentine writers who followed Perón. Critics seldom express disapproval if a writer is a Trotskyist, a Stalinist, or a Castroite, but the few writers who accepted Perón ruined their reputations.

Buenos Aires and Montevideo are peculiar in that they are the most Europeanized of Latin American capitals, and they turn their backs on the countryside. The whole of the *Sur* group (named after the title of its magazine), led by Victoria Ocampo, was closely tied with the intellectual life of England and France. Jorge Luis Borges is intellectually a European, a specialist in English literature. He is one of the few writers today who is not "engaged" in the Latin American social struggle. His concern with style and fantasy is a throwback to the last century. Another member of the *Sur* group is Eduardo Mallea, whose most famous novel is *History of an Argentine Passion* (1935). All of the group were liberal democrats. Even though they were scarcely political activists, Perón persecuted them because they refused to accept him.

Two novelists concerned themselves with Spain. *The Glory of Don Ramiro* (1908) by the Argentine Enrique Rodríguez Larreta is commonly interpreted as a eulogy of the Spain of Philip II and of the city of Avila, but it is clear that the author, who was really a French-style skeptic, preferred the sensual tradition of the Arabs and regarded the Christian Castilians as fanatics. *The Spell of Seville* (1922) by the Uruguayan Carlos Reyles enjoyed quite a vogue for some time, but it must be admitted that it is a very superficial description of the colorful Andalusian capital.

The contrast between city and rural life appears in the novels of the Andean countries, although it varies according to the nature of the countryside and its population. In Venezuela, Rufino Blanco Fombona wrote novels like *The Man of Gold* (1920), an attack on the political life of Caracas, where the dictator and his friends conspire with the agents of U.S. imperialism. The countryside is the wild plain of the Orinoco, where, in the famous novel *Doña Barbara* (1929) of Rómulo Gallegos, an embittered half-savage woman dominates a whole area and expands her holdings ruthlessly, even resorting to witchcraft to eliminate her neighbors. Her power is broken, and she disappears when a young man symbolizing the technical enlightenment of Caracas arrives on the scene. Further up the Orinoco, where Venezuela, Brazil, and Colombia meet, we come to the jungles which are the scene of *The Whirlpool* (1924) of the Colombian José Eustasio Rivera. In the first part of the century this area attracted rubber seekers, both the middlemen who made fortunes (it was men like this who made Manaus, Brazil, a tropical Paris) and the poor devils who lived in virtual slavery in the forest, where they tapped the scattered rubber trees (jungle trees, not plantations).

In the Indian countries (Bolivia, Ecuador, Peru) a favorite theme is the oppression of the Indian peasants by the landowners. One of the first of these novels was *Race of Bronze* (1919) by the Bolivian Alcides Arguedas, which, like *The Whirlpool*, describes the misery of the rubber collectors, this time in the Acre territory. The plight of these workers became an international scandal as a result of a report written by a British diplomat, Sir Roger Casement. For curious reasons, Ecuador is the country where writers have become most politicized; a majority are Socialists or Communists. The well-known novel *Huasipungo* (1934) by Jorge Icaza, which has the usual theme of the exploitation of the Indians by the local oligarchy and U.S. corporations, has as its title a typically Ecuadorian word. Indeed, these Indianist novels are hard to read because of the local vocabulary, usually of Indian origin. They certainly do not give a balanced picture, since they do not recognize the contributions the oligarchy and foreign corporations have made to their countries. Perhaps the best known of these Indianist novels is *Broad and Alien Is the World* (1941) by the Peruvian Ciro Alegría.

While some Chilean novels describe the misery of peasants and miners, the dichotomy between city and countryside is not as marked as it is in the Indian countries. Indeed, the most famous novel of all, *Brother Ass* (1922) by Eduardo Barrios, has quite a different theme. It is a naturalist novel whose protagonist, a Franciscan living in a Santiago convent, seems to be a model of all Franciscan virtues; however, his "brother ass" (the body) is passionately sensual and more powerful than the chastity he has vowed to observe.

The Mexican novel is a phenomenon apart, since so often the theme is the Revolution which began in 1910. The classic work of this kind is *The Underdogs* (1915-16) of Mariano Azuela. Azuela was a revolutionary leader, but when Carranza triumphed he fled to El Paso, Texas, where he wrote this novel, which reveals his disillusionment. It is the story of the life and death of a revolutionary peasant leader who was killed by his rivals. The Revolution began as an ideal, but it quickly degenerated into a ruthless struggle for power among rival revolutionary bosses. *The Eagle and the Serpent* (1928) of Martín Luis Guzmán is also a famous revolutionary novel, but because Guzmán has become a propagandist for the official party, he is incapable of criticizing the Revolution. The official party has bestowed its blessing on Pancho Villa, transforming the bandit into a revolutionary hero. Guzmán has published some rather fanciful memoirs which he attributes to Pancho Villa.

Some younger Spanish American writers are enjoying quite an international vogue, but it is too early to say how history will judge them. The best known are: the Mexican Carlos Fuentes, author of *The Death of Artemio Cruz* (1962), whose denunciations of U.S. policies have gained him a certain notoriety; the Argentinian Julio Cortázar, author of *The Rewards* (1961); the Peruvian Mario Vargas Llosa, whose novel *The Green House* (1966) satirizes traditional Peruvian life; and Gabriel García Márquez, who, in *A Hundred Years of Solitude* (1967), gives a haunting description of a Colombian village.

The theater is of secondary importance in Spanish America. The movies, which are closer to the techniques and the mentality of today, had considerable success in Mexico and Argentina, but in the last few years they have been sterile because of censorship and economic problems. Television could be the artistic medium characteristic of our age, but outside of Cuba, where it is a state monopoly subject to official censorship, it is in the hands of the same economic interests which in the United States use it as disguised commercial propaganda. The governments of Chile and Peru are slowly taking control of television, but it is too early to say what the results will be. In the Soviet-bloc countries, including Cuba, government-controlled television appears unbearably boring and dogmatic to a Westerner.

In general it may be said that the literature of imagination is losing prestige in Spanish America, as elsewhere. Gone are the days when poets and other authors were great national figures whom the governments honored by naming them ambassadors. Pablo Neruda, former Chilean Ambassador to France, may be the last of this species, but in any case, he is a career diplomat, and there have been other diplomats who have been better known as writers.

Brazilian Literature

Brazilian literature is a world apart. In Brazil there is no interest in Spanish American literature, and vice versa. However, since independence, Brazilian literature has followed primarily French models, and in this there is a parallel with Spanish American literature.

The colonial literature of Brazil is modest. In general, cultural life did not develop as it did in Spanish America, and some of the most famous authors, such as the Jesuit Antônio Vieira, were born in Portugal. Whereas there were several universities in colonial Spanish America, there was none in Brazil; the young Brazilians who wanted to get an advanced education had to go to Coïmbra in Portugal. The most important Brazilian poet of the seventeenth century, Gregório de Mattos, studied in Coïmbra, and he would have remained in Portugal had not the government exiled him because of his scandalous life; he went first to Bahia, then to Angola in Africa, and finally to Pernambuco. It is interesting to compare the outlook of Vieira with that of Mattos. The first saw in the history of Brazil a manifestation of the Divine Will expressed in the victories over the Dutch heretics in the Northeast of Brazil. Mattos shows us the other side of this picture: the corruption of the Church, the venality of public officials, and the injustices of the social system.

Like the baroque literature of Spanish America, much of the colonial literature of Brazil has no relationship with American reality. While life in Brazil was a ruthless struggle to get rich by exploiting sugar and mining, the intellectuals of Bahia met in academies and wrote pseudo-Italian literature. Nevertheless, in the second half of the eighteenth century, when the center of gravity of Brazil moved south to the Minas Gerais-Rio de Janeiro axis, a literary school developed in Ouro Prêto which expressed the Brazilian aspirations and grievances that led to the 1789 conspiracy known as the *"Inconfidência Mineira"* (the declaration of no-confidence of Minas Gerais). In addition to complaints about taxation and censorship, there was hatred for the "Green Book," the brutal penal and administrative code of the diamond-producing area. The conspirators viewed the American and French revolutionary movements as leading the way to the future. The conspiracy marked the beginning of the independence movement.

There is a whole literature about the *Inconfidência Mineira*. The Governor of Minas Gerais was attacked in an anonymous work, the *Chilean Letters* (1786), supposedly criticizing the government of Chile but clearly aimed at the local government. The work has been attributed to one of the conspirators, Thomaz Antônio Gonzaga, who told his experiences in *Dirceu's Marília* (1792). Dirceu (the pen name used by Gonzaga) fell in love with Marília, but, when they were about to get married, he was arrested for his part in the *Inconfidência Mineira* and exiled to Angola, where he died.

The Minas poet José Basílio da Gama, who studied in Portugal and Rome, wrote *The Uraguay,* which was published in Lisbon in 1769. It describes the struggle between the Portuguese and the Indians of Uruguay a region much vaster than present-day Uruguay); da Gama accuses the Jesuits of having stirred up the Indians against the governments of Spain and Portugal. It is essentially a propaganda work reflecting the policy of Pombal, who expelled the Jesuits from the Portuguese Empire.

The Lusiads of Camoens describes the first Portuguese sea voyage to India. The corresponding work for Brazil is *Caramurú* (1781) of the Minas poet Santa Rita Durão. While the exploits of Vasco da Gama were epic, there is something picaresque in the adventures of the hero of *Caramurú*. He was a Portuguese sailor, Diogo Alvares Corrêa, who accidentally discovered the bay (Bahia) where the city of Salvador (also called, like the state,

Bahia) now stands. With six other sailors he escaped from a shipwreck. Cannibal Indians ate the six but spared Diogo Alvares Corrêa because he was so sick that they though he would taste bad. With a shotgun he had salvaged from the shipwreck, he killed a bird, and with this magic he so impressed the Indians that they gave him the title "Caramurú," dragon of the sea. They accepted him as their chief, and he married the daughter of another chief. Husband and wife went to Europe, where she was baptized and where they gave the Portuguese king the sovereign rights over their lands. The king then sent out an expedition to establish the city of Bahia.

When the Portuguese court moved to Rio de Janeiro in 1808, the city became the cultural capital of Brazil. The first printing press and the first newspaper, *A Gazeta do Rio de Janeiro*, were established, followed by the National Library, the National Museum, and the Botanical Garden. The intellectual and political life of the period was dominated by José Bonifácio de Andrade e Silva; a man of great vision, he combined political, scientific, and literary activities. He served Emperor Pedro I, but later broke with him and was exiled. His poetry, written after he was disgraced, expresses both the Byronic ideal of liberty and his resentment of the imperial tyranny.

The most popular romantic poet was Antônio Gonçalves Dias, whose "Song of Exile" is a favorite Brazilian poem. Every school child knows the verses, mentioned earlier, which begin, "My land has palm trees where the sabiá sings." The long-drawn-out emancipation movement which brought slavery to an end in 1888 had its literary accompaniment, similar to *Uncle Tom's Cabin* in the United States. The poet of emancipation and republicanism was Antônio de Castro Alves, whose poetry has lost interest since both of these objectives were achieved.

Just as it has become routine to say that Rubén Darío is the greatest Spanish American poet, so we are told that Joaquim Maria Machado de Assis is the greatest Brazilian writer. He was without doubt a literary leader, despite his modesty. He founded the Brazilian Academy of Letters, and a bust of him stands in front of its building in Rio de Janeiro. His poetry has been compared with that of Rubén Darío, and both are characterized by a flight from reality to the world of pure poetry. He is better known for his novels like *Braz Cubas* (1881), *Quincas Borba* (1890), and *Dom Casmurro* (1900), which are psychological studies of individuals who live in a world of unreality. Critics who hail them as universal masterpieces claim to see in them intuition and subdued humor; several of the novels have been translated into English, but they are of little help for those seeking in literature a representation of Brazilian reality.

Most writers lived in Rio de Janeiro, and the dichotomy between city and hinterland we have observed in Spanish American literature is evident also in Brazil. At first, writers had no clear vision of the countryside; they saw it through the rose-colored glasses of romanticism. Little by little writers became conscious of the national reality, and in modern literature there are some brutal descriptions of rural Brazil, which, with the exception of the coastal strip, is forbidding and monotonous. The romantic interpretation of primitive life is given in the novel *Iracema* (1865) of José de Alencar, which describes in sentimental terms the love of a young Indian girl, Iracema, for a Portuguese conquistador. The story, which ends with the death of Iracema, is bucolic in the manner of the European romantics, but at least it conveys the charm of the Brazilian coast.

The Brazilian novel became a vehicle for the description of basic themes: the countryside, from the tropical jungle to the dry and inhospitable backlands of the Northeast; the inhabitants, especially the mixed breeds of the backlands and the blacks of the sugar and cacao plantations and also of the slums of the Northeast; and the role of the oligarchy, the government, and the army in the destinies of the backward regions of the interior. Regional literature concentrates on the Northeast, which has also been the focal point of Brazilian national concern. São Paulo and the prosperous south, as well as empty Amazonia, have inspired far fewer literary works.

The common belief that blacks and whites have cohabited happily in Brazil is not in accord with the facts as described in the novel *The Mulatto* (1881) of Aluísio de Azevedo. The hero is a cultured mulatto, the illegitimate son of a local landlord and a slave girl. Educated in Portugal he returns to São Luis do Maranhão, where he falls in love with the daughter of a white uncle and wants to marry her. The girl's family objects to the marriage for racial reasons, and finally a priest who is a friend of the family arranges to have the mulatto killed. The girl marries an unimpressive white employee in her father's store.

The most important literary work about the interior of Brazil is *Rebellion in the Backlands* (1902) by Euclides da Cunha. It is not a novel but a true account of a historic episode. It is what we would today call a report in depth, although it has none of the agility of modern reporting. It is a long and heavy work, and the first part, which describes in detail the geology of the Northeast, would discourage most readers. The book deals with a religious fanatic, Antônio Conselheiro, who gathered in Canudos, a miserable village in the backlands of the Northeast, a group of ignorant and traditionalist peasants who believed that the republic, being anticlerical, was the work of the devil. An old Portuguese tradition had survived among them about King Sebastian, who disappeared in Africa in 1578 fighting against the Moors. Thus ended the old Portuguese dynasty, which was succeeded in 1580 by Philip II of Spain. The Spanish domination of Portugal continued until 1640. During these years of the "Babylonian captivity," the legend arose that Sebastian was not dead and that he would return to save Portugal. Antônio Conselheiro told the peasants that Sebastian would have to return to save Brazil from the republican government. To persuade Sebastian to come back, the peasants sacrificed many babies, bashing their heads against a sacred stone (an African, not a Portuguese rite). Confronted with this barbarous and subversive spectacle, the government in Rio de Janeiro decided to send a military expedition against Canudos. Two expeditions failed, but the third crushed Canudos, of which nothing remained. The government had won a civil war, but educated Brazilians began to wonder if brute force was the only way to assure the allegiance of the peasants of the interior. The episode shook Brazil somewhat as Vietnam has shaken the United States, and the book was an enormous success.

Psychologically, Brazilians float between two extremes. On the one hand they believe, as the Brazilian proverb runs, that "God is a Brazilian." On the other hand they despair about Brazil. *Rebellion in the Backlands* reflects the pessimistic phase, as does the novel *Canaan* (1901) of Graça Aranha. The title—Canaan, i.e. the promised land—is ironical. Two German immigrants arrive in Brazil, believing that it is the land of hope. The novel describes their disillusionment. In a way, the novel is a defense of Brazil, since one of the two Germans has a Nordic disdain for Brazil and simply does not adjust himself to his new country.

From the numerous writings of Gilberto Freyre, we get a historical and sociological picture of the Northeast. Freyre has devoted his life to the study of the Recife region. Conservative and pro-Portuguese, he has developed the theory of "Lusotropicalism," according to which Portugal has shown a special aptitude for colonizing the tropics. He has thus won the appreciation of the Portuguese Government, which enjoys little support among the intellectuals of the world because of its policy in Angola and

Mozambique. After reading *The Masters and the Slaves* (1933) and his other works, we wonder what Freyre means, since he seems to destroy his own thesis by depicting the Portuguese society which lived on the plantations exploiting the labor of the slaves as lazy, sensual (there is a great sexual preoccupation in the works of Freyre), uneducated, and superstitious. Freyre wrote a book for Americans, among whom he has many admirers: *Brazil, An Interpretation* (1945).

Among the many novelists who have described the Northeast, the best known is Jorge Amado, several of whose works have been translated into English. *Gabriela, Clove and Cinnamon* (1958) tells of the love life of the "Turkish" owner of a café and his cook, but it gives us a false idea of Amado's work. He was, like many Brazilian intellectuals, a Communist; the novels in which he attacks the oligarchy (sometimes quite unfairly) have made him wealthy, but novels like *The Dead Sea* (1943) display the bitterness which has never left him.

The modern art movement, which began in São Paulo in 1922, left its mark on literature as well as on the other arts. However, it was essentially internationalist in character, and the works it produced, in general, are of little interest for those seeking a picture of Brazil.

Travel Literature

Actually, the best picture of Latin America may be obtained from travel books by foreigners. The early chronicles of Spanish explorers and Conquistadores are remarkable, but since then Spaniards and Portuguese have written little about Latin America. However, one fascinating book is *My Childhood and Youth* (1901) by the great Spanish scientist and Nobel laureate Santiago Ramón y Cajal. He tells of his experiences in Cuba during the 1898 war, a war we know almost exclusively from U.S. sources. For Americans it was a "glorious little war," but for Spaniards it was a national tragedy. Out of it was born the Generation of '98, whose great concern was the destiny of Spain. Ramón y Cajal's autobiography gives us an unforgettable picture of the tragedy as seen firsthand by a sensitive and intelligent young Spaniard.

There are numerous German works about Latin America. Alexander von Humboldt, whom we have already mentioned, wrote in French. The first German work of any importance on Latin America was the *True History of His Captivity* (1557) by

Hans Staden. The book is generally known by this title, but the original title, which is very long, gives some idea of the contents. It begins "The true history . . . of the wild, naked, fierce cannibals of the New World . . ." The scene of Hans Staden's adventures was Brazil, but not until the nineteenth century was that vast country explored scientifically. There is an important work about a scientific mission by J. B. von Spix and C. F. P. von Martius, *Travels in Brazil in the Years 1817-1820, Undertaken by Command of H.M. the King of Bavaria.* In the modern period the best-known German work about Latin America is the *Travel Diary of a Philosopher* (1925) by Count Hermann Keyserling, a close friend of the Argentinian intellectual leader Victoria Ocampo, with whom he broke after a spectacular argument.

It is curious that, despite all the French propaganda about "Latin" America, there are few French books about that continent. Perhaps the most interesting is the *Picturesque and Historical Journey to Brazil* (3 vols., 1834-39) by Jean Baptiste Debret, who went to Brazil with a cultural mission in 1816 and spent fifteen years in Rio de Janeiro. The naturalist Auguste de Saint-Hilaire wrote numerous works, especially about Brazil, but they are out of print. Of all Latin American countries, France has had by far the closest relations with Brazil. In the modern period this interest is reflected in such works as *Tristes Tropiques* (1955) by the structuralist Claude Lévy-Strauss.

In the nineteenth century the English wrote a great number of books on Latin America. The most important is *The Voyage of the Beagle* (1839) by Charles Darwin, who tells with fascinating details the story of a scientific cruise around South America to the Galápagos Islands, where he collected much of the information which was to serve as confirmation of his theory of evolution. Two naturalist colleagues of Darwin, Alfred R. Wallace and Henry W. Bates, wrote important works on Amazonia, entitled respectively *Narrative of Travels on the Amazon and Río Negro* (1853) and *The Naturalist on the Amazons* (1863). The great Alpine climber Edward Whymper, the first man to climb the Matterhorn in Switzerland, went to Ecuador to climb the Chimborazo, then thought to be the highest mountain in the world. He described his experiences in *Travels amongst the Great Andes of the Equator* (1892). A very amusing yarn is *The Sea and the Jungle* (1912) in which Henry M. Tomlinson tells the story of a freighter which carried railroad ties up the Amazon to the Acre territory, where the Madeira-Mamoré railway was being built. James Bryce, the distinguished British Ambassador in Washington who wrote the

This engraving by R. T. Pritchett is reproduced from Charles Darwin's *The Voyage of the Beagle*; it shows H.M.S. "Beagle" in the Straits of Magellan, with Mount Sarmiento in the background. (From Ronald Hilton, *The Scientific Institutions of Latin America*.)

classic study of the United States *The American Commonwealth*, traveled around South America and recorded his impressions in *South America, Observations and Impressions* (1912). Among the modern English books about Latin America, we may mention *Beyond the Mexique Bay* (1934) by Aldous Huxley, who views the landscapes of Central America with the admiration of an artist and the life there with the irony of a satirist.

There is an abundant U.S. literature about Latin America. Some books describe archaeological expeditions, primarily those to Mexico and Guatemala. The classic work of this kind is *Incidents of Travel in Central America, Chiapas and Yucatán* (1841) by John L. Stephens and Frederick Catherwood, an English artist who accompanied Stephens and drew the engravings for the work. Some books are related to scientific expeditions. Two young navy lieutenants, William Lewis Herndon and Lardner Gibbon, were sent on an exploration trip up the Amazon as far as Peru and Bolivia. They wrote an important report, *Exploration of the Valley of the Amazon* (1853-54). Some of the books are based on military campaigns, like *The Rough Riders* (1899) in which Theodore Roosevelt described the invasion of Cuba in a somewhat less than impartial manner. President Roosevelt, a great hunter, narrated his wanderings through the South American jungle in *Through the Brazilian Wilderness* (1914). The development of Brazil was predicted by Roy Nash, who, in *The Conquest of Brazil* (1926), foresaw that the interior of Brazil would have to be developed from the highlands, i.e. the area where Brasília is located; only from there would it be possible to open up Amazonia. Some American books about Latin America were inspired by missionary, usually Protestant, efforts. A number of missionaries lost their lives at the hands of savages such as the Jívaros of Ecuador, who were notorious headhunters. Books about proselytizing efforts in eastern Ecudor are *Mission to the Headhunters* (1961) by Frank and Marie Brown, and *Through Gates of Splendor* (1957) by Elizabeth Elliott, whose husband was killed by the Jívaros. Political reporting from various areas of the world was the special field of John Gunther, whose *Inside Latin America* (1940) had a great success when, during World War II, there was a sudden surge of interest in our neighbors to the south.

Curiously, there is practically no literature about a Latin American country by a writer from another Latin American country. A notable exception is *The Cosmic Race* (1925) by the famous Mexican José Vasconcelos, describing a journey he made through Argentina, Uruguay, Paraguay, and Brazil. Moreover, in his five-volume autobiography Vasconcelos describes a number of trips he made through Latin America. Vasconcelos wanted to make Mexico the spiritual center of Latin America, where he thought the "cosmic race"—a mixture of white, "yellow," and black—would develop. As president of the University of Mexico, he gave it a coat of arms with a map of Latin America and the motto "Through my race the spirit will speak." The lack of books by Latin Americans about sister republics indicates a lack of interest, and this is the basic reason why Latin American organizations have failed to develop. A fairly reliable indication of the interest of one country in another is the number of books it publishes about it. This criterion raises serious doubts as to whether "Latin America" exists, even though from the outside we may see it as a unit.

Architecture and the Arts

City planning is a major concern of the contemporary world. Everywhere cities face disaster, and Latin America is no exception. Historically, cities were centers of civilization (city-ness); today, they are rather centers of barbarism.

In the pre-Columbian period, American cities were primarily centers of civil and ecclesiastical power, and only in a secondary way human agglomerations. Now, this relationship has been reversed. Tenochtitlán, Teotihuacán, Chichén Itzá, and Uxmal in Mexico, like Cuzco and Machu Picchu in Peru, developed around immense religious monuments. In Mexico these monuments had the shape of a pyramid, and this has given rise to some curious theories about links between Egypt and Mexico. Some prehistorians assert that the Phoenicians reached the New World and left their imprint here. In Peru the buildings were megalithic. Pre-Columbian architecture was primitive, in the sense that no Indian civilization developed the true arch, which appeared quite early in the history of Old World architecture. At the same time, it is astonishing that, without iron tools the Indians could carve stone with such perfection. The bas-reliefs in Mexican, especially Mayan, architecture are remarkable. Inca architecture was much cruder than Mexican, but it is almost impossible to understand how the Incas could carve the immense stone blocks of their buildings so precisely; their irregular forms fit so perfectly that a knife blade cannot be inserted between them. While the temples and the palaces were spectacular, the common people lived in simple huts. The only places in the New World where the pre-Columbian civilizations created important centers were Mexico, Guatemala, and Peru. In other areas, life was quite primitive.

In a way the Spaniards continued the urban tradition of the Indians. The principal buildings were those of the ecclesiastical and civil authorities. The urban population was small, but in each city, as in the pre-Columbian period, there was a large open market to which the peasants of the area came to buy and to sell. The markets are still common today, although for hygienic reasons the authorities now prefer that trading be conducted in stores or closed markets. The old-fashioned market place is disappearing in Europe, and it scarcely exists in the United States. Within a few decades it will probably disappear from Latin America.

The elements of the pre-Columbian and colonial cities were similar but the disposition was new. The great tragedy of U.S. cities is land speculation; throughout the world there is a movement to end this kind of speculation, which prevents the aesthetic development of cities. In pre-Columbian and colonial cities the ecclesiastical and civil powers were so strong that speculation had very little influence on the shape of cities. In Mexico, above all, pre-Columbian Indians created grandiose civic centers. For example, in Teotihuacán there was an immense esplanade between the pyramids of the Sun and the Moon. The Indians built such structures only in parts of Mexico, Guatemala, Peru, and Bolivia. During the colonial period monumental centers arose over a much wider area. Public buildings, especially churches, were monumental because the Spaniards understood the importance of buildings in the religious and civic formation of people.

The Spaniards introduced two new factors into American cities. The first factor was the Roman concept of a city built around a square *(plaza mayor)*. In Spain the main squares of Madrid and Salamanca are perhaps the most beautiful. The square was the religious, civic, and social center of the city. The Laws of the Indies established this plan as the basic element for American cities. In the colonial cities of Spanish America there is always a square in the center; on one side is the cathedral or church, on another the civil government. The most grandiose of these squares is the Zócalo in Mexico City. Portuguese authorities did not impose this plan, and it is for this reason that Brazilian cities grew in a haphazard way, like English and U.S. cities.

The second factor introduced by the Spaniards and also by the Portuguese was architecture imitating Peninsular models. The Jesuits, in particular, built grandiose churches "Ad majorem Dei gloriam" (AMDG—to the greater glory of God). The Church had at its disposal masses of Indians (and in Brazil, of blacks) to do the manual labor, while the whites supervised the work. Frequently, the plans came from Spain, but the workmen added details drawn from their own tradition. Thus was born Hispanic American art, in which the designs came from Europe and the execution and details from the native tradition.

When the Spaniards conquered the New World, Gothic architecture still survived in Spain. In Mexico and Cuba there are some examples of late Gothic architecture. In the first years of the Conquest, there was a danger of Indian attacks, and many fortress churches were built. These were churches which could also serve as fortresses; the outer walls were thick, with battlements on top, and practically without windows. In Spanish America there are also some examples of plateresque architecture; this was a Spanish Renaissance style in which the stone was carved in bas-relief to imitate silver work—hence the name plateresque *(plata* means silver in Spanish).

The Counter Reformation was a reformation within the Roman Catholic Church. It followed the example of the Protestant Reformation in sponsoring an almost puritanical religious architecture, without that ostentatious display of images and artistic objects which the Protestants denounced as manifestations of idolatry. In Spain the Escorial is the most famous specimen of the architecture of the Counter Reformation. There are some examples of this style in Spanish America.

Nevertheless, the typical art of the colonial period was baroque, which was a reaction against the austerity of previous styles. Baroque, with its wealth of ornamentation, had a greater success in Latin America than in Europe. This was partly because of the Jesuits, who virtually sponsored baroque architecture, but also because there seems to have been a correspondence between the genius of baroque art and the genius of Latin America. Baroque was a way of life. The good manners which still characterize the Latin American oligarchy seem to be a baroque heritage, as well as the cult of images in folk religion. Baroque was a dramatic art, full of movement, in which whenever possible the curve replaced the straight line. For the Jesuits this architecture was a means of propagating the faith; the architectural drama should appeal to the imagination of the people. The Puebla region in Mexico is full of baroque art. In South America we may mention the Jesuit church in Quito.

Portuguese baroque is different from Spanish baroque because the Portuguese are different from the Spaniards. The Portuguese is an introvert, the Spaniard an extrovert. To a foreigner the extreme examples of Spanish American baroque appear in bad taste, while Portuguese baroque is more refined and sober. Large wall spaces are simply painted white, without any ornamentation, so that Portuguese churches do not have the cluttered appearance of many Spanish American churches. Frequently, instead of the frenzied sculpture of Spanish American baroque, Portuguese baroque featured pictures painted on tiles. Painted tiles are typical of Moorish architecture and, under Moorish influence, tile-making developed in Spain and Portugal. In Spain, Talavera was famous for its tiles, and Talavera skills migrated to Puebla in Mexico. In Puebla there is a profusion of polychrome tiles, which give the city an almost oriental appearance. However, the Portuguese tiles are something different. They are usually just blue on white and, rejecting completely the Moorish hostility to the representation of living things, the Portuguese used panels of tiles to depict animals, people, and even social scenes. The Portuguese sometimes covered whole walls with these tile pictures, which had a function similar to that of tapestries in Spain. Since Castile is much colder than Portugal and since it was sheep country, it was natural that the art of tapestry-making should have developed there, while in Portugal tile-making flourished in a remarkable way. Tile-making developed in hot Arab lands, and when the Portuguese tile art migrated to tropical Brazil, it almost seemed to have come home.

Portugal had the reputation of being a very intolerant country, and, indeed, in Lisbon there were impressive ceremonies in which heretics were burned before the ecclesiastical and civil authorities. These ceremonies, which were even more spectacular than those in Spain, became so famous that even in English the Portuguese name, auto-da-fé, is used. Nevertheless, the genius of Portuguese baroque art is amiable and quiet, without any trace of violence or fanaticism.

We must assume that Portuguese fanaticism was superficial and that there was more true religious fervor in Spain, since the ecclesiastical architecture of Portugal and Brazil is less religious than that of Spain. With their square and simple forms, the baroque churches of Brazil often look like civilian buildings. The decoration may be of pagan inspiration, with little Christian sentiment. In the famous church of St. Francis in Bahia, which is indeed heavily ornamented, the predominant theme consists of angels who look like bare-breasted nymphs. In the cloister there is a whole series of tile paintings depicting the social life of the aristocracy. We should note that, despite Portuguese autos-da-fé, Brazil has always been tolerant in religious matters. In Minas Gerais there are many centers of baroque art: the old capital of Ouro Prêto, Congonhas, Sabará, São João del Rei, Tiradentes, and Mariana. Only by visiting these places can we appreciate the architecture and sculpture of O Aleijadinho and his contemporaries.

In Spanish American colonial cathedrals, as in those of Spain, it was necessary to extend the choir to accommodate the numerous clergy, so that the central nave for the public was taken over by the choir. These choirs, with their ornate ironwork, are often artistic masterpieces, but the sociological implication of the separation of the clergy from the faithful by an iron work screen is the clericalism that triggered anticlericalism. Moreover, these choirs block the interior view of the churches and hide the beauty of the structures. This is true of many of the great churches of Spanish America, including the cathedral of Mexico, the largest in the Western Hemisphere. Another feature of Spanish American churches is that behind the altar the wall was blocked by a *retablo*, a screen with painted wooden statues of saints. The

colonial churches were often decorated with large religious paintings. Some of these came from Spanish workshops, such as that
of Zurbarán, but others were the products of American workshops; those of Quito and Cuzco were especially famous.

The exuberance of baroque architecture provoked the neoclas-
sic reaction. Architecture became classical and sober. Neoclassi-
cism produced a few great monuments in Latin America; the
cathedrals of Mexico City and Puebla are predominantly neo-
classical.

Following the Conquest there seems to have been an almost
complete break in the musical tradition. We know little about
pre-Columbian music; a Mexican musicologist claims that in pre-
Columbian Mexico there was a great musical tradition but that,
unfortunately practically all the instruments disappeared during
the violence of the Conquest. This reflects the Mexican tendency
to aggrandize the native tradition, as, for example, in the assertion
that the Aztecs had a developed philosophy. In Peru some native
music survives, but the instruments, such as the flute, are extremely simple. Latin American popular music is derived almost
entirely from Spain and Portugal, although, of course, the African
tradition is strong in the Caribbean and in the Northeast of
Brazil. It was thought earlier that Paraguayan music was of
Guaraní origin, but it has now been proved that, like the gaucho
music of Argentina, it came from Spain. The string instruments
typical of Latin America are all of Peninsular origin; the Indians
had wind instruments and the Africans percussion instruments
In places where there was little wood but where there were
animals of the armadillo family, the shell was used to make the
sound box of the guitar. Instruments of the violin family are of
Italian origin and arrived in Latin America later. Some modern
composers, like the Brazilian Heitor de Villa Lobos, have attempted to create an American music by using native melodies,
but these efforts have had only a modest success.

The Jesuits understood the importance of music in religious
life, and under their influence large baroque organs were installed
in churches which themselves were often baroque. There is a
correspondence between baroque architecture and baroque music.
The convolutions in the melodies recall the convolutions in the
stone—architecture has been described as frozen music. Pale-
strina had a great influence in Spain, and in general Spanish and
Latin American music followed the development of Italian music.
There were talented composers during the colonial period; one
of the great musical centers was the Mexican city of Morelia.

Native art has survived best in pottery. The Indians of the coast of Peru made *huacos* (pots) of great artistic value. Mochica *huacos* in the university museum of Trujillo in northern Peru represent men, women, and animals with incredible realism; nearby are the vast ruins of Chan Chan, and the *huacos* give us some idea of the vitality of the Indians who created that civilization. During the colonial period European techniques and styles were adopted. Mass-produced porcelain, glass, and metal vessels have largely eliminated high quality handmade pottery. Most pots are now made for kitchen use or for sale to tourists. Some governments are making an effort to revive folk arts, but once a craft is gone, it is hard to bring it back artificially.

Museum collections give us some idea of the wealth of the artistic tradition of the pre-Columbian and colonial periods. Mexico is one of the leading countries in the world in museum development; it has established museums which tell the history of Mexico for the common people, for children, and for tourists. In comparison the great museums of the United States and Europe seem unimaginative. In Mexico City there are many noteworthy museums. In the old castle of Chapultepec there is the National Museum of History, and on the hillside below is the "spiral staircase" which takes the visitor from the courtyard of the history museum down to the street level. As he walks down, the whole history of Mexico unfolds before his eyes. Nearby stands the new and world-famous National Museum of Anthropology, where the history of Mexican Indians is illustrated in spectacular fashion. The art of the colonial period is best represented at the Colonial Museum in the old Jesuit convent at Tepozotlán.

After independence Latin America became attuned culturally to France. Its nineteenth-century art reflected French fashions and has only a relative interest. The most valuable French contribution was in urbanism. The Latin Americans who visited France returned with a vision of its beautiful cities, with their boulevards, their fountains, their parks, and their esplanades along river banks and seashore. The Avenida de la Reforma in Mexico City, the Malecón in Havana, and Palermo in Buenos Aires all reflect the influence of French urbanism. Unfortunately, in recent years the beautiful cities of Latin America have been invaded by desperate peasants who have seized vacant lots and built there ugly and unhygienic shacks. Cities like Rio de Janeiro, Buenos Aires, and Mexico City are carrying on active campaigns to get rid of these warts.

During the modern period, without doubt the most interesting painting is that of the Mexican school of the Revolution. The great figures of this school are Diego Rivera, José Clemente Orozco, and David Alfaro Siqueiros. Rivera, who was a vocal but rather unorthodox Communist, depicted not only the events of the Mexican Revolution but all the evolution of Mexico, with a realism bordering on caricature. Most of his work is in Mexico City—in the National Palace, in the Ministry of Education, in the Hotel del Prado, and elsewhere. The great mural which is the feature of the lobby of the Hotel del Prado created a scandal because Rivera painted Ignacio Ramírez, a philosopher of the Reformation, holding up a paper inscribed, "God does not exist." Proclerical elements tried to destroy the mural, until Rivera agreed to eliminate the offending phrase and replace it simply with the date of Ramírez's atheistic declaration. Conservatives dislike Rivera's work because Cortés, the Conquistadores, and the Spanish priests are depicted as monsters. American tourists are shocked to see U.S. businessmen and diplomats represented as ogres or birds of prey. Rivera has the doctrinaire leftist interpretation of Latin American history: the Indians and the common people are good, but until the Revolution they were oppressed by the oligarchy — landowners of Spanish origin, Spanish-style priests, gross army officers, unscrupulous businessmen, and rapacious foreign capitalists.

Orozco, whose principal works are in Guadalajara, has the same interpretation of history, but his work does not have the comic-book character of Rivera's. Rivera recalls the satirical Mexican engravers of the nineteenth century, whereas Orozco reminds us of Michelangelo. Siqueiros is the most violent of the three— in politics, in art, and in life. He had serious trouble with the government, which jailed him for several years.

The burst of mural art in Mexico was rather a special phenomenon. Mural paintings had been important in pre-Columbian art—witness the murals of Bonampak—and the Revolution sought to rediscover the art of ancient Mexico. Moreover, the mural movement received a strong impulse from José Vasconcelos, who believed that mural art should bring the story of Mexico and its revolutionary ideals to the people, just as medieval murals indoctrinated Europeans with Christian dogmas. As Minister of Education, he gave Rivera and other painters fellowships to go to Italy to study the great mural artists. Partly as a result of the mural movement, Mexicans have come to view their history through the spectacles of the Revolution, although the obligatory, government-approved textbooks have also been an important factor.

The only other country where there was a mural movement of any importance was Brazil, where Cândido Portinari, another Communist, painted murals, some of which may be seen in the Hispanic Foundation of the Library of Congress in Washington. Since the colonial period, Quito has had an important tradition of painting, and today it has a school of painting of Communist or Socialist tendencies. The most famous of the modern painters is Oswaldo Guayasamín.

There has been a reaction against didactic, or "socialist," art (the Communists assert that art must serve a social purpose), and for some years it has been fashionable to belittle Rivera and the muralists as provincial. In painting and sculpture, abstract or nonrepresentational art dominates, and Latin American artists want to keep up with world trends. The biennial São Paulo exhibition is the mecca for those interested in the latest world art movements. While this biennial is world-famous, the art it generates is international, and it ceases to interest those looking for specifically Latin American art as a manifestation of Latin American history and personality.

The same may be said of modern architecture, of which there are many examples, especially in Brazil, where the influence of Le Corbusier may be clearly seen. Modern architectural styles were adopted much faster in Brazil than in the United States. Several Latin American architects have achieved international fame, notably Oscar Niemeyer, who was one of the architects of the United Nations building in New York. His best known building was erected in Rio de Janeiro as the Ministry of Education, but since the capital moved to Brasília, it is now simply a local office of the Ministry. Niemeyer decorated it with Portuguese-style tiles, so it has a traditional touch about it. Brazilian architects also adopted with some success the fixed concrete screens Le Corbusier recommended to keep out the sun, the wind, and the rain, but to allow the air to circulate. Unfortunately, many modern buildings are simply boxes which noisy air-conditioning keeps so cold that a person coming in from the tropical outdoors can easily catch a cold; if the air-conditioning breaks down, he asphyxiates. Although air-conditioning can help to make life pleasant in hot regions, it is in some ways less satisfactory than the air-conditioning which the massive structure of some colonial buildings created.

Latin American governments wish to leave a record of monumental construction, and this often benefits the cities. Brasília is an assemblage of modern architecture probably unique in the

world, but President Kubitschek was accused of sacrificing everything to build a monument to his administration. The physical
appearance of Brasília has aroused both criticism and praise. The
surrounding countryside is flat and monotonous, with only scrub
vegetation. An artificial lake gives the city a charm hitherto lacking. The city itself is the creation of a group of architects, city
planners, and landscape architects; some of them, such as the
architect Oscar Niemeyer, are internationally famous. The master
plan of the city is impressive and modern; there are no intersec-
tions, so the traffic flows freely, but the distances are such that
to go from one point to another is a veritable expedition. Some
buildings, like the presidential palace, are beautiful, while others,
like the ministries and apartment blocks, are ugly boxes. At first
the government rejected the proposal to have a university in the
capital, since it feared that student violence would prevent the
government from working efficiently. However, it gave in to pressure, and it may since have had reason to regret it.

Thanks to oil money, Venezuelan cities have been transformed.
Both Caracas and Maracaibo have developed from shabby little
towns into modern cities in a few decades. Even though it was a
mistake to build a modern metropolis on a filled-in lake bed in a
valley where smog inevitably collects, Mexico City is an impressive combination of architecture, old and modern. Guadalajara
has become a spectacular city. However, in the cities of Latin
America, as elsewhere, deterioration seems to be taking place
faster than improvement. It is too early to say if Latin American
cities are caught in an almost irreversible decline. It is certain
that the intense concern Latin Americans felt for art has diminished. Ariel has left Latin America. Where has he gone?

Science and Technology

Only since World War II have Latin American governments fully
realized that science and technology are keys to national development, although the Positivists and the Mexican "scientists" were,
in theory at least, very conscious of this, so much so that the
University of Mexico was abolished for some time in the belief
that individual science faculties could operate more effectively
than a tradition-bound university. When José Vasconcelos tried to
make the reestablished University of Mexico the intellectual center of Latin America, he was thinking in terms of the humanities.
Buenos Aires was the great science center in Latin America and
attracted students from many other countries. It is no coincidence

that two Argentine scientists have won Nobel Prizes, Bernardo Houssay in Medicine and Luis Leloir in Chemistry. The Peronista regime was obscurantist in its attitude toward science; Houssay was dismissed from his post at the University of Buenos Aires, and it was largely American help which made it possible for him to continue his work.

Brazil, likewise, has a noteworthy tradition in medicine and the natural sciences. Oswaldo Cruz has given his name to the most famous Latin American institute in the field of tropical medicine and biology. The Instituto Butantan in São Paulo is similar, but it is better known because of its spectacular snake farm. Chapingo, near Mexico City, has become a world-famous center for agricultural research, thanks largely to the Rockefeller Foundation-supported International Maize and Wheat Improvement Center, where U.S. agronomist Norman E. Borlaug did the research which won him the Nobel Peace Prize. Scientific institutions have sprung up all over the continent, but most of them are inadequate in terms of facilities, library, and staff. Cuba has followed the Soviet model; the Academy of Sciences, which occupies the old capitol, controls scientific research throughout the island. The former close scientific ties between the United States and Cuba have been swept away. Pure science has largely been supplanted by applied technology, with Soviet specialists playing a rather uneasy role.

In the eighteenth and especially the nineteenth centuries Latin America had a great interest for European naturalists, as is evident in the explorations and research of men like the Spaniard José Celestino Mutis, the German Alexander von Humboldt, the Frenchman Aimé Bonpland, and the Englishman Charles Darwin. However, such taxonomic exploration is no longer on the frontiers of science, which is now occupied by molecular biology and similar laboratory subjects requiring advanced equipment and modern information facilities. The contemporary interest in ethology has led to a focusing of interest in central Africa, where baboons and other primates are being studied in order better to understand human behavior. The belief that man may be of African origin has also led to a concentration of scientific efforts in Africa. In botany and geology, South America is still a focal point for research.

The lack of adequate recognition of the needs of science, combined with political unrest, have led to an exodus of scientists from Latin America, which can ill afford such a brain drain. Argentine science has been especially badly hit. Latin American

This sketch of Darwin by George Richmond was made in 1839. Charles Robert Darwin (1809-82) traveled around South America to the Galápagos and on around the world back to England as a young naturalist attached to H.M.S. "Beagle" on its voyage of exploration which lasted from 1831 to 1836. This was the most important scientific journey in history, since during it Darwin matured the theory of evolution which found its classical expression in The Origin of Species (1859). Darwin told the story of his journey in a book commonly known by an abridged title, The Voyage of the Beagle (1839). It is still the best travel book about South America.

governments are usually willing to provide millions for the latest military equipment, but not the relatively small amounts for scientific literature. The left and the right are equally to blame. Castro's Cuba is now the most militarized country in Latin America, but there is not an adequate science library in the island. Universities and science have been crippled both by intensive politicization and by the authoritarian repression which so frequently comes as a reaction.

Conclusion

Despite all the doubts and uncertainties, Latin America still offers a fascinating cultural picture. We in the United States are now so concerned with Puerto Ricans and Chicanos that we forget the vast area to the south which has its own cultural existence. Although we talk about Latin America as our backyard, Rio de Janeiro, São Paulo, and Buenos Aires are as far away from the United States as Moscow or Tokyo, not to mention Western Europe. We should ban the expression "our backyard" from our political jargon. The bibliography at the end of this volume shows that in recent years U.S. scholars have produced many volumes on Latin American economics, sociology, political science, and history, but very little on Latin American culture, despite a modish enthusiasm for a few modern authors whose works have not yet withstood the test of time. If we are to understand Latin America, we desperately need not only the specialist who knows one tree but the generalist who can understand the incredible variety of cultural flora which flourish in the immense sector of America south of the Tropic of Cancer.

Bibliography

This bibliography lists only selected general works in English which have appeared since 1960 and which may be presumed to be in print. Some are new editions or reprints. The latest U.S. edition is given. For more detailed bibliographical references, consult the bibliographies in the various works. An excellent source of critical information about books is the quarterly *Hispanic American Historical Review*, now edited at the University of Texas and published by Duke University Press. For brief references to books and to articles, consult the annual *Handbook of Latin American Studies*, published by the University of Florida for the Hispanic Foundation of the Library of Congress. Other useful bibliographies are:

Bayitch, Stojan A., ed. *Latin America and the Caribbean. A Bibliographical Guide to Works in English.* Dobbs Ferry, N.Y.: Oceana, 1968.

Griffin, Charles C., ed. *Latin America. A Guide to Historical Literature.* University of Texas Press, 1971.

Gropp, Arthur E. *Bibliography of Latin American Bibliographies.* Metuchen, N.J.: Scarecrow Press, 1968-71.

Weaver, Jerry L., ed. *Latin American Development: A Selected Bibliography 1950-1967.* Santa Barbara, Calif.: ABC-CLIO, 1969.

Among the general books on Latin America are:

Arciniegas, Germán. *Latin America.* New York: Knopf, 1967.

Clissold, Stephen. *Latin America. A Cultural Outline.* New York: Humanities Press (Hutchinson), 1970.

238 • *The Latin Americans*

Mitchell, Sir Harold. *Caribbean Patterns.* New York: John Wiley, 1972.

South American Handbook. Distributed by Rand McNally, annual.

Veliz, Claudio, ed. *Latin America and the Caribbean: A Handbook.* New York: Praeger, 1968.

Wilgus, A. Curtis. *Historical Atlas of Latin America.* New York: Cooper Square, 1967.

Chapter 1. A WORLD OF REGIONS: LATIN AMERICA, THE NAME AND THE PLACE

Butland, Gilbert J. *Latin America: A Regional Geography.* New York: John Wiley, 1966.

James, Preston. *Latin America.* New York: Odyssey, 1969.

Webb, Kempton E. *Geography of Latin America.* Englewood Cliffs, N.J.: Prentice-Hall, 1972.

Chapter 2. THE POPULATION

Bates, Margaret. *Migration of Peoples to Latin America.* College Park, Md.: McGrath, 1970.

Beyer, Glenn H. *The Urban Explosion in Latin America.* Cornell University Press, 1967.

Chaplin, David. *Population Policy and Growth in Latin America.* Lexington, Mass.: Heath, 1971.

Cole, John P. *Latin America: An Economic and Social Geography.* Totowa, N.J.: Rowman, 1971.

Harris, Marvin. *Patterns of Race in the Americas.* New York: Walker, 1964.

Heath, D. B., and Richard N. Adams, eds. *Contemporary Cultures and Societies in Latin America.* New York: Random House, 1965.

Lipset, Seymour M., and Aldo Solari, eds. *Elites in Latin America.* Oxford University Press, 1967.

Salzano, Francisco M., ed. *Ongoing Evolution of Latin American Populations.* Springfield, Ill.: C. C. Thomas, 1971.

Wolf, Eric R., and Edward C. Hansen. *The Human Condition in Latin America.* Oxford University Press. 1972.

Chapter 3. HISTORY AND GREAT MEN

Bailey, Helen M., and Abraham P. Nasatir. *Latin America: The Development of Its Civilization.* Englewood Cliffs, N.J.: Prentice-Hall, 1968.

Bennett, Wendell C., and Junius A. Bird. *Andean Culture History.* New York: Doubleday (Natural History Press), 1964.

Crow, John A. The Epic of Latin America. Garden City, N.Y.: Doubleday, 1971.

Diffie, Bailey W. Latin American Civilization: Colonial Period. New York: Octagon, 1967.

Fagg, John E. Latin America: A General History. New York: Macmillan, 1970.

Gibson, Charles. Black Legend. New York: Knopf, 1971.

————. Spain in America. New York: Harper, 1966.

Herring, Hubert. History of Latin America. New York: Knopf, 1968.

Madariaga, Salvador de. Rise of the Spanish American Empire. New York: Free Press (Macmillan), 1965.

————. Bolívar. University of Miami Press, 1967.

Martin, Michael R., and Gabriel Lovett. Encyclopedia of Latin American History. Indianapolis: Bobbs Merrill, 1967.

Reed, Alma. The Ancient Past of Mexico. New York: Crown, 1964.

Stein, Stanley J. and Barbara H. The Colonial Heritage of Latin America. Oxford University Press, 1970.

Thompson, John Eric. The Rise and Fall of the Maya Civilization. University of Oklahoma Press, 1966.

Worcester, Donald. Makers of Latin America. New York: Dutton, 1966.

Worcester, Donald, and Wendell G. Schaeffer. The Growth and Culture of Latin America. Oxford University Press, 1971.

Chapter 4. THE ECONOMY

On land problems, see the publications of the Land Tenure Center, University of Wisconsin.

Anderson, Charles W. Politics and Economic Change in Latin America. Princeton, N.J.: Van Nostrand-Reinhold, 1967.

Baer, Werner, and Isaac Kerstenetzky, eds. Inflation and Growth in Latin America. Yale University Press, 1970.

Baerresen, Donald W., Martin Carnoy, and Joseph Grunwald. Latin American Trade Patterns. Washington, D.C.: Brookings Institution, 1965.

Benham, Frederic C., and H. A. Holley. Short Introduction to the Economy of Latin America. Oxford University Press, 1960.

Dell, Sidney. A Latin American Common Market? Oxford University Press, 1966.

Glade, William P. The Latin American Economies. Princeton, N.J.: Van Nostrand-Reinhold, 1969.

Gordon, Wendell C. *The Political Economy of Latin America.* Columbia University Press, 1965.

Grunwald, Joseph, and Philip Musgrove. *Natural Resources in Latin American Development.* Johns Hopkins University Press, 1970.

Krause, Walter, and John Mathis. *Latin America and Economic Integration.* University of Iowa Press, 1970.

Landsberger, Henry O., ed. *Latin American Peasant Movements.* Cornell University Press, 1969.

Nisbett, Charles T. *Latin America, Problems in Economic Development.* New York: Macmillan, 1969.

Prebisch, Raúl. *Change and Development: Latin America's Great Task.* New York: Praeger, 1971.

Ross, John B. *The Economic System of Mexico.* Stanford, Calif.: California Institute of International Studies, 1971.

Smith, T. Lynn, ed. *Agrarian Reform in Latin America.* New York: Knopf, 1965.

Stokes, Charles J. *Transportation and Economic Development in Latin America.* New York: Praeger, 1968.

Teichert, Pedro C. M. *Latin America's Basic Resource and Development Background.* University of West Florida, 1970.

Wionczek, Miguel S., ed. *Latin American Economic Integration.* New York: Praeger, 1966.

Chapter 5. THE PRESS, POLITICS, AND THE LAW

Alexander, Robert J. *Today's Latin America.* New York: Praeger-Doubleday, 1968.

———. *Latin American Politics and Government.* New York: Harper, 1965.

Burnett, Ben G., and Kenneth F. Johnson, eds. *Political Forces in Latin America.* San Francisco: Wadsworth, 1968.

Calvert, Peter. *Latin America: Internal Conflict and International Peace.* New York: St. Martin, 1969.

Chilcote, Ronald H. *The Press in Latin America, Spain, and Portugal.* Stanford, Calif.: California Institute of International Studies, 1963.

———. *Revolution and Structural Change in Latin America. A Bibliography.* Stanford, Calif.: Hoover Institution Press, 1970.

Geyer, Georgie Anne. *The New Latins.* Garden City, N.Y.: Doubleday, 1970.

Hanke, Lewis. *Contemporary Latin America.* Princeton, N.J.: Van Nostrand-Reinhold, 1968.

Lambert, Jacques. *Latin America: Social Structures and Political Institutions.* University of California Press, 1967.

Lieuwen, Edwin. *Arms and Politics in Latin America.* New York: Praeger, 1961.

Needler, Martin C. *Latin American Politics in Perspective.* Princeton, N.J.: Van Nostrand-Reinhold, 1968.

————, ed. *Political Systems of Latin America.* Princeton, N.J.: Van Nostrand, 1964.

Sigmund, Paul E., ed. *Models of Political Change in Latin America.* New York: Praeger, 1970.

Silvert, Kalman H. *The Conflict Society: Reaction and Revolution in Latin America.* New York: Harper and Row, 1968.

Szulc, Tad. *Latin America.* New York: Atheneum, 1966.

Whitaker, Arthur P., and D. C. Jordan. *Nationalism in Contemporary Latin America.* New York: Free Press (Macmillan), 1966.

Williams, Edward J. *Latin American Christian Democratic Parties.* University of Tennessee Press, 1967.

Chapter 6. RELIGION AND PHILOSOPHY

Crawford, William R. *A Century of Latin-American Thought.* Harvard University Press, 1961.

Kadt, Emanuel de. *Catholic Radicals in Brazil.* Oxford University Press, 1970.

Pike, Frederick B., ed. *The Conflict between Church and State in Latin America.* New York: Knopf, 1964.

Read, William R., Victor M. Monterroso, and Harmon A. Johnson. *Latin American Church Growth.* Grand Rapids: Eerdmans, 1969.

Schmitt, Karl M., ed. *The Roman Catholic Church in Latin America.* New York: Knopf, 1972.

Turner, Frederick C. *Catholicism and Political Development in Latin America.* University of North Carolina Press, 1971.

Chapter 7. INTER-AMERICAN RELATIONS

Bemis, Samuel F. *The Latin American Policy of the United States.* New York: Norton, 1967.

Burr, Robert N. *Our Troubled Hemisphere: Perspectives on United States-Latin American Relations.* Washington, D.C.: Brookings Institution, 1967.

Connell-Smith, Gordon. *The Inter-American System.* Oxford University Press, 1966.

Gauld, Charles A. *The Last Titan, Percival Farquhar.* Stanford, Calif.: California Institute of International Studies, 1972.

Gil, Federico G. *Latin American-United States Relations.* New York: Harcourt Brace Jovanovich, 1971.

Goldenberg, Boris. *The Cuban Revolution and Latin America.* New York: Praeger, 1965.

Hilton, Ronald, ed. *The Movement toward Latin American Unity.* New York: Praeger, 1969.

Lieuwen, Edwin. *U.S. Policy in Latin America: A Short History.* New York: Praeger, 1965.

Ronning, C. Neale. *Intervention in Latin America.* New York: Knopf, 1970.

Slater, Jerome. *The OAS and United States Foreign Policy.* Ohio State University Press, 1967.

Trask, David F., Michael C. Meyer, and Roger R. Trask. *A Bibliography of U.S.-Latin American Relations since 1810. A Selected List of Eleven Thousand Published References.* University of Nebraska Press, 1968.

Wagner, R. Harrison. *United States Policy toward Latin America: A Study in Domestic and International Politics.* Stanford University Press, 1970.

Whitaker, Arthur P. *The Western Hemisphere Idea.* Cornell University Press, 1965.

Wood, Bryce. *The Making of the Good Neighbor Policy.* Columbia University Press, 1961.

Chapter 8. WORLD RELATIONS

Bailey, Norman A. *Latin America in World Politics.* New York: Walker, 1967.

Jackson, D. Bruce. *Castro, the Kremlin and Communism in Latin America.* Johns Hopkins University Press, 1969.

Johnson, Cecil. *Communist China and Latin America, 1959-1967.* Columbia University Press, 1970.

Oswald, J. Gregory, and Anthony J. Strover, eds. *The Soviet Union and Latin America.* New York: Praeger, 1970.

Pike, Frederick B. *Hispanismo, 1898-1936.* University of Notre Dame Press, 1971.

Zea, Leopoldo. *Latin America and the World.* University of Oklahoma Press, 1969.

For current relations between the Soviet Union and Latin America and the Soviet interpretation of developments in Latin America, see the quarterly *World Affairs Report* of the California Institute of International Studies.

Chapter 9. THE LANGUAGES

There is no general book in English (or in any other language) on the total language picture in Latin America. Still useful for the Indian languages is:

Boas, Franz, ed. *Handbook of American Indian Languages.* Washington, D.C.: Smithsonian Institution, 1911; reprinted 1969.

Chapter 10. LITERTURE, THE ARTS, AND SCIENCE

Anderson-Imbert, Enrique. *Spanish-American Literature. A History.* Wayne State University Press, 1969.

Bushnell, Geoffrey H. *Ancient Arts of the Americas.* New York: Praeger, 1965.

Cohen, John M., ed. *Latin American Writing Today.* Baltimore, Md.: Penguin, 1967.

Franco, Jean. *An Introduction to Spanish-American Literature.* Cambridge University Press, 1969.

————. *The Modern Culture of Latin America: Society and the Artist.* Baltimore, Md.: Penguin, 1970.

Harris, Walter D. *The Growth of Latin American Cities.* Ohio University Press, 1971.

Hilton, Ronald. *The Scientific Institutions of Latin America.* Stanford, Calif.: California Institute of International Studies, 1970.

Kelemen, Pál. *Baroque and Rococo in Latin America.* New York: P. Smith, 1966.

Kubler, George. *Art and Architecture of Ancient America.* Baltimore, Md.: Penguin, 1961.

Robertson, Donald. *Pre-Columbian Architecture.* New York: Braziller, 1963.

Torres-Rioseco, Arturo. *The Epic of Latin American Literature.* University of California Press, 1961.

————. *Aspects of Spanish-American Literature.* University of Washington Press, 1963.

Wolfe, Bertram. *Fabulous Life of Diego Rivera.* New York: Stein and Day, 1963.

Index